Sports
Broadcasting

About the Author

John R. Catsis has been an assistant professor in the School of Journalism and Broadcasting at Oklahoma State University since 1990. He created the school's first full-credit course in sports broadcasting, at which time he learned that no textbook on the subject existed. This text fills that gap.

Professor Catsis has had more than thirty years of broadcast experience, following his graduation from Northwestern University, where he received two degrees from the Medill School of Journalism. He first went on the air at the age of seventeen in his home town of Evanston, Illinois, handling the play-by-play of three area high schools' football and basketball schedules. Later, he handled the play-by-play of Northwestern University football and basketball teams, plus other major college teams and tournaments.

His broadcast sports experience continued at KYW-AM, the all-news radio station in Philadelphia, and KPRC-AM-TV, the NBC affiliate in Houston. Professor Catsis has also worked for KHOU-TV, Houston, and was news director of Houston's all-news-and-talk AM station, KTRH. Later, he served as executive producer of WMTW-TV, Portland, Maine, and became owner and manager of three radio stations and one television station, all in New Mexico.

In each of these capacities, Professor Catsis was actively involved in the creation and production of various sports broadcasts. This text combines this knowledge and experience into a very readable and clearly understandable work that only a broadcaster with his depth could create.

Sports Broadcasting

John R. Catsis
Oklahoma State University

Nelson-Hall Publishers/Chicago

Project Editor: Rachel Schick
Production Design Manager: Tamra Phelps
Typesetter: E. T. Lowe
Printer: Capital City Press
Illustrator: Bill Nelson
Cover Painting: *Football* by Cissy Allweiss

Library of Congress Cataloging-in-Publication Data

Catsis, John R.
    Sports broadcasting / John R. Catsis.
      p. cm.
    Includes bibliographical references and index.
    ISBN 0-8304-1379-0
    1. Radio broadcasting of sports—United States—History.   2. Television broadcasting
of sports—United States—History.   I. Title.
    GV742.3.C38   1995
    070. 4'49796'0973—dc20   95-1215
                                                                                CIP

Manufactured in the United States of America

10   9   8   7   6   5   4   3   2

TO CONNIE,
What a fan!

Contents

1. *The History of Radio Sports*   1

2. *The History of Television Sports*   27

6. Radio Technology   101

7. Television Technology   107

8. Producing   143

9. Sportscasts   167

10. Play-by-Play Preparations   197

11. *Play-by-Play and Color* 223

Preface: The Pregame Show

"Good afternoon, ladies and gentlemen, and welcome to *Sports Broadcasting,* the book that brings you the excitement—and complexity—of the world of radio and TV sports. It's a beautiful day in America. The weather is ideal, and from our vantage point it appears that everyone is ready for this long-anticipated event."

First, a little background. Broadcast sports has become a multibillion-dollar business and touches nearly every American. For example, the 1994 Winter Olympic games in Lillehammer, Norway, was the most watched event in U.S. television history, seen by an estimated 92.5 percent of all Americans. The broadcasting of sports has spread from the major professional leagues to the grass-roots level, such as Little League or the local golf course. On the fairway or elsewhere, personal camcorders are prevalent, and any of these cameras is capable of capturing what could become the play of the day or the play of the year.

Thanks to the sports media, virtually every American has heard of Michael Jordan. When Jordan announced his first retirement from basketball in 1993, the story was considered so big that CBS news anchor Connie Chung and NBC anchor Tom Brokaw covered the news conference. Nearly three-quarters of a century earlier, Babe Ruth became a household name, largely because of broadcasting. These examples are but two of many, with many more certain to follow in the coming years.

The most significant reason for the growth of sports in radio and TV is that it makes money. Lots of it. WFAN, an AM sports talk station in New York City, was the second-highest billing radio station in America in 1994, generating an estimated $33 million in revenues. And it attracts the right kind of viewers; folks with money to spend. For example, according to one study, most of those who watched the 1994 Super Bowl on television had a higher educational level than the average American.

There are plenty of places to advertise to the affluent viewer. According to *Satellite TV Week,* a dish owner in 1993 could have watched 800 NHL games, 1,000 NBA contests, 1,400 major league baseball games, 250 pro football games, and 3,500 college football contests. As unbelievable as some of these numbers may seem, they are certain to grow even more. This is because of a new technology called DBS, which in 1994 began providing what is expected to be up to 500 channels of TV to the home of any American who wanted it.

More than 60 percent of U.S. homes have cable. Nearly half (48 percent) can pick up twenty channels or more. Multi-set ownership is growing, and four out of five homes have a VCR. You can bet that many of the shows watched are sports programs.

At the same time, viewing habits are changing. Baseball is no longer television's most watched sport. It's football. Viewers say they now prefer watching football on TV by a margin of more than 2–1 over baseball. Basketball is a close third, and if present trends continue, it will surpass baseball and become the second most watched sport on television by the end of the century.

"We've sold our soul to television," says Jim Garner, former athletic director at Oklahoma State University, and now an executive with the Shreveport Pirates of the Canadian Football League. His statement was less of a complaint and more of an expression of how things are. Garner pointed out how willingly schools will reschedule games to suit a network's scheduling convenience. The reason is easy to comprehend: healthy rights fees.

"Anytime a game is on TV, TV orchestrates all, including the pre-game events," says Kent Houck, a Big 8 Conference football official. Again, the reason is clear, and the reason is the same—money. The sale of broadcast rights is a major source of revenue for many colleges, and certainly for most pro teams, as well. Both professional and amateur sports have only three ways to generate income. On the collegiate level, they are fund-raising, ticket sales, and broadcast rights. On the pro level, they are merchandise licensing, ticket sales, and broadcast rights. For many teams broadcast rights represent the largest single source of income.

Broadcasting means more than money. It also means exposure, which translates into athletic success. For example, at the college level, radio and television are attracted to schools with good athletic teams. The better schools, legitimized by broadcasting, attract the most talented high school athletes. After all, these youngsters want to be on TV and take part in bowl games, the College World Series, or NCAA championship playoffs. Thus, largely due to broadcasting, the best athletic programs get even better. By getting better, they get increased exposure. This, in turn, results in greater revenue.

Sports broadcasting has other benefits as well. For individuals like you, it's an opportunity for a satisfying profession and life-style. For some former coaches who become broadcast analysts, it may be part of a hidden agenda; their real aspiration is not to broadcast but to get another coaching job. Other broadcasters may impact sports in different ways. Most bring credit to themselves and to the events they cover. Some can actually bring about change. One such example was ESPN's Beano Cook. In 1993, he complained about the condition of the Penn State University playing field, on which the Nittany Lions were playing Rutgers. A few days later, the university said it was re-sodding the field for the next home game.

All announcers do not get the respect they think they deserve. Jim Rome was assaulted during an ESPN2 interview show by New Orleans Saints quarterback Jim Everett in 1994. Two years before, a Texas A & M University radio announcer was ejected from a baseball game by official Brian Stout. The ejection was the apparent result of ongoing harassment of Stout by the announcer.

The 1993 attacks on tennis great Monica Seles and American figure skater Nancy Kerrigan prompted several athletes to request bodyguards. But the protection was not limited to athletes. ABC announcer Julie Moran asked for a bodyguard while covering the figure skating event at the 1994 Olympic games in Lillehammer, Norway.

Despite these isolated incidents, sports and the broadcasting of them are events that millions of persons around the world anticipate. Who would have thought that a drawing to determine the order of a yet-to-be-held NBA draft selection would become a television event? Who would have envisioned that schools would televise the opening of college basketball practice, live at midnight? Who would have predicted that the Professional Bowlers Tour on ABC, first started in 1960, would be the second-longest live network sports series on TV, surpassed only by college football?

That last example shows the staying power of a sport that many consider "minor." The fact is that more people (42.5 million) actively take part in bowling than the so-called Big 3: baseball, basketball, and football. Even so, bowling is not the most popular participation sport. That honor goes to fitness walking, with 68 million persons taking part. The producer who can create an interesting and entertaining program on fitness walking has the potential of attracting a massive audience!

Americans who bowl and walk also listen to or watch sports on radio and television, and that's what this textbook is all about. It's about a unique and specially trained unit: the broadcast team. Individuals who make up these teams work behind the scenes and in front of the microphone to bring the excitement of athletic participation to radios and television sets everywhere.

A recent study at Ball State University in Muncie, Indiana, found that watching sports events helps older people feel better about themselves. Another found that 32 percent of sportswriters and broadcasters ranked watching a live sports event as more fulfilling than sex.

With that, we welcome you to the wonderful world of sports broadcasting!

"Now, ladies and gentlemen, let's take a break. We'll be back in a moment, with today's MVP lineups."

Acknowledgments: The Textbook Hall of Fame

Like any successful endeavor in the world of sports, this textbook is the result of a team effort. The individuals who helped with this difficult and time-consuming project are very special persons. I call them my MVPs: Most Valuable Professionals.

Three stand out. One is *Dr. Marlan Nelson,* director of the School of Journalism and Broadcasting at Oklahoma State University. Not only was he instrumental in helping me to cross the line into academics, he also acknowledged and supported the value of this project.

Next is *Dr. Harry Heath,* the previous director of the School, who is now retired. A former sportswriter in his own right, Dr. Heath turned out to be my cheerleader, spurring me on when I became otherwise distracted.

Unknowingly, *Dr. Ed Paulin* contributed to the creation of this work by recommending that I continue what he had started at OSU; a sports announcing practicum. This extracurricular activity, involving a handful of motivated students, evolved into a permanent sports broadcasting class, which led to this book.

At the end of each chapter, the reader will find the names of other MVPs, who reviewed or contributed to the success of that chapter. A very special thanks goes out to them.

Additionally, I would like to thank *Elizabeth Beal,* who performed the darkroom work on many of the photographs, and to a number of students in my classes who helped with the editing of the manuscript. They include *Rafael Denson, Stephanie Guthrie, Kyle Haley, Teah McDugle, Andrea Murdock,* and *Cary Taylor.*

Finally, I would like to thank many other professional broadcasters, sports officials, sports executives, and coaches who provided valuable information and insight.

Broadcasters include: *Brian Barnhart,* Oklahoma City '89ers baseball; *Bob Barry,* Sports Director, KFOR-TV, Oklahoma City; *Dean Blevins,* Sports Anchor, KOCO-TV, Oklahoma City; *Mick Cornett,* Sports Director, KOCO-TV, Oklahoma City; *Bob Costas,* Sports Announcer, NBC-TV; *Tom Dirato,* Color Analyst, Oklahoma State University broadcasts; *Al Eschback,* Sports Talk Radio Host, WWLL, Norman, Oklahoma; *Ron Franklin,* Play-by-Play Announcer, ESPN; *David Garrett,* Play-by-Play Announcer, New Orleans Saints; *Curt Gowdy,* Former NBC-TV Play-by-Play Announcer; *Rex Holt,* Sports Director, KSPI Radio, Stillwater, Oklahoma; *Keith Jackson,* Sports Announcer, ABC-TV; *Larry Reece,* Play-by-Play Announcer, KSPI Radio, Stillwater, Oklahoma; *Bill Simonson,* Sports Talk Radio Host, KTOK, Oklahoma City; *Dick Stockton,* Sports Announcer, Fox TV; *Bill Teegins,* Play-by-Play Announcer, Oklahoma State University broadcasts; *Lesley Visser,* Sports Announcer, CBS-TV; and *John Walls,* Sports Director, KOTV, Tulsa, Oklahoma.

Coaches include: *Steve Anthis,* Oklahoma State University basketball; *Kendall Cross,* Oklahoma State University wrestling; *Randall Dickey,* Oklahoma State University basketball; *Paul Graham,* Oklahoma State University basketball; *Henry P. Iba* (deceased), Oklahoma State University basketball; *Pat Jones,* Oklahoma State University football; *Bill Miller,* Oklahoma State University football; *Russ Pennell,* University of Mississippi basketball; *Tony Purler,* Oklahoma State University wrestling; *Bill Self,* Oral Roberts University basketball; *Jim Shields,* Oklahoma State University wrestling; *John Smith,* Oklahoma State University wrestling; *Eddie Sutton,* Oklahoma State University basketball; and *Gary Ward,* Oklahoma State University baseball.

Game Officials include: *Jim Byers,* Central Hockey League; *Kent Houck,* Big Eight football conference; *Duane Smith,* Big Eight basketball conference; and *Bob Wedlake,* Central Hockey League.

Managers and Professors include: *Robert Burton,* NCAA Compliance Officer, Oklahoma State University; *Steve Buzzard,* Sports Information

Director, Oklahoma State University; *Bob Dellinger,* Executive Director (retired), U.S. Wrestling Hall of Fame; *Tony Linville,* Executive Director, U.S. Wrestling Hall of Fame; *Steve Edwards,* Sports Psychologist, Oklahoma State University; *Jim Garner,* Vice President, Shreveport Pirates, Canadian Football League; *Brad Lund,* General Manager, Oklahoma City Blazers Hockey Club; *Dave Martin,* Interim Athletic Director, Oklahoma State University; *Steve Smethers,* Assistant Professor, Oklahoma State University; and *Michael Strauss,* Associate Director of Sports Information, Oklahoma State University.

Broadcast Engineers include: *Joe Commare,* Chief Engineer, EBU International, Atlanta; and *Bill Hodges,* School of Journalism and Broadcasting, Oklahoma State University.

Finally, a word about our guest speaker. I'm not ashamed to say it. Curt Gowdy is my hero. I believe he represents the finest that sports broadcasting and sports announcing has to offer. During his many years before the microphone, he has exhibited the skill, the knowledge, and perhaps most importantly, the class to inform and entertain sports fans in a manner that few people have ever been able to do.

Curt Gowdy may be an unfamiliar name to some readers. To a mature audience, however, he is recognized as one who helped set the standard for today's generation of sports announcers. Not all of them, just those whose professional and non-frenetic delivery emulates the style of the "Cowboy from Wyoming."

I first became aware of Curt Gowdy when he was calling American Football League games in the early 1960s. He had already achieved success as the voice of the New York Yankees and Boston Red Sox. As a Chicago-area native, I had not heard of Mr. Gowdy until NBC hired him to cover the AFL.

His professional approach to sports broadcasting was clearly apparent. And as the appendix to this book illustrates, Curt Gowdy was honored by the National Academy of Television Arts and Sciences in 1991 for a lifetime of achievement in his craft. He also has been named National Sportscaster of the Year on three different occasions. He is the recipient of the Ford Frick Award, which is given by the Baseball Hall of Fame, and the Pete Rozelle Award, which is given by the Professional Football Hall of Fame. In 1970 he was honored with the George Foster Peabody Award for high achievement in radio and television. He is the only sports announcer ever to earn the Peabody.

Ladies and gentlemen, I'm proud to present the individual who has covered more major sports events than anyone else in the history of sports broadcasting: Curtis Gowdy, Sr.

Introduction
by Curt Gowdy

I wish I had had this book when I was starting out in the business. But then, this book would not have been possible, because the business was still defining itself. Everything about it was easier then. For one thing there was less pressure because sports broadcasting had yet to be associated with big money. For another, covering a game on radio or television was far simpler. Technology consisted of little more than a couple of microphones and a couple of cameras. Graphics, instant replay, and super slo-mo hadn't been invented.

Heck, when I started out, the six-man high school football game I covered didn't have what everyone now takes for granted: yard-line markers on the field and numbers on the uniforms. There weren't even any rosters available. I did what any green kid from Cheyenne would do. I made up the names. But instead of getting disciplined after the game, I was complimented. Station Manager Bill Grove was delighted and called me "a natural."

Can you imagine someone trying the same thing today? I guarantee you, he or she would get fired. Today, even at the high school level, the importance of presenting a positive image during a sports broadcast is well recognized. That's why even the smallest sports organization will exert maximum effort to provide the broadcaster with the necessary tools to air a quality show.

But I was lucky. I didn't get fired, and two years later, in 1945, I was "discovered" while working for KFBC in Cheyenne. It was like a Hollywood movie script. Ken Brown, the general manager of KOMA-AM in Oklahoma City, was on vacation, and he heard me doing a basketball game. At the time, he was also looking for someone to broadcast University of Oklahoma football and basketball games. I was hired on the spot. I'd spent most of my life in Wyoming, but now I was going to head for the big time and major college broadcasting.

Sure, it was luck. But I don't think I would have had any chance at all if it hadn't been for my Mom. When I was in high school, she insisted I take elocution lessons. You can imagine how a teenage boy would react to that! But I did it. Then Mom insisted I learn how to type. I was the only boy in my high school typing class. If you think I got teased, you're right. But if it weren't for Mom's insistence, I'm convinced I would not have achieved the success that I did. That's because good writing goes hand in hand with clear speaking. That combination also helps a person to think more intelligently. The result is greater self-confidence.

Anyway, I got hired by KOMA and for nearly five years I covered Sooners football and basketball. In 1945, Oklahoma A & M (now Oklahoma State) won the NCAA basketball title under legendary coach Henry P. Iba. As a result, I convinced management to allow me to cover both Sooner and Aggie basketball the following season. It was a great decision, because the Aggies won the national title again, becoming the first school to win back-to-back titles.

I guess you'll allow me to be a bit nostalgic when I recall this. And in a way, it's especially fitting that I contribute to this book, since much of its content is the result of Oklahoma State University athletic department folks. And like me, the author of this book moved to Oklahoma from the cold north in search of greater successes.

During those years, some of the Sooner and Aggie games were broadcast on a delayed basis. The recordings were not on tape as is the practice today, because tape hadn't been invented yet. Instead, we used 15-inch records that comprised the standard radio station recording method of the day. It was called an *electrical transcription*.

I had great fun in Oklahoma, and I learned a lot—about sports and about myself. Plus, I was fortunate to be associated with two of the greatest college coaches of all time, Bud Wilkinson in football and Henry Iba in basketball. They were marvelous in the help they gave in learning more about their respective sports.

Greater opportunity was to follow. In 1949 I was hired as part of the New York Yankee baseball games. I had been broadcasting the Oklahoma City Indians in the Texas League for three years. In the fall of 1948, I received a letter from George Weiss, the General Manager of the Yankees, stating that Russ Hodges had left the Yankees to move over to the Giants, thus leaving an opening on the Yankee broadcast team. Would I come to apply?

I sent in a recording of my work plus a resume thinking I would never hear from Mr. Weiss again. About a month later I received a telegram from Weiss inviting me for a personal interview. When I got there I found out that the Yankees had over three hundred applicants but had narrowed the choice down to three minor league play-by-play announcers.

I met Mel Allen in person, which was a big thrill, and the next day received the greatest break of my life by being named as Mel's new partner on the Yankees broadcast. He taught me the value of listening to the other's commentary, so as to complement each other on the air. I also learned that I needed two hours to prepare for each hour of anticipated play-by-play. There's no substitute for doing your homework. Another time, I learned the importance of checking and double-checking facts and pronunciations. That lesson came during an NCAA regional tournament basketball game in 1978. Al McGuire and I had been assigned to telecast the doubleheader of Arkansas versus Weber State and UCLA versus Kansas.

After the first game, Al and I had to go down to the basement of the field house to do a separate halftime show. We were late in getting upstairs for the second game and breathlessly arrived at our broadcast table just as they were tipping off for UCLA–Kansas. I had carefully prepared my identification boards with myriad notes on the players. I desperately searched for them while the play was going on. They were completely covered by sheets of stats and notes dropped on the table from the first game. My statistician had scribbled down the starting line-ups and misspelled two of the names. I kept using the wrong first names of those two players until the bell rang in my head that something didn't sound right. I retrieved my own line-ups, corrected the two names, and apologized.

But all hell broke loose the next day. The newspapers made a big thing of it. It wasn't exactly my fault but I couldn't blame the poor stat man (who was a college student).

I took complete responsibility and apologized on NBC the following week. I had learned that you take nothing for granted and how important preparation was.

That was a moment I'd like to forget, but can't. Another mistake that was more serious, but thankfully not my fault, was the now-famous NFL telecast of the "Heidi Game," which is described in this book. When NBC clipped the final minute in order to begin a broadcast of "Heidi" at the top of the hour, I naturally stopped announcing. After all, we were off the air. Later, realizing their mistake, especially in light of the game's dramatic finish, the network scheduled a taped broadcast of the final minute during the NBC evening news and the next morning's newscasts. I was asked to provide the play-by-play. You can imagine how tough it was to fake surprise and enthusiasm after the fact. Incidentally, that game changed network scheduling policies forever.

I've had a lot of memorable moments covering sports. And that includes high school and college, in addition to the pro level. In fact, some of my best memories are from the early part of my career in Wyoming and Oklahoma. They're special to me, although few readers would appreciate the excitement of a six-man football title game in one of America's most sparsely populated states, or listening to the late University of Oklahoma football coach Bud Wilkinson talk about his philosophy of coaching, or seeing Henry Iba teaching Bob Kurland, one of the first seven-footers to play basketball, how to block shots. Kurland's shot-blocking skills, incidentally, led to the rule that prohibits shots from being blocked during the ball's downward arc.

On the professional level, there've been numerous events I've broadcast that I recall with fondness. They include the 1969 World Series, when those Amazing New York Mets beat the Baltimore Orioles, four games to one, and Hank Aaron's dramatic 715th major league home run in 1974, breaking Babe Ruth's career record.

But perhaps the single most significant event I covered is Super Bowl III, following the 1968 season, when the New York Jets of the upstart American Football League beat the Baltimore Colts, 16–7. The AFL came of age on that day and I was especially pleased, because of my association with the league as its lead play-by-play announcer. I went on to broadcast a total of eight Super Bowls, along with sixteen World Series and eight Olympics. All these were certainly memorable events, but the sight of Joe Namath jogging off the field, holding his hand in the air with one finger extended in victory, is something I'll never forget. Sports memories do indeed last a lifetime.

For the young man or woman deciding on a career, I can think of few things that can equal the excitement and fulfillment that one can find in sports broadcasting. With enthusiasm and a positive attitude, one can achieve satisfaction in any facet of the business; whether it's producing, announcing, or anything else; in large markets or small; radio or television. It's a heck of a way to earn a living.

I have always been an avid reader both for knowledge and entertainment. It helps your vocabulary and gives you background. In the world of radio and TV, I discovered the written word was so important. I used to be sports editor of the Wyoming Eagle and my high school paper. Marshaling your thoughts and expressing them in an orderly, interesting fashion are priceless. Most of the great announcers I know write their own material for sportscasts and openings and closings. If I had it to do over, I would take combined courses of journalism and broadcasting in college. Even if you do not move on in a broadcast career, the time you spend in broadcasting will help you in other jobs.

I remember that one day, while serving as the Boston Red Sox play-by-play announcer, I came home after a game in a bad mood. A local sports columnist had taken a shot at me in the papers that morning, I received a couple of bad letters in the day's mail, and the Red Sox had lost the game to cap off a lousy day.

Upon arriving home, I went directly to the kitchen, took out a cold beer, and sat down at the kitchen table while my wife was fixing dinner. "You know what," I said to Jerre, "I'm going to get out of this business. Everyone is always trying to nail you." My wife replied, "Curt, I want to ask you something. I want you to sit there quietly and think...think about how many men in this country would like to have your job?"

I sat there thinking, and after a while I said, "You know what? You're right. You will never hear me bring it up again."

1 The History of Radio Sports

P heidippides was not the first broadcaster, but he could have been. He is best known in history for starting a sport and operating without a microphone. Pheidippides was a Greek runner who was sent from Marathon to Athens to convey the news that the Persian army had been defeated. Pheidippides completed his mission, presumably before a small audience, then dropped dead. Color analysts had not yet been invented, as the year was 490 B.C. The marathon race developed from that historic moment, and is now best known as an Olympic event, for which there are numerous color analysts.

Indeed, in the short span of barely a century, sports broadcasting has come a long way. Radio, television, and cable have brought millions of sports events described by millions of announcers to billions of persons all over the world. New technologies will bring even more events to more people in ways we can only imagine.

Sports broadcasting through the electronic media did not begin with the human voice, however. It began with the telegraph, which helped provide early reports of baseball games to subscribers around the nation. Even during those early beginnings, the question of rights came up. Did a telegraph company have the right to report the action on the field? Or did the teams "own" the action? In the case of one game in

1

Cleveland in 1873, the baseball team said it owned the rights to its entertainment, and denied admission to the telegrapher. But the resourceful Western Union operator didn't give up. He climbed a nearby tree, patched into a line, viewed the game, and transmitted his dots and dashes.

Often, there was a telegrapher at the other end who would read the Morse code, and then announce the play through a megaphone. Such was the case for the 1912 World Series between the Boston Red Sox and the New York Giants. Thousands of fans gathered in New York's Times Square or at various railroad stations to follow the games in progress.

April 11, 1921

When commercial radio began in 1921, sports broadcasting began right along with it. Florent Gibson, a sportswriter for the *Pittsburgh Post*, may have been the first person ever to provide a broadcast sports play-by-play. Gibson was asked to give a blow-by-blow description of a prizefight from Pittsburgh's Motor Square Garden. The date was April 11, 1921, less than six months after KDKA-AM had signed on the air. KDKA, still owned by Westinghouse Broadcasting Company, is generally acknowledged as America's first radio station, having first signed on on November 2, 1920.

The first sports event heard simultaneously on two stations occurred on July 2, 1921. The event was a heavyweight title fight held in Jersey City, New Jersey, across the Hudson River from New York City. That day, Jack Dempsey successfully defended his crown with a fourth-round knockout of Georges Carpentier. Calling the bout for New York stations WJZ and WJY was J. Andrew White, editor of a magazine called *Wireless Age*. White was assisted ringside by David Sarnoff, who later would gain fame as president and chairman of RCA, the parent company that for many years owned the NBC radio and television networks. White described the action into a telephone. At the other end was a WJY engineer, J.O. Smith. Wearing earphones, Smith heard the blow-by-blow action and repeated it into his own microphone. Although radio was less than a year old, it was estimated that 300,000 persons heard the broadcast that day. It also was credited as the first sports re-creation, a type of broadcast that would continue until the end of the twentieth century.

Tennis was the second sport to be carried on radio, when Pittsburgh's KDKA began three days of Davis Cup coverage on August 4, 1921. A day later, baseball was to begin a relationship with radio that has never stopped. That's when KDKA began carrying Pirates games. Harold

Arlin, later recognized as the world's first full-time announcer, aired that first game, between Pittsburgh and the Philadelphia Phillies. The Pirates won, 8–5.

Both New York teams won pennants that year: the Giants and the Yankees. This created a great opportunity for radio to capitalize on its growing popularity. It was a newspaper reporter, Sandy Hunt of the Newark, New Jersey *Sunday Call,* who recognized it and convinced WJZ to carry the games. But the phone company refused to install telephone lines in the press box of the Polo Grounds, the Giants' home park. Determined to cover the World Series, WJZ bought a box seat and had the phone line placed there. That's where Hunt sat, describing the action by telephone to Thomas H. "Tommy" Cowan, who was listening at the WJZ studios. He took Hunt's descriptions and repeated them word-for-word. Though they were Hunt's words, it was Cowan who received the credit as the World Series' first announcer.

At the end of that historic game, which the Giants had won, 3–0, Cowan had a sore ear and a numb hand from pressing the heavy telephone earpiece against his head. For the games that followed, Cowan was outfitted with a pair of headphones. The Giants won the Series, five games to three. The broadcasts were an immediate success, as evidenced by more than 4,000 letters the station received from listeners.

This made the 1922 World Series easier to cover. For one thing, WJZ did not have to resort to creative methods to get a phone line installed. And with the Giants and Yankees repeating as pennant winners, all games again were played in New York. That year, Grantland Rice, one of America's greatest newspaper sports reporters, handled the play-by-play. For the second year in a row, the Giants became world champions.

Later that fall, WJZ began college football broadcasts, also from the Polo Grounds. W.S. Flitcraft, another newspaperman, handled the play-by-play. The year 1922 also saw what may have been the first live broadcast of a sports event occurring hundreds of miles away from the station airing it—a football game from Stagg Field on the University of Chicago campus. Chicago's game with Princeton on October 28, 1922 was heard live over WEAF in New York.

Interviews with athletes soon became an important part of sports broadcasting. Perhaps one of the earliest examples was what became known as the "non-interview" with New York Yankee legend Babe Ruth. During a stop in Pittsburgh for an exhibition game, Ruth was invited to the KDKA studios. He accepted, but as the interview was about to begin, Ruth developed a case of mike fright. Even in those early days, reporters proved resourceful. One of those in the studio that day was a newspaper reporter who had written a speech that the Babe was to have delivered on another occasion. When it became obvious that the Bambino could not move his lips with the grace that he moved his bat, the reporter produced the speech. Announcer Harold Arlin read it. Later, the station was to receive letters commenting on the quality of Babe Ruth's voice. This may have been the first, and perhaps only, radio interview that was conducted thanks to the combined efforts of a ghost writer and a ghost speaker!

Graham McNamee

Though Gibson, Arlin, Hunt, Cowan, Rice, and Flitcraft helped to form the beginnings of sports broadcasting, it was Graham McNamee who became the first well-known play-by-play announcer. McNamee had played in five sports in high school, but his career goal was to become a singer. When he found it difficult to find employment, McNamee accepted a position as an announcer for WEAF, another New York City station. Originally, he was assigned to announcing concerts. But on August 23, 1923, he launched his sportscasting career when he was asked to handle the blow-by-blow description of a middleweight fight between champion Johnny Wilson and Harry Greb.

McNamee had prepared for this broadcast in a manner one might follow today. That is, he was organized and thorough. First, he visited both training camps. He talked with both fighters and their handlers. On the day of the broadcast—again from the Polo Grounds—McNamee arrived early, as final preparations were being made. Because of his dedication and personal experience as a boxer, McNamee easily described the various types of punches and blocks. He was commended by the station manager for doing a great job, and reassigned to covering sports full time. McNamee was on his way to making a name for himself as America's first outstanding sports announcer.

His next major assignment was the 1923 World Series, once again between the Giants and Yankees. But this time, McNamee was told he would be the color commentator, talking only between innings. The play-by-play was to be handled by yet another newspaper sports reporter, William O. "Bill" McGheehan of the New York *Tribune*.

By the third game of the series, however, McGheehan decided he'd had enough of this newfangled invention and went back to his typewriter. McNamee was again responsible for the entire broadcast. But he soon realized that baseball was not like boxing. Action was not continuous. McNamee soon developed techniques for sustaining interest by talking about the crowd, celebrities in the audience, signs from the dugout, pitchers in the bullpen, and so on. Again, the broadcasts proved successful, as evidenced by nearly 1,700 letters received by the station.

TIME-OUT 1.1

Graham McNamee . . . On the Air

Radio held the fascination of America for many years. When Graham McNamee became a popular sportscaster, the *New York Times* transcribed and published an entire broadcast. What follows is a brief excerpt of a New York Yankee-St. Louis Browns game of October 7, 1926:

Hafey is batting. One strike, just over the inside corner, a fast ball almost shoulder high. A fly to Babe Ruth. Can't tell yet. Babe got it! One of the prettiest catches you ever saw in your life. A foul ball that was over the barrier, and Babe ran and slammed up against the barrier, got his hand over, almost touching the populace inside the grandstand, and took the foul with his gloved hand.

I hope to tell you that was a catch! It wasn't only a hard catch, but it was the danger of running into that heavy barrier out there in right field at the same time. It took nerve to go and get that ball.

O'Farrell is up. On an attempted steal they put him out, catcher to short. The throw was a little low. Quite low. It touched the ground before Koenig caught it, but he made the put-out very nicely.

The crowd over by the Yankee dugout is giving Ruth a fine hand as he comes in, following his circus catch out in left field.

Ted Husing

Barely a year after Graham McNamee made his mark in radio as the industry's first true sports announcer, Edward Britt "Ted" Husing went to work at WJZ, a New York City station owned by RCA. Husing loved to read, to learn new words, and to talk. When he answered a newspaper ad announcing the WJZ opening, Husing was one of six hundred applicants. Then, as now, broadcast openings attracted a tremendous number of applications. But because Husing had practiced and rehearsed before the audition, he got the job. Having previously worked as a carnival barker probably helped as well.

Later, Husing was to broadcast Braves baseball games for WBET in Boston, followed by Columbia University football for WHN in New York. Husing rapidly gained a reputation as a good sports announcer. In fact, some considered him better than Graham McNamee.

In 1925, Husing and Phil Carlin formed a team known as "The WEAF Twins" to broadcast major college football games. Each week the two men would alternate between play-by-play and color chores. However, the "color" portion of the announcing was not as we would define it today. It more closely resembled the job of a spotter, who would identify the runner and the name of the player who made the tackle. The play-by-play announcer described the play, including down and yards gained.

Broadcast Sports Comes of Age

The 1925 World Series marked a turning point for both sports and broadcasting. The American people began to depend upon the four-year-old medium to provide instantaneous information and entertainment. Nowhere did these two elements blend so well as in sports. When Graham McNamee provided the drama of a seven-game series between Pittsburgh and the Washington Senators (won by the Pirates), station WEAF received 50,000 letters from listeners, and McNamee went on to win the *Radio Digest* magazine award as the most popular announcer in America.

The Cubs

The year also was marked by the extension of sports broadcasting to America's heartland. Phillip Wrigley was one of the first major league baseball owners to recognize the value of live coverage. He believed the broadcasts added to the popularity of the sport, and certainly to his team, the Chicago Cubs. WMAQ, then owned by the *Chicago Daily News,* began covering Cubs baseball from Wrigley Field on June 1, 1925, with Harold O. "Hal" Totten handling the play-by-play. But WMAQ did not have an exclusive. WGN, owned by the *Chicago Tribune,* also covered the Cubs and the White Sox. Probably because he worked both teams, Quinlan Augustus "Quin" Ryan quickly became Chicago's best-known sports broadcaster. By the late 1920s, the Cubs became the first team to allow broadcasts of all games, and by 1934, any station that wanted to air Cubs games could, provided the station ran at least five promotional announcements before the game started.

The Cubs, steeped in baseball tradition, have been blessed by two other announcers following Hal Totten. Bert Wilson and Harry Caray often were more recognizable than the players they covered. In the decades that followed World War II, Wilson was the voice of the Cubs. He is best remembered for his trademark slogan: "We don't care who wins, as long as it's the Cubs." Wilson was one of sports broadcasting's most enthusiastic "homers." His colorful and passionate delivery left no question as to which team he was rooting for, because he was an unabashed fan of the Cubs. As the twentieth century ended, Harry Caray staffed the play-by-play mike. He is perhaps best known as the song leader for "Take Me Out to the Ball Game" during the seventh-inning stretch. When the Cubs actually won a game, during this usually lackluster period in Wrigley Field history, Caray would utter, "Cubs win, Cubs win," at the final out.

Long-Distance Broadcasting

Many early radio stations were owned by electronic manufacturing firms. The reason was simple; by offering programming the American people wanted, there would be a demand for radio receivers. Thus, most of those who started stations were more interested in selling equipment than in providing music or sports. Examples were RCA, Westinghouse, Crosley, and AT&T. The latter, through its subsidiary, Western Electric, owned WEAF in New York. Western Electric used WEAF as a laboratory to show other broadcasters that long-distance broadcasting, using the telephone, of course, was feasible.

WEAF was thus at the forefront of providing long-distance broadcasting, and the most logical of programming was sports. It started with college football. In Chicago, WGN broadcast University of Illinois football from Champaign, 137 miles to the south, plus the Indianapolis 500 and the Kentucky Derby.

Re-Creations

Another form of distance broadcasting involved what is known as re-creations. Re-creations were different from live broadcasts in three major ways: (1) instead of a telephone line, a telegraph wire was used; (2) instead of reporting from the event, the announcer was in a radio station studio; and (3) instead of immediate reporting, broadcasts could be delayed minutes, hours, and in a few instances, decades.

Re-creations were devised as an economical method of covering events many miles away from a broadcast station. By doing so, a station saved money by avoiding the costs of: (1) expensive telephone lines; (2) travel, hotel, and meal expenses for its announcer; and (3) overtime pay for the announcer. Other broadcasters were forced to adopt re-creations, because some teams would not permit live coverage.

For all broadcasters, there was a side benefit. Because games could be delayed, scheduling could be streamlined. For example, WJJD in Chicago would schedule a White Sox-Red Sox broadcast from Boston to

TIME-OUT 1.2

Code Talkers

Western Union play-by-play was initially sent to a radio station in Morse code. By the late 1920s, when the teleprinter was developed, telegraphic play-by-play was delivered in the form of printed letters and numbers. This meant a person familiar with the dots and dashes of the Morse code no longer was required at a radio station to decipher the transmission. By either system, the information was sent as a form of shorthand. For example, this is how the plate appearance of a typical batter might have been sent by a telegrapher:

Code	*Explanation*
BONDS UP—BATS RIGHT	Announcer expected to know first name
B1 LO OS	Ball one, low and outside
S1 C	Strike one called. Count is 1 and 1
S2 S	Swung and missed. Strike 2
B2 HI IS	Ball, high and inside. Count is 2 and 2
F1 TO RF FENCE	Long fly, foul, toward right field fence
B2 IN DIRT	Ball 3, low in dirt. Full count
S3 C	Bonds called out on strikes

air between 3:00 and 4:30. In reality, the game might have begun at 12:30, Chicago time, and would certainly be over by 3:00 in virtually all instances (at that time, baseball games were played more quickly than they are today). Announcers would then re-create the game at a pace faster than reality. It was always interesting to note that hitters hit the first ball pitched more frequently in re-creations than they did in home games carried live. That was one technique for speeding up action. Today, of course, a play-by-play announcer would face severe criticism, and perhaps discipline, for not reporting the action accurately.

Faking live coverage was commonplace. In 1930, for example, Harold Carter, an Englishman who called himself Boake Carter on the air, was hired by WCAU in Philadelphia to broadcast an Oxford-Cambridge boat race. In reality, he was not in England but in the United States, broadcasting from a studio and playing a record of crowd noise.

The system for re-creating games was simple. Western Union telegraphers already were based at a ballgame, providing reports to other clients. It was thus a simple matter for a station to subscribe to the service at nominal cost. In addition to the announcer at the studio, the station also had to hire a telegrapher who could read the dots and dashes. But this pay was minimal compared to the other costs listed above.

With a minimum of information coming to them by telegraph, announcers drew upon their own creativity to embellish a baseball broadcast. They found ways of creating the sound of bat hitting ball, generally by slapping a wooden ruler against the top edge of a desk. Crowd noise, recorded earlier at the local ballpark, was played back as background noise. Whenever an exciting play occurred, the volume was increased for a few seconds.

Education

Educators embraced the new medium early in its history, and began offering courses at the university level for students wishing to pursue careers as announcers. Although Northwestern, Missouri, and Columbia were mentioned most prominently, none of these is believed to have been the first to launch a course in radio broadcasting. That credit goes to Washington State University, which began, as early as 1926, what some claim was the first course in radio broadcasting. A student who was enrolled at the time was young Egbert Roscow Murrow, a native of Polecat, North Carolina. Egbert aired a few sportscasts for campus station KWSC during his college career. Later, he would change his name and devote himself to exclusively covering the news as Edward R. Murrow.

A Landmark Year

The year 1927 was one of the most significant in the histories of both sports and sports broadcasting. On New Year's Day, NBC launched its first coast-to-coast broadcast of any kind, with coverage of the Rose Bowl game from Pasadena, California. Graham McNamee handled the play-by-play of the game between Stanford and Alabama. The 7–7 tie confirmed a game with little action. And, as a result, McNamee met with some criticism. He was accused of sacrificing accuracy in the interest of excitement in his game descriptions. But McNamee had no apologies, saying enthusiasm was what his broadcasts were all about.

The year also is remembered for Babe Ruth's record of sixty home runs, and for a controversial heavyweight title fight between Gene Tunney and champion Jack Dempsey. The bout, known as "the long count," occurred in Chicago on September 22, 1927. McNamee also covered this event, which is considered the highlight of his career, although his broadcast performance also had its detractors. Through the first few rounds, Dempsey seemed to be on his way to defending his crown, but after knocking Tunney down in the seventh round, Dempsey did not go to a neutral corner, as the rules required. As a result, the count did not begin until he had. This gave Tunney what is estimated as four extra seconds to regain his senses and his feet. Hence the term "long count." Tunney recovered and won the title by a unanimous decision.

When Tunney finally go up, McNamee said so, but many listeners insisted he had said "out" instead of "up." A recording of the broadcast confirmed that McNamee had said "up." Probably what McNamee should have said, for clarity, in those days of scratchy reception, was "Tunney is back up on his feet."

First known as the Columbia Broadcasting System, CBS began operations in 1927. The network became a leader in sports broadcasting on radio and later, television. CBS hired Ted Husing as its first and principal sportscaster.

The Megaphone

Some early broadcasters first developed their skills by working as public address announcers. Their only equipment was the megaphone. This limited tool required both clarity of voice and volume. In 1928, Tom Manning became the first play-by-play announcer for the Cleveland Indians, after eight years as the team's PA announcer. On his first radio broadcast, Manning talked so loudly that reports said he blew station WJAY off the air.

The Derby of 1929

Early sports broadcasts often saw more than one station or network covering the same event. The Chicago Cubs broadcasts were one such example. Another was the Kentucky Derby of 1929, when both CBS and NBC covered the race. Ted Husing worked alone for CBS, the station he had joined only two years before. Clem McCarthy, who was to make a name for himself as America's most recognized horse race broadcaster, had a crew of thirteen. Each announcer declared a different winner, but it was Husing, working alone, who turned out to be right, by calling Clyde Van Dusen the winning horse.

A major crisis in the development of broadcast sports was narrowly averted that year. That's when American League club owners, at their annual meeting, gave serious consideration to banning all radio coverage.

THE HISTORY OF RADIO SPORTS

St. Louis Browns owner Phil Ball declared that he would prohibit broadcasts of any of his team's games the following year. Even though the ban was not approved as league policy, owners recognized that broadcasters were making money from their games. This would soon lead to the payment of rights fees.

The Early 1930s

Barely ten years after the introduction of radio, it had become an important part of the American way of life. By then, most families had a radio that served as the centerpiece of the living room, much as a television set does today. Families would gather around, listening to music and drama in the evening; and on weekends, they would hear broadcasts of various sports events.

TIME-OUT 1.3

Network Rules

By the mid-1930s, barely ten years after radio had started, stations and networks had defined the role of the announcer. As a result, audition scripts had become part of the application process. When they were hired, announcers were required to follow some basic rules. For example, one network, now extinct, had these posted policies:

- Don't smoke in the studio.
- Don't worry.
- Don't change your natural style.
- Don't fail to rehearse your show.
- Don't touch the microphone.
- Don't drink liquor, beer, milk, or soft drinks before going on the air.
- Don't eat ice cream or a heavy meal within an hour of your broadcast.
- Don't go on the air if you don't live up to these don'ts.

These rules may seem humorous as written, but they are just as valid today as they were sixty years ago. Any professional sports announcer abides by these rules as a matter of course.

The prohibition against certain drinks is just good sense. Dairy products such as milk, ice cream, and even artificial powdered coffee creamers can cause severe throat congestion that may take an hour or more to clear. Carbonated soft drinks can result in an embarrassing on-the-air belch!

The early '30s also saw technology enter the broadcast booth, with the invention of the electric football spotting board. Developed by Ted Husing and named "The Annunciator Board," it listed eleven players for each team, with a light bulb by each name. The spotter would activate any of the twenty-two lights to indicate which player had made the run or tackle. This board may have worked well when the game had players who played both defense and offense, but probably was doomed when free substitutions and two-platoon football came into vogue. Besides, it's just as easy to point to a name as flip a switch.

As broadcasting became more sophisticated, so did requirements for employment. Applicants for NBC positions faced a rigorous audition, which included a test of their ability to read the following without stumbling: "The seething sea ceaseth, and thus the seething sea sufficeth us."

"Dutch" Reagan

In 1932, a young man named Ronald Reagan was graduated from Eureka College in Illinois, where he had played football. He borrowed the family car and drove to Davenport, Iowa, telling the program director at WOC he wanted to be a sports announcer. The PD had Reagan pretend to broadcast a fictitious football game. Apparently, he did well enough, because he was hired to do the remainder of the University of Iowa football season at a starting salary of $5 a game.

The following year, Reagan was promoted to WOC's co-owned WHO in Des Moines, a much larger city, after convincing management he was capable of covering track meets. Track meets attracted more interest then, compared to the present day. With the promotion, his salary had tripled to $75 a week. At the same time, he changed his air name to Dutch Reagan, because he did not believe the name Ronald worked for a sports announcer.

Later, as president, Ronald Reagan enjoyed telling reporters and others about his days in sports broadcasting, especially the techniques employed in sports re-creation, when he would air the Chicago Cubs over WHO. For example, in 1935, WHO lost telegraphic service from Chicago in the bottom of the ninth inning, with the score tied. Reagan had the batter hitting foul balls for six and a half minutes before the line was restored and Dutch learned the batter had popped out. Two years later, Reagan would leave broadcasting for the movies, when Warner Brothers signed him to a $200-a-week contract. This came following a successful screen test while Reagan was covering the Cubs spring training on Catalina Island, off the California coast from Los Angeles.

The Called Shot

The early part of the 1930s saw Graham McNamee involved in yet another broadcast that was to be argued for many years. McNamee was behind the microphone that autumn day in Wrigley Field in 1932 when Babe Ruth supposedly pointed his bat toward the bleacher seats a moment before hitting a home run there. It was the famous "called shot" that was discussed and debated for decades to follow. The incident was more memorable than the Yankees' four-game sweep of the Cubs in the World Series.

From Jock to Mike

Until 1933, play-by-play and color announcers came from various walks of life, but none of them had been renowned athletes. Norman Ross may have been the first to make the jump. Ross was a world-class swimmer, competing internationally, including the 1932 Olympic games in Antwerp, Belgium. Soon after he retired from athletics, Ross worked briefly for the Chicago *Daily Journal,* and then was hired by WIBO to work a World Series game. By late 1933, Ross became a member of the NBC broadcast team.

Jocko Maxwell, a former high school athlete, may have been the first black sports announcer. He went to work in 1935 for WHOM in Jersey City, New Jersey.

Bill Stern

In the fall of 1934, Bill Stern was working as an assistant stage manager at Radio City in New York, the home of NBC. Stern had had some experience broadcasting sports in Rochester during the mid-1920s. With this background on his resume, he convinced NBC officials to give him the opportunity to provide two minutes of play-by-play for three football games Graham McNamee was assigned to cover. He did well and the network told him he could do the Army-Illinois game by himself. Stern was so excited that he asked friends and relatives to send telegrams to the network, saying what a great job he had done. One problem arose, though: the telegrams arrived two days before the scheduled game, and Stern was fired before the broadcast.

That, plus the loss of a leg in a traffic accident, were only temporary setbacks for Stern. By 1935, he was broadcasting Southwest Conference football games, and two years later was rehired by NBC. He would go on to enjoy a long career in sportscasting, which also included television. He had a reputation for using colorful words and colorful language. At times, it is said, he embellished the facts. Nevertheless, he was highly popular with listeners, and in 1939, a *New York Telegram* editor's poll selected Stern as the best sportscaster.

Barber and Brickhouse

Stern was one of the first sports announcers to make the transition from radio to television. Two other early notables were Jack Brickhouse and Red Barber. Brickhouse developed his skills in 1934, when he became sports editor for WMBD in Peoria. He then moved to Chicago and covered a variety of sports for WGN-TV, most notably Cubs and White Sox baseball. Barber joined WLW in Cincinnati as voice of the Reds, for

TIME-OUT 1.4

Purple Hearts

Sports announcers have always sought to be close to the action. This need for nearness, plus the sometimes aggressive style of some broadcasters, has led to a few close calls.

Graham McNamee, who always seemed to find himself in the thick of the action, no matter what it was, got more than he bargained for on August 11, 1935, when he was covering a Soap Box Derby from Akron, Ohio for NBC. During one race, a young driver lost control of his gravity-powered vehicle and crashed into McNamee. He was knocked unconscious. Another broadcaster, Tom Manning of WTAM, Cleveland, suffered two broken vertebrae.

Two years later, Frank Austin was covering a wrestling match for KDKL in Salt Lake City when he found himself in a headlock. One of the wrestlers had been tossed out of the ring by his opponent. The wrestler grabbed Austin in a headlock and dragged him to the ring before realizing his mistake. He later apologized, saying he had suffered a crack on the head that left him temporarily dazed.

Sometimes broadcasters bring it upon themselves. For example, on April 6, 1994, ESPN2 interviewer Jim Rome was taunting New Orleans Saints quarterback Jim Everett during a talk show, by calling him "Chris Evert," an apparent reference to the female tennis star. Everett stood up, pushed a table over on Rome, and then jumped him. Instant replay then shows studio personnel jumping in to separate the two men before any major injury could occur.

$25 a week. In 1935, he and Bob Elson handled Mutual's first World Series broadcasts. Two years later, Elson became the voice of the Chicago White Sox for WGN. On January 1, 1937, Barber broadcast the Villanova-Auburn football game for Mutual, from Havana, as part of Cuba's National Sports Festival. Barber went on to broadcast Brooklyn Dodgers and New York Yankees games. Fans in the New York area loved the rich accent of the Mississippi native. Later, Barber won a Peabody for his commentaries on National Public Radio and became, with Mel Allen, the first two broadcasters to be honored in the Baseball Hall of Fame.

Ford Frick

Ford Frick became president of the National League in 1934, just four years after starting a sportscasting career. He worked first for WOR in New York, and later for WINS. Even after he joined major league baseball, Frick moonlighted by airing college football games in the New York City area.

During the early '30s, Ted Husing, Graham McNamee, and Ford Frick were considered the best of the best, usually ranking in various popularity polls in the order shown above. The next generation, however, soon took over.

UP and INS

The development of regular sports news programming to complement play-by-play coverage took a giant leap on May 15, 1935. That's when both United Press (UP) and International News Service (INS) began offering both news and sports news to radio stations. Acceptance by radio stations was slow because of the cost, but within a few years many stations came to depend upon the news wires. Later, UP and INS would merge and become UPI.

A young reporter by the name of Walter Cronkite left his job with the UP bureau in El Paso, Texas, in 1936 to broadcast football games for WKY in Oklahoma City. Cronkite had previously covered sports for KCMO in Kansas City. He would later gain fame as one of America's best known TV anchors for CBS.

Rights Fusses

Although by the mid-1930s many broadcasters were paying fees for the rights to cover sporting events, others believed they had a duty to cover an event even though team owners denied them access to the stadium.

TIME-OUT 1.5

Remote Remotes

Dave Garroway is best known for hosting the *Today Show* on NBC-TV for many years. Yet, he created several innovations in remote sports broadcasting. Perhaps the most significant was the time in 1938 when he reported a golf tournament for KDKA in Pittsburgh. What was unusual about it was that Garroway was playing in the tournament at the same time! He provided stroke-by-stroke coverage, including his own, through a portable transmitter strapped on his back. In those days of delicate vacuum tube-powered equipment, the heavy transmitter was certain to have affected Garroway's golf score, which was not recorded for posterity.

For example, in 1934, KGHI in Little Rock wanted to broadcast the Traveler baseball games, but was unable to obtain permission from the Southern Association team. Ever resourceful, announcers Waymond Ramsey and Leon Sipes broadcast from a tree located about 500 feet from home plate. A wooden platform had been erected in the tree, and a telephone line installed. Team management went to court, and after a few weeks, the broadcasters were permanently evicted from their perch.

By 1936 it had become clear that baseball did own the rights to its games. This was established as the result of a lawsuit against a station in Jamestown, New York. The suit accused the station of re-creating play-by-play action of the 1934 World Series (between the St. Louis Cardinals and the Detroit Tigers) by listening to the game over another station. The Federal Communications Commission also reinforced the court decision by warning station owner A.E. Newton that any subsequent violation would result in the loss of his broadcast license. It was now clearly established that sports teams could legally sell broadcast rights to their games.

Baseball's property rights were further confirmed in 1938 when a federal court ruled that KQV in Pittsburgh had acted illegally in re-creating Pirates games by listening to two other Pittsburgh stations—WWSW and KDKA. The suit had been filed not only by the baseball team but also by the sponsors of the broadcasts.

In addition to rights, major league baseball team owners faced a second concern involving game broadcasts. Many were afraid the broadcasts resulted in lower attendance. Even minor league owners believed broadcasts of major league games had that effect on their attendance. After all, they reasoned, who would want to see a minor league game when they could hear a big league game on the radio, and at no cost or inconvenience? As a result, in 1936, baseball commissioner Kenesaw Mountain Landis ordered major league teams to restrict authorizing additional coverage of their games.

New York, New York

By 1939, every one of the sixteen major league teams was airing regular season games. The last three holdouts were the New York City teams: the Giants, the Yankees, and the Dodgers. Red Barber left Cincinnati to become the first broadcast voice of the Dodgers, and was heard over WOR and WHN. Al Helfler, who became his assistant, went on to become the lead announcer on other major league team broadcasts.

Arch McDonald won out over six hundred applicants to become the play-by-play announcer for both the Giants and the Yankees home games. This was not as difficult as it may seem, since one team was always on the road when the other played at home. McDonald was helped by a young Southerner named Mel Allen. A year later, Allen replaced McDonald as the chief play-by-play announcer for both the Yankees and the Giants. Allen was to become a prominent sports voice for most of the last half of the twentieth century.

Although they never gained national fame, the Laux brothers did earn the distinction of becoming the first brother sports announcing team on radio. Edward was chief announcer at WAAT in Jersey City. Roger was the sports announcer for WCBS in Springfield, Illinois, and France was chief announcer and sportscaster at KMOX in St. Louis. France was awarded the *Sporting News* trophy as radio's outstanding baseball announcer in 1938.

TIME-OUT 1.6

"She Died Happy"

By 1941, Red Barber and his Southern accent had become an established part of the Brooklyn Dodgers and their broadcasts. Red was earning $15,000 a year for his play-by-play work at a time when many persons were lucky to make one-fifth of that salary. He earned an additional $15,000 for a daily sports show and sports commentary for Pathé News, which was a film production company that provided newsreels for movie theaters.

Listeners had confidence in what he said, and his mail averaged five hundred letters a week. One man wrote: "My wife was a semi-invalid. Yesterday, she began to sink, but she heard the last out. She died happy."

The 1940s

On April 24, 1942, Graham McNamee died at the age of fifty-two. This may have marked the beginning of the end of the early era of sports broadcasting in America. The days of McNamee, Ted Husing, Tommy Cowan, Harold Arlin, and Grantland Rice were ending. They were being replaced by Mel Allen, Red Barber, Clem McCarthy, Lindsay Nelson, and Bill Stern. These would become the dominant national voices of sport for the next thirty years.

TIME-OUT 1.7

Sports and Disasters

Rain during a baseball game is the most common interruption of a sports event. Baseball and other sports events occasionally experience additional weather factors that can postpone, cancel, or prematurely end a game. Although football is often played under less than ideal weather conditions, some games have been called because of deep snow or extreme cold. Golf tournaments are delayed because of thunderstorms. Warm weather can cause fog to form in an indoor ice rink, forcing postponement of a hockey match. Every year, some sort of weather phenomenon affects sporting events around the country.

In the history of sports, however, natural disasters and armed conflicts have had the greatest lasting imprint on broadcast coverage, while also impacting world history.

On December 7, 1941, at 2:26 P.M., Eastern Time, WOR-AM in New York interrupted a Dodger-Giant football game to read a flash that the Japanese had attacked Pearl Harbor, Hawaii. The surprise attack marked the beginning of World War II. A "flash" is the wire service's most urgent of all news stories. Use of a flash occurs very rarely in the news business.

On September 5, 1972, a group of Arab terrorists took ten Israeli athletes hostage at a housing compound in the Olympic village in Munich, Germany. ABC-TV sports announcer Jim McKay informed the world of the activities throughout the day and night. The incident ended tragically with the deaths of all ten athletes, their coach, and three of the terrorists.

On October 17, 1989, the second-worst earthquake in American history struck San Francisco at 5:04 P.M., Pacific Time, just as a World Series game between the Giants and the Oakland Athletics was about to begin. Because of the extensive ABC-TV remote television equipment in place at Candlestick Park for the game, early news pictures were seen across America. Instead of baseball action, play-by-play announcer Al Michaels described the human drama of devastation and death.

Before his death, McNamee listed his eleven greatest moments in sports. What was unusual about the list was not his first choice, but the fact that he mentioned nine different sports; boxing, baseball, football, auto racing, horse racing, swimming, tennis, track, and crew. This shows the early diversity of early radio sports coverage, a tradition that continues in television to this day.

McNamee claimed his most memorable event was the 1927 Dempsey-Tunney long count heavyweight championship fight. Babe Ruth's "called shot" in the 1932 World Series ranked sixth. The other events, while significant in the 1920s and 1930s, are now an obscure part of history, surpassed by present-day "games of the century" every year in collegiate and professional sports. As in McNamee's time, only a few of these present-day "games of a lifetime" will truly live up to their billing and be remembered in the twenty-first century.

Another turning point in sports coverage was marked by the outbreak of World War II, as many of America's future leading sportscasters went into the service of their country. Leading this corps was Lt. Bob Elson, the first serviceman to broadcast a major sports event. While on leave from the Navy, he and Red Barber covered the 1943 World Series between the New York Yankees and the St. Louis Cardinals. Elson would later become the radio voice of the Chicago White Sox. A year later, Sgt. Mel Allen would broadcast sports programs overseas via shortwave.

When the war ended, America began a frantic but happy period of overindulging following the four years of sacrifice. New radio stations popped up throughout America, many in small towns never before served by a radio voice. As a result, new opportunities opened up for coverage of local sports events.

Nationally, television had been developed but was yet to be a force in America's communications picture. Radio was still king, however, and on June 15, 1945, the Blue Network became the American Broadcasting Company. The Blue Network had been part of the NBC radio network.

The year 1945 also was marked by radio's first coverage of basketball; college doubleheaders from New York's Madison Square Garden. Behind the mike was Marty Glickman, a former football star at Syracuse, who broke into broadcasting in 1937. He was the first well-known athlete to make the transition from sports to play-by-play, although Norman Ross had preceded him by four years. Glickman later made the transition into television, where he enjoyed success for many years.

New York City, which was the last town to experience regular coverage of home major league baseball games, in 1946 became the first to air away games live. Before then, games had been covered on a re-creation basis.

Gordon McLendon

Major league baseball was limited in its geographic scope after World War II. No teams were farther west than St. Louis or farther south than Cincinnati. This imbalance was not lost upon Gordon McLendon, a young Texan who started a new AM station in Dallas—KLIF. Choosing to ignore the latest FCC and court rulings, McLendon hired a reporter in 1948 to monitor WABC in New York and send the information by teletype to the KLIF studios, where the game was aired on a re-creation basis.

First to complain was the minor league team in Dallas. It went to court to stop the broadcasts, arguing that radio coverage of a major league game would hurt local attendance. But the suit was dropped when McLendon offered to pay the team $500 for the rights to cover its games. The team took the money and McLendon never aired the minor league games.

The major league broadcasts were so popular that other stations asked for feeds. McLendon formed Liberty Broadcasting System, and by 1952 it had become the second largest radio network in America, with 458 affiliates. Only Mutual was larger. But barely a month into the 1952 season, Liberty was out of business. That's because many of the affiliates were in the northeastern part of the United States, where the major league teams were located. Owners successfully prevented Liberty from airing any games there. Unable to attract sufficient advertising as a result, the network went bankrupt on May 15.

Though bitter and angry, McLendon, who called himself "The Old Scotsman," did not give up. Two years later he announced plans for another network, initially with 175 affiliates. Among the games that would be carried were those of the Chicago Cubs, then heard on KYA in San Francisco. But a California federal district court ruled in favor of both KYA and the Mutual Network. Mutual provided the Cubs broadcasts to KYA and other stations as part of its "Game of the Day" broadcasts, which had begun in 1950. For the first time, the court ruling clearly stated that baseball had the ultimate control of its broadcast distribution rights.

By this time, broadcast rights fees had escalated to about $200,000 a year per team. This was mainly due to the Mutual broadcasts.

The Golden Age of Re-Creation

The 1940s and '50s saw significant increases in baseball re-creations. There were several reasons for this: (1) it was cheaper than sending an announcer to a distant game for live coverage, (2) it cost less to use

Western Union telegraph than AT&T telephone lines, (3) more local stations were beginning to air minor league games, and (4) games could be aired at times more convenient to the station and its audience.

In 1949, Western Union typically charged a station less than $20 to provide coverage of a baseball game. But by 1959 the fees had tripled. This proved to be too expensive for many stations. At that time many of them were charging less than a dollar for a one-minute commercial. A more economical method of getting play-by-play information had to be found. Broadcasters found it in the telephone.

A newspaper reporter, or for that matter, anyone in the pressbox who had a phone handy, would call a station every two innings with a play-by-play synopsis. The sequence of pitches, however, was normally not part of the phoned report. The announcer would add his own balls and strikes, based on his own vivid imagination. This development, therefore, saw the end of accurate baseball reporting, and the beginning of creative play-by-play. The better the theatrical ability of the announcer, the better the game sounded to the fan at home. The telephone also

Bob Robertson of the Tacoma Tigers broadcast team aired the last re-created game in the United States in 1991. (Source: Courtesy of the Tacoma Tigers Baseball Team)

meant that game action might be described half an hour or more after the actual event. Additionally, it soon meant that Western Union was experiencing a decrease in clients subscribing to its complete, pitch-by-pitch service. On September 9, 1979, Western Union discontinued the service, a victim of broadcast economics.

But re-creation would continue well beyond that time. In fact, baseball was not the only sport covered on a re-creation basis. Football, basketball, boxing, and tennis were popular re-creation events. So were soccer and ice hockey, but to a limited degree. The age of re-creation

TIME-OUT 1.8

Re-Creation Hijinks

Re-creation involved high levels of creativity to make the broadcast sound like it was real. Even though FCC rules required a disclaimer announcement, this did not prevent announcers from doing their best to make the broadcasts sound as real as possible.

Sound effects were the single most important element in adding realism. Slapping a ruler against the desk simulated the crack of a bat. For home runs, one announcer would drop a water glass on the table. The resulting shatter would sound like a window breaking, presumably in a building far beyond the outfield fence. Other announcers struck their fist against a wallet to replicate the sound of ball hitting glove. Public address announcers could be faked by simply talking into a waste basket, slightly off mike.

Crowd noises were important elements in most re-creations. The simplest form was to play a single audio tape of crowd murmur and raise or lower the volume, depending on the action. However, simply increasing the gain (volume) of murmur did not sound realistic. That's why many broadcasters utilized more sophisticated sound effects, involving different kinds of crowd noises for different game situations. When audio cart machines became commonplace in the mid-1960s, realism was further expanded to include sounds of refreshment salesmen, boos and hissing, thunderstorms, and even planes and trains.

Other techniques involved tipping off friends and bosses whenever a home run was about to be hit, or, if the game had already ended in real time, disclosing the winner. This was done through code words while describing non-action activity. For example, talking about warm or cold weather might signify whether the home team had won or lost the game. Other codes would disclose an impending home run.

Radio rapidly gained a reputation for mobility and timeliness, even during the early years. (Source: Courtesy of Hubbard Broadcasting)

Remote coverage often involved utilizing whatever equipment was available, such as this baby carriage. (Source: Courtesy of Hubbard Broadcasting)

FIGURE 1.1: Chronology of Radio Sports Broadcasting

1873	Telegraphic reports of National League baseball games become an accepted part of sports reporting.
1921, April 11	The first sports broadcast, a boxing match, is aired on KDKA, Pittsburgh.
1921, July 2	The first sports broadcast heard on two stations, a heavyweight fight, is heard on WJZ and WJY, New York.
1921, Aug. 4	The first tennis match ever broadcast airs on KDKA, Pittsburgh.
1921	The first World Series (New York Giants and New York Yankees) is aired. Tommy Cowan is the first World Series announcer.
1922	The first college football game to be broadcast is aired from the Polo Grounds in New York.
1922	The first long-distance sports broadcast is heard on WEAF, New York, from Chicago, where the University of Chicago football team played Princeton.
1923, Aug. 23	Graham McNamee, America's first true sports announcer, begins his career by reporting a boxing match.
1924	Ted Husing is hired by WJZ, New York.
1926	Washington State University offers the first college broadcasting course in America.
1927, Jan. 1	The first coast-to-coast broadcast of any kind features the Rose Bowl football game.
1927 (?)	The Chicago Cubs become the first major league team to allow broadcast coverage of all games.
1927, Sept. 22	Graham McNamee broadcasts the historic Dempsey-Tunney "long count" heavyweight fight.
1929	American League owners reject a proposal to ban all radio broadcast coverage of AL games.
1932	Ronald "Dutch" Reagan is hired by WOC, Davenport, to air University of Iowa football games.
1932	Graham McNamee broadcasts Babe Ruth's "called shot" during the Yankees' World Series game with the Cubs in Chicago.
1933	Norman Ross becomes the first athlete to become a sports announcer.
1935, May 15	UP and INS begin offering sports news to radio stations.
1935	Jocko Maxwell, the first black sports announcer, is hired by WHOM, Jersey City, New Jersey.
1935	Mutual Radio Network covers its first World Series, with Red Barber and Bob Elson as announcers.

FIGURE 1.1 (*Continued*)

1936	Courts and FCC rule that baseball owns the rights to its games.
1937, Jan. 1	The first international sports broadcast is aired, featuring a football game between Villanova and Auburn, from Havana, Cuba. Red Barber is the announcer.
1939	All major league baseball teams now permit broadcast coverage of regular season games.
1941, Dec. 7	Dodgers-Giants football game is interrupted by a news bulletin of the Japanese attack on Pearl Harbor.
1943	Lt. Bob Elson becomes the first serviceman to air a major sports event—the World Series.
1946	New York's major league baseball teams begin live coverage of all away games.
1948	Gordon McLendon begins re-creating baseball games on KLIF, Dallas.
1952	Liberty Broadcasting System, owned by McLendon, becomes the second largest radio network in America, with 458 affiliates.
1952	Liberty Broadcasting System files for bankruptcy.
1959	The telephone replaces the telegraph as the main source of acquiring information for re-creation.
1979, Sept. 9	Western Union discontinues telegraphic play-by-play service.
1991	Tacoma Tigers and announcer Bob Robertson discontinue re-creation at the conclusion of the season, becoming the last team to do so.

came to an end with the conclusion of the 1991 baseball season for the Tacoma Tigers of the Pacific Coast League. Bob Robertson, the voice of the Tigers, was the last to voice re-creation on American radio. Now, he travels with the team and covers each away game live.

Packaging

The early resistance to radio coverage of sports events, especially baseball, began to melt in the late 1940s. Not only did major and minor league teams allow broadcasts, they began producing them themselves. There were two reasons for this. First, the teams could earn additional income above and beyond what they might otherwise have earned from simply selling broadcast rights. By also selling advertising and creating a network of several stations, they expanded coverage and interest in the team. Second, some stations simply did not want to go to the expense of airing games. As a result, teams were forced into producing broadcasts if the games were to be heard by a radio audience. Thus, producing games became a matter of necessity.

By the mid-1950s, radio coverage of sports had not only become commonplace, but also reached a level of sophistication that is not much changed to this present day. The last forty years were marked by the creation of thousands of radio stations throughout North America, most of which carried games of local teams—a trend that still continues. This period also was marked by several notable moments. On April 15, 1965, Johnny Most, the venerable voice of the Boston Celtics, uttered his famous phrase, "Havlicek stole the ball," as the Celtics went on to win another NBA title. Simulcasting became popular. Audiences would tune to their favorite radio sportscaster on the radio and watch the game on television after first having turned down the TV volume.

One of the strangest events to mark the history of radio sports broadcasting occurred during 1994. On August 12, when major league baseball players went on strike, WJMP-AM in Kent, Ohio, began playing "Take Me Out to the Ball Game" continuously. Although the station vowed to program only that one song until the strike was settled, the protest ended on October 19, after 57,161 performances. By the end of the year, the station even dropped its sports/talk format.

Despite these minor distractions, radio sports is stronger than ever. It is also different, basing most of its popularity and strength on the coverage of local teams and local events (see figure 1.1 for a chronology of radio sports broadcasting). The spirit of "localism" as envisioned and espoused by the Federal Communications Commission and the Communications Act of 1934 is alive and well in radio sports. However, television has become the medium for national and international sports events.

The MVP for This Chapter

Dr. Steven Smethers, of the School of Journalism and Broadcasting at Oklahoma State University is recognized as America's leading authority on sports re-creation. Much of the material on that subject in this chapter is the result of his original research. I consider him an expert, colleague, and friend.

2

The History of
Television Sports

Radio was barely a teenager when television became a reality in 1939. That's when NBC's New York City station became the first to provide sporadic programming to a handful of set owners. The station first was known as WNBT, and operated on channel 1, before the FCC deleted the channel from the TV spectrum. Later, WNBT moved to channel 4 and became WNBC-TV, where it remains today. NBC was then owned by RCA, the Radio Corporation of America. As in radio, the initial concept of programming was as a promotional tool for the sale of receivers. RCA, Westinghouse, DuMont, and others were in the business of selling radio and TV sets. Programming was only a secondary consideration. Yet, without these companies, broadcasting would not have grown into the multibillion-dollar business it is today.

Within weeks of transmitting the first TV signal, NBC broadcast the first sports event. The date was May 17, 1939. It was a baseball game between Princeton and Columbia. Only one camera was used because that's all NBC owned at the time. Reception was poor, and the camera—mounted on a platform near third base—covered interviews and mostly infield play. At the time only about four hundred TV sets existed in New

The first sports telecast was aired by NBC-TV on May 17, 1939, and featured a college baseball game between Columbia and Princeton. One camera handled the entire game, including interviews. (Source: Courtesy of NBC-TV)

Early sports television coverage had limited equipment and was broadcast in black and white. (Source: Courtesy of ABC-TV)

York City. It probably was fortunate, because this first attempt at covering sports resulted in negative newspaper reviews.

With limited equipment, limited skills, and limited ability to cover games utilizing large areas such as baseball and football stadiums, television executives quickly realized they needed to cover sports that were confined to smaller areas, which could be handled easily by one or two cameras. Boxing and wrestling were ideal, and these events were to become regular fixtures in the early years of sports television. In fact, the first boxing match covered by television was aired only a few weeks after the Columbia-Princeton baseball game. Red Barber called the match, featuring heavyweight fighter Max Baer.

On August 26, Barber announced the first televised major league baseball game. Between innings he handled his own commercials, which included pouring a bowl of Wheaties. He also continued his practice of flipping a three-minute egg-timer, which he used as a reminder to give the score. Fans had convinced Barber early in his career of the importance of giving the score frequently. The admonition is as true today as it was then.

Postwar Development

Television grew slowly, and when World War II broke out, research was suspended for more pressing needs. It was not until 1946 that scientists went back to work improving cameras, transmitters, and the TV sets that quickly would become a significant element in the American way of life. That same year, NBC televised the Joe Louis-Billy Conn heavyweight title fight on a four-city hookup and watched by an estimated 100,000 fans. It would not be until many years later that these matches would become the mainstay of pay per view. In sharper contrast to the bad review of the Columbia-Princeton baseball game seven years earlier, the *Washington Post* said "television looks good for a 1,000 year run."

That year, program schedules were expanded on the few stations then on the air. Even so, most signed on early in the evening, and often went off the air before midnight. Boxing, professional wrestling, bowling, basketball, and roller derby became regular sports features. In the 1948–49 season, 30 percent of prime time programming consisted of sports. During the late 1940s there was more boxing on television than football games today. Some of the earliest shows were *Wrestling from St. Nicholas Arena* and the *Gillette Cavalcade of Sports*. Gillette became the first advertiser to recognize the impact that television would have.

As in the development of radio, there were no set rules or procedures governing television. Broadcasters learned as they gained experience. When Dennis James was assigned to handle pro wrestling telecasts, he tried to make the shows more interesting by adding sound effects. This was achieved with a whistle, which could produce a variable tone. He would blow it in certain situations, such as when one wrestler would throw another to the mat.

Dennis James was one of the first sports announcers who became recognized solely for his work in television. Others had gotten their start in radio. In fact, many continued to earn their principal income in radio while covering the occasional televised sport. Among those who made the early transition to TV were Bill Stern and Red Barber.

Another was Clem McCarthy, who was best known for covering horse races. History repeated itself in 1947, when McCarthy called the wrong winner of a race during a telecast of the Preakness. He had done the same thing eighteen years earlier while working a radio broadcast of the Kentucky Derby.

In 1947, NBC televised the World Series for the first time. As in radio twenty-six years earlier, both teams were from New York. As the Yankees went on to defeat the Brooklyn Dodgers, 4 games to 3, 3.9 million persons watched at least part of the seven games. The overwhelming majority (3.5 million) watched from bars and taverns. That's because high prices for television sets made private ownership unreachable to all but the wealthiest persons.

Even so, bars were the single biggest contributor to the interest in, and sale of, television sets. Television also helped attract more customers to bars that had sets. It soon became apparent that if a tavern were to survive, it had to have a television set, and it had to advertise that fact. For those who did not frequent bars or taverns, stores that sold televisions would display operating sets in shop windows, even when the stores were closed. Audio was piped to an outside speaker. It was not unusual for dozens—sometimes hundreds—of persons to gather around a store window on a cold, dark evening to watch a favorite show.

While these entrepreneurs were making money, other established businesspersons were not. Because television was so good at covering intimate sports such as boxing and wrestling, it was blamed for the demise of nearly three hundred fight clubs around the country. This would not be the only time sports television would be accused of contributing to a drop in attendance at actual sports events.

By 1948, television was available in most of America's biggest cities, although live network programming was yet to become a nationwide reality. Boston, New York, Philadelphia, and Washington were linked by coaxial cable; the first method of providing a clean signal between distant towns. Other stations either did without network programs—all of which originated in New York at the time—or relied upon a kinescope.

The Kinescope

A kinescope essentially involved taking a motion picture of a TV screen as a show was presented live. The resulting "recording" was at best fuzzy, but it was the only technique available at the time for making a permanent record of a television program. The kinescope film was then developed and duplicated in a motion picture processing laboratory. Copies, called "dubs," were then made and shipped by commercial airlines to any TV station that wanted them, often airing days or weeks after the actual event.

This also was the method used to supply news and sports video to network-affiliated stations. Only a few stations could get same-day service. It helped if the town was within a few hours commercial airline flying time from New York. Motorcycle couriers were employed to shorten the delivery time between the location airport and the television station. Other stations had to wait until the next day or the day after to air filmed highlights of a major news or sports event. The American people readily accepted the delay, because television was still new and exciting.

Coast-to-Coast

Even though only 9 percent of American households had television sets by 1949, network programming expanded greatly that year. Construction of the coaxial cable was well under way. Every week, a new town became linked to New York City. Just as the railroad unified America when the first transcontinental service began in 1869, live television became a coast-to-coast reality in September 1951. It now was possible for persons in Los Angeles to see a major league baseball game played in the East Coast. New Yorkers could see a football game featuring California schools. The year also saw the introduction of color broadcasts. That year, more than one-third of the American homes had television sets. Prices began to drop, making ownership for more families a reality.

Despite this, television remained a novelty for most Americans. Radio was still king, commanding sports rights fees triple those of TV. Teams that wanted to be on television sometimes found it difficult to convince a station or network to carry a schedule. In at least one instance, the Chicago Bears paid a station to carry a game. Fortunately for team owners, this situation would not last long.

TIME-OUT 2.1

The Growth of Television Households

Each year, television executives eagerly look forward to two sets of figures.
One is ratings, and the other is the number of TV homes in America.
Both are important to the financial success of programs, stations, and networks.
The growth of TV homes results in a corresponding overall increase in
television viewing. What follows is a historical perspective. From 1950 to 1969,
NBC tabulated the growth of television homes. Since 1970, Nielsen Media
Research has done that job.

TV Season	Total U.S. Households	Total TV Households	Percent with TV
1949–50	43,000,000	3,880,000	9.0%
1954–55	47,620,000	30,700,000	64.5
1959–60	52,500,000	45,750,000	87.1
1964–65	56,900,000	52,700,000	92.6
1969–70	61,410,000	58,500,000	95.3
1974–75	70,520,000	68,500,000	97.1
1979–80	77,900,000	76,300,000	97.9
1984–85	86,530,000	84,900,000	98.1
1989–90	93,760,000	92,100,000	98.1
1994–95	97,009,000	95,400,000	98.3

Note: All years prior to 1988–1989 excluded Alaska and Hawaii.
Source: Courtesy of Nielsen Media Research

The Videotape Recorder

By 1956, nearly four out of five homes had a television set. For sports
fans, the year was marked by the telecast of Don Larsen's perfect game in
the World Series on October 8. Larsen and the Yankees defeated the
Dodgers that day, but Brooklyn went on to win the Series. Though
Larsen's performance was a memorable moment in the history of sports
television, it was overshadowed that year by the announcement that the
Ampex Corporation had developed the world's first successful videotape
recorder. This development was the first of two major technological
breakthroughs that would change the face of television, and especially
sports coverage. The other, as will be discussed shortly, was satellite
transmission.

The first videotape recorder was large—about the size of a double-wide refrigerator—and heavy—weighing as much as a piano. It was powered by vacuum tube technology and the picture was in black and white. The tape was two inches wide, and a tape and reel weighing nearly ten pounds was required to record a one-hour show. Because of its high cost, not all television stations could afford to purchase an Ampex VTR.

Despite these apparent limitations, the videotape recorder proved to be an instant hit. Duplication now became easy—provided a station had two recorders—and certainly quick, because messy and time-consuming film laboratory work was eliminated. The biggest bonus was the enhanced image clarity over the primitive kinescope method.

Within five years, Ampex introduced the color videotape recorder. This prompted NBC to offer a growing number of programs in color, far outdistancing ABC and CBS. The reason was clear. By 1960, nearly 90 percent of America's homes had television sets, and virtually all of them were black and white receivers. If the saturated TV market were to grow, it would have to be through the introduction of color. And that's why NBC parent RCA decided to promote a growing number of sports and entertainment shows in color. Of the three network giants, only NBC was linked to a company that made TV sets. Once again the desire for increased set sales dominated programming decisions. The strategy worked.

Television Goes Portable

During the late 1950s, equipment was beginning to get smaller. Cameras could now be carried on aircraft. In 1959, CBS introduced the first live shot from a blimp, paying $3,000 to install a camera in the Goodyear Blimp, which then flew over Miami's Orange Bowl. Following the first Olympics ever televised—the 1960 Winter Games from Squaw Valley, California, hosted by news anchor Walter Cronkite—CBS went on to cover the Summer Games in Rome that year. That's where the portable color camera was introduced. Utilizing a heavy backpack in addition to the camera, photographers were able to get extreme closeup shots, adding to the emotion and human drama of sports. Soon, portable cameras were everywhere. And as they became smaller, tiny unattended models were placed anywhere a producer thought coverage of a sports event would be enhanced. With the portable camera, television entered a new era of sports coverage, where reaction shots would become as important as the action of the event itself.

*Early studio sports programs involved sets that were simple by today's standards.
(Source: Courtesy of CBS Sports)*

Wide World of Sports

April 1961 saw the first telecast of *Wide World of Sports* and the creation
of ABC Sports. The show was intended originally as a summer replacement
geared toward a male audience. After taking a few months off, it came
back in January 1962. *Wide World* would go on to become the longest-
running sports program on television. A young announcer from Baltimore,
James K. McManus, was hired by producer Roone Arledge to be the
host. McManus eventually changed his name to Jim McKay, a name that
has become linked inexorably to the show and to Olympic coverage as
well. For decades, when viewers thought of ABC Sports, they would
think of McKay, Arledge, and *Wide World of Sports*.

Described as an anthology program, it brought unusual sports
from unusual locales around the world to viewers at home. One did not
necessarily have to be a sports fan to enjoy the program. Because of the
nature of the events, they could be filmed or taped and played back in
edited form days, weeks, or even months later. The stories still had a
freshness about them because they were more than just events; they

often represented dramatic moments staged before a sports backdrop. As McKay would often say, drama was important to sports, because announcers are in the business of "telling stories."

Satellites

The Chicago Cubs helped to usher in the TV satellite age in 1962. The Cubs were playing a traditional afternoon game in Wrigley Field on July 16 when NBC News anchor Chet Huntley announced on an evening newscast that Europe was at that moment linked for the first time to America, Chicago, and the Cubs by means of the recently-launched Telstar satellite; the first satellite expressly designed to provide commercial television pictures. Within a short time the Grand Prix of LeMans become the first live European sports event seen by American viewers.

The development of satellite technology—coupled with the invention of the videotape recorder—has had a profound effect on television sports coverage. Satellites provided two distinct program advantages:

1. *Programming choices.* As these first satellites were launched, it become possible to provide TV coverage from virtually any spot on the globe. This ability was enhanced by the development of portable satellite trucks that could deliver a live television picture from anywhere there was a navigable road.

2. *Programming flexibility.* With what seemed to be a limitless number of signals, networks had the opportunity, for example, to give viewers expanded coverage of National Football League games. No longer were fans relegated to watching games that held little interest. They now had the opportunity to see games involving home teams, even if those contests were held thousands of miles away. Until the age of satellite transmission, local TV stations often got the games network sports executives in New York decided they should get. Sometimes this was dictated by the limitations imposed upon the land-based microwave transmission system. Although it had come to replace the coaxial cable and provide a better picture, microwave transmission had limited signal capacity. If the featured national game of the day became a blowout, it was generally difficult, if not impossible, to switch to a more interesting one. Satellites changed that, providing instantaneous switches. With the later advent of "squeeze zoom," viewers could see two games at the same time, displayed on opposite corners of their picture tube. This has become a popular technique for telecasts of the NCAA basketball playoffs, for example.

Satellites also would usher in the era of cable networks and what is sometimes referred to as the wired nation. Before 1962, the three established broadcast (over-the-air) networks (ABC, CBS, NBC) attracted more than 90 percent of all television viewing. A few independent and noncommercial stations shared the remainder. The average home could receive four or five channels. In 1975, cable programming expanded rapidly with the launching of the RCA Satcom I satellite, which carried a variety of cable networks. As more and more cable networks were created, broadcast network viewership eroded. With the recent addition of Fox, four broadcast networks now share about 72 percent of the total viewership. More than 61 percent of American homes have cable television, which means most of these homes are capable of receiving dozens of channels from one of more than 9,500 cable systems.

Instant Replay

Sports often served as the proving ground for new technology. In fact, networks that obtained rights to either Winter or Summer Olympic coverage often introduced pace-setting equipment or methods of coverage not seen before. One of the exceptions, however, was instant replay. The occasion was not the Olympics but the 1963 New Year's Eve football classic between Army and Navy. Lindsey Nelson, who had broken into sports broadcasting by serving as a spotter for Bill Stern, was calling the game that day. In his earphone the director told him that they were going to attempt to replay a touchdown that had just been scored. Nelson told his audience they were going to try something new...that they would see the touchdown being scored a second time. As he would say later, "by golly, it worked."

Instant replay would be expanded and improved. Instead of just one camera and one recorder, sports events today now have several camera-recorder combinations dedicated for instant replay purposes. Soon, replay in real time would be enhanced by the ability to show the action in slow motion and super-slow motion. This capability is further enhanced by the capability of freezing any action into a single picture.

The First Super Bowl

In early 1967, seven months after agreeing to merge, the AFL and NFL scheduled what was then called the World Championship Game. It would not be called the Super Bowl, complete with Roman numeral designations, for another three years. Both CBS and NBC covered the game, pitting the Green Bay Packers against the Kansas City Chiefs. The contest was several years away from capturing the imagination of the American people and becoming the nation's most popular single sports event. In fact, it wasn't until Super Bowl VI in 1972, when Dallas beat Miami 24–3, that the game came of age. On that day, it became the most watched American TV show of all time. Since then, other programs, including more Super Bowls, have surpassed that record, dropping Super Bowl VI to twenty-ninth place on the all-time list.

The Heidi Game

It didn't take a Super Bowl to underscore the impact of sports on television. That became apparent on November 17, 1968, during an American Football League regular season game between the Oakland Raiders and the New York Jets. The game was running longer than expected. With one minute left to play and the Jets leading, NBC-TV suddenly cut away and switched to its prime-time feature presentation of *Heidi*, scheduled for the top of the hour. NBC received thousands of irate phone calls that night. Clearly, the network had blundered by not carrying the game to its conclusion.

The following evening, during the Huntley-Brinkley national newscast, NBC played the missing minute of action. By then most viewers knew they had missed a lot, because Oakland had scored two touchdowns during the final sixty seconds to come from behind and defeat the Jets, 43–32, in what would always be known as "The Heidi Game."

This memorable event helped to underscore the policy of all networks to carry sports events to their conclusion, even if other programming would not begin as scheduled.

Monday Night Football

Pro football gained new fans and popularity when ABC-TV began *Monday Night Football* telecasts in 1970. The show, developed by Roone Arledge, was intended to bridge the gap between sports and entertainment. It achieved that with the first regular three-person announcing team in history. Keith Jackson was the original play-by-play announcer, succeeded a year later by Frank Gifford, who became teamed with the outspoken and often controversial Howard Cosell and the irrepressible and often humorous Don Meredith. Cosell had traded a law profession for the microphone, gaining early recognition while covering the fights of a young Cassius Clay, including his bouts with Selective Service. Clay, who would change his name to Muhammed Ali, claimed he was a conscientious objector and refused to be called to duty during the Vietnam war. Meredith and

Cosell would often get into verbal fights on *Monday Night Football* and the public loved to hear Meredith win an argument. The announcing trio came across as three guys one might find in a tavern watching a game on TV. When the outcome of a game was no longer in doubt, Meredith would break into song, singing "turn out the lights, the party's over."

Monday Night Football also introduced elaborate musical beginnings to the show. Best known was "Are You Ready for the Football?" sung by Hank Williams, Jr. The song has become part of American folk history. *MNF* also witnessed technological advancements such as slow motion and stop action. It also introduced the "reverse angle" camera, which was placed on the side of the field opposite from the others. Sparingly used, it was employed specifically for replay situations, especially to catch action that could not be seen by other cameras.

Monday Night Football gained the added distinction of becoming solely responsible for sociological change by helping to curtail crime. New York City police revealed that reported crimes had dropped 16 percent on the nights the show was aired.

The 1972 Olympics

The 1972 Olympics in Munich, West Germany, was broadcast almost entirely in prime time. However, it is best remembered for the tragedy that saw ten Israeli athletes, a coach, and three terrorists shot and killed following an attack on a room in the Olympic village. Jim McKay reported the incident to the world for ABC Sports. The network later won twenty-nine Emmys for its coverage of the tragic drama, as well as the games themselves. This Olympics also witnessed the improbable scene of an impostor running into the Olympic stadium near the conclusion of the marathon, seemingly the surprise leader. He was quickly identified as a phony and pulled off the track, allowing the marathon to conclude properly.

Phyllis George

Crowned as Miss America in 1971, Phyllis George became part of *The NFL Today* on CBS in 1975. She thus became the first woman network sports announcer, teamed with Brent Musberger, Irv Cross, and Jimmy the Greek. George often received poor reviews for her work, but she did remain a fixture on the show until 1984. She helped pave the way for other women to become part of what had been a traditionally male-dominated profession. Because of her and others, sportcasting opportunities are now available to more women than ever before.

ESPN

On September 7, 1979, ESPN made its debut as a total sports cable network, exactly fourteen months after the service was first announced by William F. Rasmussen and his son Scott. Within a year, ESPN (Entertainment and Sports Programming Network) was operating twenty-four hours a day and was covering college basketball in addition to college football.

TIME-OUT 2.2

ESPN Firsts and Notables

No network—cable or broadcast—has achieved so much in covering sports in such a short period of time. A brief list of ESPN's major achievements includes the following:

1979, Sept. 7	ESPN debuts with *Sportscenter*, the first national sports news program.
1980, March	First electronic cut-in format utilized, featuring the NCAA men's basketball tournament.
1980, Apr. 29	First-ever telecast of the NFL Draft.
1980, Aug. 3	First-ever telecast of the Baseball Hall of Fame induction ceremonies.
1982, Apr. 22–26	First-ever coverage of all four rounds of a PGA golf event— the USF&G from New Orleans.
1982, November	ESPN begins its coverage of NBA games.
1983, Apr. 26	Ten-hour telecast of NFL Draft becomes the longest live sports program in American history.
1984, Apr. 16	Boston Marathon receives live national coverage for the first time.
1984, Apr. 30	ABC becomes sole owner of ESPN.
1985, July 25	Three-year deal announced with National Hockey League.
1987, June	First cable network to reach 50 percent of all American television households.
1987, Aug. 16	First cable telecast of an NFL game—Chicago at Miami.
1990, April	ESPN begins coverage of major league baseball.
1994, Nov. 7	ESPN purchases controlling interest in SportsTicker from Dow Jones.

Olympic television coverage has reached a new level of sophistication. Here, Bryant Gumbel covers the games in Seoul, South Korea, in 1988. (Source: Courtesy of NBC-TV)

From Miracle to Boycott

Al Michaels says the U.S.A. team victory over the Soviet Union in the 1980 Olympic hockey tournament at Lake Placid, New York, transcended sports. It certainly was a memorable moment in sports television history, made famous by Michaels' excited utterance in the closing seconds: "Do you believe in miracles? Yes!" The event helped Michaels' sportcasting career. Six years later he became the play-by-play voice for *Monday Night Football* on ABC. In 1990, he signed a six-year contract that would pay him $15 million, surpassing Brent Musberger's five-year, $10 million pact signed the year before. It wasn't long before these seemingly extravagant totals were significantly surpassed.

The summer following the Lake Placid Olympics, NBC-TV was scheduled to carry the Summer games from Moscow. The network had paid $80 million for the rights, but when the Soviet Union invaded Afghanistan, President Jimmy Carter ordered a U.S. boycott of the Olympics. This included television. The Olympics went on, but without participation by American athletes or TV coverage. NBC-TV later claimed it had gotten most of its deposit back.

The Growth of Cable

The rapid success of ESPN was followed by the creation of regional sports cable networks. These networks proliferated during the early 1980s. There are now about two dozen, each covering college and professional sports in specific regions of the country. Viewers are attracted to these networks because they are more local in nature. For example, viewers in Texas and Oklahoma rely on HSE (Home Sports Entertainment) to carry Texas Rangers and Houston Astros baseball during the summer; Rockets, Spurs and Mavericks NBA games during the winter; Dallas Stars NHL hockey; plus college football and basketball, featuring Texas and Oklahoma schools.

As these networks were developing, other national networks and so-called "superstations" were expanding their coverage of sports. Most notable among the superstations carried on most of America's cable systems are WTBS in Atlanta, owned by Turner Broadcasting, which airs Braves baseball and Hawks basketball; and WGN-TV in Chicago, which has been carrying Cubs, White Sox, and Bulls contests for decades.

Established networks tried to strengthen their niches. ABC was the most successful, purchasing ESPN, as mentioned earlier in this chapter. NBC bought SportsChannel America in 1990. All three major broadcast networks attempted to diversify further by creating and owning their own sports and events such as *Battle of the Network Stars* and beach volleyball, among others.

A Question of Rights

For more than forty years, CBS had been one of the leaders in sports television. It had NFC football, NBA basketball, and major league baseball, plus the NCAA basketball tournament and major golf tournaments. In 1988, CBS-TV again showed its apparent dominance by signing a five-year contract with major league baseball for $1.06 billion. The deal proved to be a major mistake.

Unable to support its extravagant spending habits, the CBS Sports empire began to crumble. In rapid succession the network lost the NBA, baseball, and the NFC, along with two of America's most popular announcers: John Madden and Pat Summerall.

In 1993, baseball formed a new partnership with ABC and NBC called "The Baseball Network." For the first time since radio sports broadcasting had begun nearly three-quarters of a century earlier, no rights fees would be paid. Instead, all three partners would share the financial risk . . . and the profits. The 1994 season was to include an extra

FIGURE 2.1: Chronology of TV Sports Broadcasting

1939, May 17	NBC televises its first sports event: college baseball game between Columbia and Princeton.
1939, Aug. 26	First telecast of a major league baseball game.
1946	Boxing and wrestling become regular prime-time sports shows.
1947	First World Series telecast: New York Yankees and Brooklyn Dodgers.
1951, Sept.	Network television reaches the West Coast.
1956	Ampex introduces the videotape recorder.
1959, Jan. 1	First live TV pictures from a blimp: Orange Bowl, Miami.
1960	CBS-TV is first to air Olympics; the Winter games from Squaw Valley, California.
1961, April	*Wide World of Sports* makes its debut on ABC-TV.
1962	First satellite TV program of any kind transmitted to Europe, featuring Cubs game from Wrigley Field in Chicago.
1963, Dec. 31	Instant replay makes its debut at Army-Navy football game.
1967, Jan.	CBS and NBC air first championship game pitting AFL and NFL teams; to be called "Super Bowl" three years later.
1968, Nov. 17	"Heidi Game" played, in which the final minute of the NFL contest is not aired until following night on NBC newscast.
1970	*Monday Night Football* telecasts are launched by ABC.
1972	ABC Sports covers the terrorist attack on Israeli athletes at the Olympic Village in Munich, West Germany, in which fourteen persons are killed.
1975	Phyllis George becomes the first regular female host of a network sports program, *The NFL Today*.
1979, Sept. 7	ESPN makes its debut as the first all-sports TV network.
1980	Millions of viewers watch the United States defeat the Soviet Union in Olympic ice hockey.
1980	The United States boycotts the Summer Olympics in Moscow, terminating NBC's coverage plans.
1982, Jan. 24	Super Bowl XVI becomes the highest-rated sports show of all time, with a rating of 49.1 and a share of 73.
1983, Apr. 26	ESPN airs the longest live sports program in TV history: ten hours of the NFL Draft.
1984	ABC introduces stereo audio to sports broadcasts at the Olympic games.

FIGURE 2.1 (*Continued*)

1989, Oct. 17	An earthquake hits the Bay Area, as San Francisco prepares to play Oakland at Candlestick Park in the World Series.
1993	ABC, NBC, and Major League Baseball announce a unique partnership, called "The Baseball Network," to market and televise games.
1993	Fox outbids CBS for coverage of NFC football.
1994, Jan. 24	John Madden signs four-year, $30 million contract, becoming the highest paid sports announcer in history.
1994, Feb. 23	Women's figure skating becomes the most watched single Olympic event in history.
1994, July	World Cup soccer games shown in high definition television (HDTV) format in Los Angeles theaters and European cable systems.

round of playoffs, and a limited number of popular regional games, similar to what the NFL has carried for many years. Only a few regular season games were telecast before the players went on strike and the baseball season ended prematurely.

Violence and Ratings

The essence of sports is confrontation; the attempt by one athlete or team to defeat the other. The essence of sports also requires that this be done within the rules, and without causing malicious injury. Such was not the case in 1993, when two women became victims of separate, malicious attacks. The attacks and their aftermath were played and replayed prominently on television around the world.

Tennis star Monica Seles was stabbed in the back during a tournament in Hamburg, Germany, by a spectator. The attacker, Gunther Parche, said he wanted Seles out of tennis so Steffi Graf could retain her number one world ranking. Later that year, American figure skater Nancy Kerrigan was attacked and struck on a knee by a man linked to fellow skater Tonya Harding. Three months after the attack, at the Winter Olympics in Norway, both women competed against each other for the first time since the attack. The notoriety associated with the incident made the February 23, 1994, Olympics coverage the sixth-most-watched TV show of all time and the single-most-watched Olympic event ever. Two days later, with Harding far behind in the competition, viewer interest waned. Even so, the finals of the women's figure skating competition took the thirtieth spot on the all-time list. Kerrigan went on to win a silver medal.

The Fox That Roared

For most of the 1980s Fox Television was struggling to earn a foothold with viewers. As late as 1992, the Federal Communications Commission, in an effort to help the fledgling operation, officially declared that Fox was "not a network." Because of this unique FCC policy position, Fox was not required to follow the same rules as ABC, CBS, and NBC. By late 1993, Fox had ended all speculation on the question of its survivability when it outbid CBS and won the rights to televise NFC football, beginning with the 1994 season. The four-year contract was worth $1.58 billion. The action stunned CBS, which fully expected to continue what it had been doing for the previous thirty-eight years. This was only the beginning. Two weeks after taking the NFL from CBS, Fox also took its two leading announcers, John Madden and Pat Summerall. Madden signed a contract that would pay him $30 million over four years, making him the highest paid sportscaster of all time. In mid-1994, Fox began expanding its affiliate members by signing up local CBS stations; several in major markets. Later in the year Fox signed a five-year contract for $150 million to carry the National Hockey League. Because of sports, and specifically the NFL, Fox had become a major player...and a major network. The FCC could no longer claim that Fox was "not a network."

The Future

As the twentieth century nears its end, television seems to have taken the kinks out of how it covers sports (see figure 2.1 for a chronology of TV sports broadcasting). Coverage is professional and predictable. The future will likely see more channels, with more sports choices. Technology will improve to levels we can only dream about. In the final analysis, however, sports television history will continue to be made by memorable games and by the men and women who can show them and talk about them in a skillful and interesting way.

3 Opportunities in Sports Broadcasting

Job opportunities in sports broadcasting are growing at a rapid pace. This means jobs are opening up for announcers, producers, and technicians at a rate never before seen in the broadcasting industry. There are several reasons for the growth: (1) the dramatic increase in the number of radio and television stations; (2) the emergence of all-sports regional and national cable networks; and perhaps most important (3) the realization by both broadcasters and sports team executives that big money can be made by covering games. At one time, team owners feared that broadcast coverage—even radio—would result in diminished ticket sales. Certainly the opposite has been the case. Broadcasting—especially television—has increased interest in and attendance at many sports events. Even more significant are the rights fees that team owners earn; amounts that exceed what might be earned through ticket sales.

This heightened awareness is evident from extensive coverage of what once may have been considered sports of minor interest, such as Little League or American Legion baseball on radio. Television also has extended coverage by creating or helping to support new sports leagues such as arena football, beach volleyball, and indoor soccer, along with new sports competitions such as the Skins golf matches; all for the exclusive coverage by network television.

Numerous opportunities are available to persons aspiring to a career in sports broadcasting. Here, a photographer, soundman, and floor producer work a college football game. (Source: From the collection of John R. Catsis)

Historical Perspective

In the mid-1960s, sports coverage was severely limited. Local radio stations covered high school and college football and basketball, but probably ignored high school and college baseball when spring came around. Often, the only professional sport covered on radio was baseball, and even then most road games were re-created. Other professional sports were all but ignored. In Chicago, for example, Blackhawks hockey was only covered at home, with the broadcast beginning at 10:30 P.M., two hours after the game had started. This meant play-by-play was usually limited to just a portion of the third period. Away games were not broadcast at all. The announcer was Bob Elson, who earned his major income handling the play-by-play of the Chicago White Sox. At this time, the National Hockey League consisted of only six teams. Four were in the United States, and the farthest west franchise was in Chicago.

Radio sportscasts were virtually nonexistent. WIND, the Chicago station that carried the Blackhawks, provided a brief segment within its nightly 11:00 P.M. five-minute newscast to give scores of games played that night. A regularly scheduled sportscast that dealt with scores and stories in depth simply did not exist. WMAQ, the NBC radio station in Chicago, provided some limited coverage on the weekends in a show called *Monitor*. When the show eventually died, so did sports coverage. Fans again found it necessary to receive the bulk of their information a day later from the city's three major newspapers.

Even so, radio broadcasters probably thought they were providing adequate amounts of sports coverage, and to some degree that was true. After all, FM radio was just beginning to develop. There were very few receivers and even fewer stations; all of which were struggling to survive. Even with AM radio, there were far fewer stations than there are now. Radio was just beginning to develop different music formats to suit different listening tastes. Until that time, all radio stations sounded pretty much the same. They tried to be everything to everyone; playing middle-of-the-road music, providing noontime remotes featuring live bands, offering soap operas and children's programming during the day, plus adding a little news and weather. With this kind of schedule, there wasn't much time for sports.

Television coverage was not much better. On a typical fall weekend, only one network carried college football. And coverage was limited to one game. The only time more than one game was seen was when all three networks covered the major bowl games on January 1 of each year. College and professional basketball was limited to a "game of the week," with no provision for regional coverage. Major league baseball had the same arrangement. In a few large markets, however, independent television stations began to recognize the value of sports programming. These stations aired many of a team's home games. Like radio, the cost of covering away games live was considered prohibitive.

Sportscasts on television, however, were well established, though limited in technical capability. Fans turned to TV ahead of radio to get the latest scores. But that's about all they got. Because of technical limitations, highlights were rarely shown. Most of a sportscast consisted of seeing the sports anchor read from a script. The "visual" part of the telecast usually consisted of scores posted with press-on numbers and letters that were photographed with a studio camera. Once in a while, a local film might be shown. National sports news was frequently old, often shown many hours or even days after the event.

Radio Opportunities

Most of today's "big-name" television play-by-play announcers got their start in radio. Thanks to escalating rights fees, the financial opportunities in radio sports are growing at a rapid rate. The total dollars may not compare with rights paid for television coverage, but the cost of production is far less expensive. This can result in a handsome profit for radio broadcasters. As a consequence, there are now more opportunities for newcomers to enter the radio sports arena than ever before. In some cases, there also are increased opportunities for seasoned professionals to earn a good living by concentrating on radio sports. Beyond the obvious play-by-play opportunities, there are two major reasons for this: (1) the proliferation of sports talk shows on radio stations throughout America, and (2) the trend to all-sports formats by some stations in major markets. By 1994, there were more than seventy-five such stations. Chicago had two competing against each other; WMVP and WSCR. While there may be some openings for producers on talk shows and game broadcasts, these positions are generally filled by staff employees. The majority of the sports broadcast opportunities in radio involve play-by-play announcers. Even color analysts are hired on a per-game basis.

For the person with no experience, offering to work as a spotter or statistician can be an excellent opportunity to prove one's value. Both small and large stations can use these persons, but not all offer any pay. Even so, the experience and contacts a newcomer obtains are invaluable. Statistician and spotter opportunities are most prevalent in football. To get started, contact your local station, in person, at least two months before the season is scheduled to begin. And be prepared. You should be neatly dressed and display enthusiasm. By discussing intelligently the information contained in this textbook, you will demonstrate that you have the ability and qualifications the station is seeking.

As a spotter or statistician you will gain a greater understanding of how a broadcast is created, plus the roles that engineers, producers, and announcers play. This often leads to opportunities later on. In fact, many persons who started as spotters or statisticians have been promoted to producers and announcers.

The value of a strong formal education cannot be emphasized enough. While it is true that some broadcasters have become successful without a college degree, the overwhelming number have been graduated from a college or university. Many employers will not consider an applicant if the resume does not show evidence of a degree. A recent survey of fifty-five of ESPN's announcers and analysts, for example, shows that forty-two have degrees and five others attended some college. Only eight did not have higher education experience.

Announcer salaries can range from minimum wage at the smallest radio stations in America to $100,000 a year or more for those who host sports talk shows on major market radio stations. The average salary for a full-time employee of a medium market station is around $20,000 a year. The reader should be aware that these figures are merely guidelines.

Popularity of the program, acceptance of the announcer, commitment by management, and size of the broadcast market are all factors in determining a person's salary. In a few cases, union pay scales may dictate what the employee earns. In small markets the sports director may be called upon to perform any of a number of additional duties. This may include news reporting, disc jockey work, or sales.

Television Opportunities

Television provides well-paying employment for the greatest number of individuals who enjoy involvement with sports. They include play-by-play and color announcers, producers, and technicians. Part-time positions include statisticians or spotters. As in radio, these two jobs are acknowledged as excellent ways to break into broadcast sports. Some of the biggest names in broadcast sports got their start in this manner. Nothing can beat knowing persons in hiring positions, no matter what the profession.

Part-time spotter and statistician jobs can lead to full-time producer positions, especially at a local television station. In other cases, a person who has experience as a newscast producer is reassigned to play-by-play production. The same qualifications are required for both positions, including a creative mind, a high degree of organizational skill, the ability to act and react quickly, a willingness to take on any kind of job function, leadership skills, and the ability to work harmoniously with others. Television sports producers have the opportunity to work on local telecasts, regional sports networks, pay-per-view, and the national broadcast and cable networks.

Color analysts and sideline announcers are generally part-time or freelance positions. If either of these assignments appeals to you, it's a good idea to have a regular full-time job to support yourself and your family. Len Elmore, who played in the NBA, later worked as a color analyst for ESPN. But he earned his major income as an attorney and agent. Fired professional and collegiate coaches in both football and basketball are often hired by networks to work as experts on pre-game and half-time shows. Some of these individuals use these programs to keep their faces before the public, and more importantly, before the owners, general managers, and athletic directors of other teams that soon may be looking for a new coach. There is some concern and controversy among some broadcasters and coaches as to the ethics of this activity. Are these coaches really interested in working in television, or are they merely promoting themselves for the next coaching opportunity? It would appear that some are self-promoters. The host must skillfully exercise some form of tactful control on that individual before the

ESPN's Dick Vitale and Ron Franklin have gained national reputations as outstanding college basketball announcers. Success did not come easily. Both had to work hard to reach the top. (Source: From the collection of John R. Catsis)

credibility of the program is brought into question. As former quarterback and Fox Network analyst Terry Bradshaw once put it: "Everyone will do their own thing. I love [Mike] Ditka [former Chicago Bears head coach]. If you listen to Mike, you'll be able to tell whether he's going back to coaching. Those that return don't burn bridges on the air."

Color analysts for play-by-play broadcasts often come from the sport itself, especially on network telecasts. Again, this presents part-time employment opportunities for former athletes and coaches, who are expected to bring a high degree of insight to the game. One of the best known of these individuals is former Oakland Raider football coach John Madden, who handled color analysis for CBS-TV for more than a dozen years before moving to Fox in 1994. His work has won him eight Emmys awarded by the National Academy of Television Arts and Sciences.

A well-known former analyst who came from the ranks of broadcasting and not athletics was Howard Cosell. An attorney by training, Cosell understood the power of the medium and used that power to create controversy by the comments he made. As a result, Cosell was either liked or disliked, but never ignored. He was best known for *Monday*

Night Football telecasts on ABC-TV. Even those who disliked Cosell would tune in to hear what he might say that some viewers would consider outrageous. Cosell believed he was the first true sports journalist, and claimed that he "has had more impact upon sports broadcast [sic] in America than any person who has yet lived."

Play-by-play announcers are often full-time employees of local stations and broadcast networks. In fact, the four major over-the-air networks—ABC, CBS, Fox and NBC—maintain a stable of sports announcers and producers who are assigned to events throughout the year. However, there is a growing trend for regional and national cable sports networks to hire freelance announcers on a per-game basis. In fact, this trend has extended to producers and some technical personnel. There are three reasons for this: (1) a network can hire persons who are especially skilled or well-known in a particular sport, which has a season lasting only a few months of the year, (2) by paying by the event, rather than by the week, month, or year, a network can exercise greater fiscal responsibility, and (3) by hiring freelancers, it can save additional money by avoiding most payroll taxes and benefits packages that are customary with full-time employees.

For most persons, however, sports television employment means working at a local station covering local sports. In some TV markets this will mean area high schools and perhaps small colleges. For those who have moved up to the top 40 markets, it means covering major league sports as well. This activity usually entails preparing and delivering twice-nightly sports reports within a station's newscast. For these persons, salaries can range from $15,000 a year at the smallest markets to $100,000 or more in major league markets. Network broadcasters earn even more. For example, in 1993, popular CBS football and golf announcer Pat Summerall was given a four-year contract worth $1.8 million a year. Less than a year later, Summerall was able to get out of that contract and sign a new one with Fox for $2.5 million a year. He thus was reunited with John Madden, who the week before had signed a four-year deal with Fox for $7.5 million a year. The January 24, 1994, signing was the biggest announcing contract in sports broadcast history.

Additional Opportunities

For some individuals who hold full-time broadcasting jobs, additional employment opportunities, usually of a freelance nature, become available. For example:

- *Announcing local teams on radio.* Well-known local sports announcers are often hired to multi-year contracts to be the "voice" of a local college or professional team. In a medium market this can pay $30,000 or more for seasons lasting only a few months.

* *Working pay-per-view games.* This is an excellent opportunity in many TV markets to serve as a play-by-play or color announcer.

* *Narrating videotapes for college and professional teams.* These tapes highlight the season just concluded and are offered for sale to the general public. This can be a valuable "off-season" source of income.

* *Authoring books and magazine articles.* Some broadcasters are so well-known that an autobiography can earn a significant income, but usually for only a brief time. Even regional "legends" can find this a lucrative way to earn additional income.

* *Going Hollywood.* Some announcers are often asked to play themselves in bit parts in movies about sports. One such example was Bob Neal of CNN Sports, who portrayed a play-by-play announcer in *The Program,* the story of a fictionalized college football team. Another was NBC baseball analyst Bob Uecker, who played the radio announcer for the Cleveland Indians in the movie *Major League,* and its sequel. The best example of a sports announcer who went on to Hollywood full time, and then to even greater heights, was former president Ronald Reagan.

Opportunities for Women

Until only several years ago, women had few opportunities to work in broadcast sports. The exceptions were appearances as guest commentators during special events such as major tennis or golf tournaments, or the Winter or Summer Olympics. And even in those instances, women were assigned only to women's events.

That changed in 1975, when Phyllis George, a former Miss America, served as a co-host on *The NFL Today* for CBS-TV. Her eight years at that position helped pave the way for other women announcers, as men suddenly "discovered" that women were fully capable of discussing men's (and women's) sports.

In 1985, golf great Judy Rankin became the first woman on-course reporter at the men's U.S. Open. Lesley Visser is one of today's better known female sports announcers covering men's sports. Her roles principally have been in the areas of interviewing and in narrating player profiles. Nanci Donnellan, of *The Fabulous Sports Babe Show* on ESPN Radio, became the first female host of a major sports talk show in America in 1994. Robin Roberts, an ESPN anchor on *Sportscenter,* may have become the highest paid female sports announcer—her 1994 salary was estimated at $265,000. Suzyn Waldman, a sports announcer for WFAN-AM in New York City, worked as a color commentator in June of 1993, when she worked a couple of New York Mets games.

That same year, the male bastion in major league public address announcing was broken when Sherry Davis was hired by the San Francisco Giants. The following year, Leslie Sterling became the first black female major league PA announcer when she was hired by the Boston Red Sox. And when the Dallas Stars of the National Hockey League launched their inaugural season in 1993 after moving from Minnesota, they also employed a female public address announcer, a Dallas disc jockey, who went by the air name of Sari.

Television Job Growth

The increase in TV job opportunities coincided with the development of satellites as a principal means of relaying television signals across great distances. Satellites contributed to increased sports coverage in four ways:

1. Sports, and for that matter any event, were now easier to cover. Technical limitations were eased because of satellites. Crews could travel to any place they wished and cover a competition live. At first, this capability was limited to networks, but as costs came down, even local stations were able to afford satellite trucks that are now commonplace all over North America.

2. Satellites allowed broadcast networks to schedule as many regional professional or college games as they wished, instead of offering a single contest to the entire country. Prior to the advent of satellites, regional telecasts were severely restricted or nonexistent. Cost and complexity were the reasons that often prevented stations from receiving the regional game of their choice. That's because TV signals traveled along the surface of the earth through complex microwave relay towers. Because there was a limit to the signals that could be carried, it might be impossible for a station to receive the game it wanted to show, even though it might be available in another part of the country... or even to another station only 100 miles away. This complexity could be overcome by either building or arranging for more lines. But networks were unwilling to expend the money because the results would not have been cost-effective. As a result, a station in Memphis, for example, might be given a National League game featuring Atlanta and Miami, when it might have preferred to receive a Cincinnati-St. Louis contest instead. These situations resulted in reduced viewership levels.

Cable networks have created numerous job opportunities for sports broadcasters. Al Bernstein and Barry Tompkins (from left to right) are America's best known boxing announcers. (Source: Courtesy of ESPN)

Now, with more regional coverage, viewership levels have risen. And because of the increased coverage, more announcers, producers, and technical personnel are required to handle these telecasts.

3. Satellites led to the creation of cable networks because it was now economically possible to transmit pictures almost anywhere from almost any place. Cable operators saw these new cable networks as a means of acquiring additional subscribers, because of the unique programming they provided. Among the early entries in cable television were CNN and ESPN. The latter, an all-sports network, contributed to hundreds of employment opportunities. These national cable networks were followed in short order by regional sports networks such as NESN (New England Sports Network), MSG (Madison Square Garden), HSE (Home Sports Entertainment), and many others. Another development was the creation of so-called "occasional" networks. These could be formed with little advance planning to cover tightly-targeted sports activity. Among the leaders are Raycom (now merged with Ellis Communications) and Prime Network. Raycom, for example, has covered Big 8 basketball for stations in markets where interest in these games is high.

4. Finally, satellite technology opened the door to pay-per-view. At first, PPV was limited to major national events, such as heavyweight title fights. Soon, promoters saw PPV as a profitable opportunity for covering games that might have great local or regional appeal. As a result, contests involving mediocre teams that have been rejected by regional networks are now available on PPV.

Retransmission Consent

A recent broadcast development that has helped sports on television resulted from the FCC's 1992 cable regulation rules. Among other things, the rules stated that local over-the-air broadcast stations could not be carried by cable operators without first working out an arrangement with the broadcaster. Stations had two choices: (1) They could require the local cable system to carry their signal. If they opted for mandatory carriage, the cable operator would not be required to pay the station for doing so. Many independent stations chose this course of action. (2) Most network-affiliated stations and a few large independents selected the second alternative called "retransmission consent." This simply meant, "if you wish to carry our station, Ms. Cable Operator, you must pay us in some manner." These stations were betting that the cable systems wanted to carry their signals, because if no satisfactory payment arrangement was reached, the signal could be dropped from the cable system. In a couple of cases, they were. Obviously, this could have disastrous implications for the station. It also would be of serious consequence for the cable operator, especially in instances where the signal might be the only off-air network station that could be viewed on the cable system. For example, if an NBC-TV affiliate were dropped by the cable operator, and she could not replace that station with another nearby NBC-TV affiliate, cable subscribers could become dissatisfied with getting less than they expected and paid for.

Even so, cable systems were hard-pressed to put out additional monies for carriage rights. As a result, some stations worked out nonfinancial arrangements. One of them was the creation of an additional cable channel for the local station. This would permit better utilization of a station's news and sports departments by providing expanded news coverage. As a result, staffs were expanded, and new programs were added. This extra local channel for a local television station thus allowed the opportunity for covering more local high school and college sports events, in effect creating more employment opportunities.

Emerging Opportunities

As explained elsewhere, satellites have done more to advance sports coverage and program flexibility than any single programming or technological development in history. Because of satellites, new services and new employment opportunities have emerged. Here is a partial list, representing just the past few years:

- In 1992, ESPN launched a radio network to supplement its already successful cable television venture of the same name.
- On October 1, 1993, ESPN launched a second network, ESPN2, which was intended to appeal to a younger audience—viewers between the ages of 18 and 34. Those are highly sought demographics by advertisers, because persons of this age group represent the most prolific consumers. Taking a page from MTV, ESPN2 often programs material that might be considered nonmainstream sports, and it does it in a more humorous or irreverent manner. At the same time, ESPN2 has further expanded sports coverage by carrying additional game broadcasts of the National Hockey League, college basketball, soccer, beach volleyball, surfing, and skiing.
- ESPN and Sony Electronic Publishing have agreed to work together to develop a series of sports video games.
- Fox became a major player in sports broadcasting when it took the NFC games away from CBS in 1993. Though Fox also recruited a number of persons away from CBS, the senior network continues to have a viable sports department.

Future Opportunities

Future opportunities in sports broadcasting are tied to the development of new technologies and new national and regional networks. For example:

- Coming to a window sill near you is the next wave of TV programming called DBS (Direct Broadcast Satellite). By the end of the century, it will be possible for homes to receive up to five hundred channels from satellites by means of a small antenna mounted on an outside window sill.
- CBS is considering the establishment of a sports network. This may or not be the result of a merger or partnership with other broadcast entities.
- Prime SportsChannel has announced plans to establish an all-sports cable network, headquartered in Clearwater, Florida.

- *Sports Illustrated* magazine has begun to develop sports television. Its first effort was a cooperative venture with HBO called *Sports Illustrated for Kids*. *SI* is serious about TV, having hired former CBS Executive Sports Producer Ted Shaker to head up its TV projects.
- Affiliated Regional Communications, the parent company for the

TIME-OUT 3.1

Emerging Cable Channels

Because of Direct Broadcast Satellite (DBS), programmers are rushing to create new networks that will utilize the expanded opportunities that DBS provides. DBS will change the face of television dramatically, even more than the growth of cable. DBS will be the "magazine rack" of tomorrow, offering numerous choices. Sports will be one of them. For example, by the mid-1990s, no less than eight new sports channels were either announced or already in operation. They include the following:

Network	Launch Date	Format
The Golf Channel	Jan. 17, 1995	Golf tournaments, tips, and talk. This is a premium channel, similar to HBO or Disney.
Classic Sports Network	early 1995	Reruns of classic sports events and documentaries.
Cable Health Club	spring 1995	Aerobics and nutrition.
Gaming Entertainment Television	mid-1995	Where legal, viewers will be able to bet by phone on horse races and jai alai.
Women's Sports Network	late 1995	Live and taped events, talk, and fitness.
Liberty Women's Sports	early 1996	Same as above.
ESPN3	1997	Continuous sportscasts, similar to CNN's Headline News.
Motor Sports Network	1997	Another ESPN project, featuring auto, motorcycle, and powerboat racing.

Not all of these announced networks may survive. Even so, it can be presumed that other entrepreneurs will eagerly jump in with additional sports programming. Possibilities include two outdoor channels; one dealing with hunting and fishing, and the other concentrating on hiking, climbing, and camping.

Prime Network, announced plans to establish its second all-sports cable network called Prime Plus. Carrying 60 percent original programming, Prime Plus could reach 8 million cable households.

- Prime Ticket Network is planning to launch the first all-sports network aimed at America's Spanish-speaking population. Prime Ticket La Cadena Deportiva would reach 8 million viewers in the western United States.

- New sports leagues are being created, which means new broadcast opportunities. Roller hockey is seeing the creation of not one but two professional leagues: Roller Hockey International and the World Roller Hockey League. The interesting part of the WRHL is that every team plays all its games in Orlando during May. The videotaped matches are then scheduled for broadcast on ESPN during July and August. Baseball has developed a Hawaii winter league, with four teams playing a fifty-four-game schedule. The league was formed to replace winter leagues in Latin American countries where civil unrest has made playing and living conditions difficult if not dangerous.

    As many as four soccer leagues either have been started or are announced, partially due to the publicity received by the World Cup competition, which was held in the United States in 1994 for the first time ever. One is the newly formed Continental Indoor Soccer League. Following a successful inaugural season in 1993, the CISL had planned to double the number of teams by 1995. Another is the American Professional Soccer League, which plays its games outdoors. It launched its inaugural season in 1994 in direct competition with the established National Professional Soccer League. But the biggest league of all is the United States Interregional Soccer League, which has more than seventy teams playing nationwide. Broadcasting soccer games in North America may be the radio and television growth industry for the twenty-first century.

- Don't overlook lacrosse, a sport best known in the northeastern part of the United States. Lacrosse is played in the summer on fields and in hockey rinks where the ice has melted. The Major Indoor Lacrosse League is big with fans, as evidenced by the 16,284 spectators who jammed an arena in Buffalo recently to watch a game.

- More made-for-TV sports events. Beach volleyball and the Skins golf games are proven winners. Dick Clark, best known in music circles, developed a series of programs that link sponsors and sport. The first was *The Chrysler Great American 18,* a tournament involving four golfers playing eighteen holes on eighteen different courses over four days.

- The Professional Chess Association was formed in 1994, largely in the hope of earning income from television.
- Syndicators are creating sports quiz shows. One example is *Sports Snapshot,* a trivia game created by GGP and Preview Media, Inc. The show has merchandising tie-ins that permit local stations to share in the profits from sales, in addition to conventional advertising within the show itself.

Summary

These opportunities are just the beginning. While some of the plans outlined above may never materialize, there are certain to be other sports and leagues that will take their place, including sports that have not yet been created. Technology and a growing interest in sports cannot halt the rapid increase in program options. This means thousands of new jobs, mostly in television, for persons seeking sports broadcasting opportunities.

At the same time, radio sports will continue to benefit from the growth of television coverage. While many professionals will enjoy rewarding careers in radio sports, many newcomers will get their start by broadcasting high school football, basketball, and baseball games. Radio is the blending of what's uniquely American in sports broadcasting.

4 Understanding Ratings

The average American household watched 178 hours of sports on television in 1992. This statistic does not include radio sports and does not include any Olympic coverage. The statistic is more amazing when the reader considers that only one person in every six is actively interested in sports news.

The most popular sports event among Americans is the NFL's Super Bowl. The Winter and Summer Olympics also draw a massive audience; next to soccer's World Cup, these are the most watched TV sports events in the world.

Television sports has had an influence on the youth of America. According to a survey of 5,000 students between the ages of nine and eighteen, 37 percent would most like to trade places with a professional athlete. Teachers and the president of the United States tied for second with 21 percent.

The vast earnings and comfortable life-style of top athletes does not go unnoticed by these youngsters. They know that at the peak of his career, Michael Jordan earned under $4 million playing professional basketball, while his outside income topped $32 million. Jordan's $20 million deal with Nike is the most lucrative endorsement contract in sports.

Great as he was as a basketball player, Jordan did not attain superstar status until Nike promoted him and its shoes on television. The Jordan name then became a household name. One did not have to follow the NBA to know who Michael Jordan was. Other players who will follow Jordan in the NBA will likely receive the same type of publicity off the court, thanks to endorsement contracts. Two such emerging NBA stars are Shaquille O'Neal and Larry Johnson.

Broadcast sports is big business. And beyond endorsement contracts, American corporations spent nearly $3.7 billion sponsoring sporting events in 1992. That's an increase of nearly one-third over the previous year. More than 2,000 companies sponsor events. Soft drink and beer bottlers are the leaders in dollars spent.

These companies are not doing this as a benevolent gesture. On the contrary, they have made what they believe are prudent investment decisions. And they have done so for two reasons: (1) TV exposure of their message is seen by millions of viewers. For example, when Al Unser, Jr., won the Indianapolis 500 race in 1992, sponsor Valvoline believed it got publicity worth $6.87 million, based on conventional TV advertising rates. Nearly $1.8 million of that was attributed to the TV camera mounted inside Unser's car, which scanned, among other things, the Valvoline logo. (2) To a significant degree, fans support the companies whose logos grace race car bodies. This support probably extends beyond the sport of auto racing, as well.

History

Broadcast sports advertising wasn't always big business. Fees paid for broadcast rights did not exist or were modest by today's standards. But both broadcasters and team owners were quick to realize the potential that sports brought to the American audience.

Radio became an advertising medium in 1922 when WEAF in New York City aired the first commercial. This occurred about a year after radio first became available to the American people. The sponsored program was a non-sports event, but broadcasters quickly recognized that sports in general, and baseball in particular, held the potential for solid advertising income. By 1929, American League owners were concerned that radio was making money from their venue. One complaint heard was that an unnamed broadcaster had sold $30,000 in advertising contracts for the 1930 season. The amount was then considered extraordinarily high. Soon, a few major league club owners demanded a rights fee; that is, payment for permission to broadcast play-by-play of their games. Some clubs prohibited radio entirely, fearing it would cut into ticket sales. Even so, by the early 1930s, each team's average rights earnings was $1,000.

By the mid-1930s, many major league club owners began to relax their resistance to coverage of their games. At the same time, recognizing a ready-made male audience, companies such as Kellogg, General Mills, Socony-Vacuum Oil (Mobil), B.F. Goodrich, and Atlantic Refining Company bought the greatest amount of advertising time.

General Mills advertised Wheaties extensively on these broadcasts, and by 1937, over $1 million was spent advertising the cereal that became known as the "breakfast of champions."

In 1937, WBBM in Chicago, whose powerful signal reached several midwestern states, paid the Cubs and White Sox $7,500 each for broadcast rights to the games. Two other Chicago stations, WIND and WCFL, both with weaker signals and smaller geographical coverage areas, paid $3,000 each.

In 1939, the Gillette Safety Razor Company got into sports broadcasting for the first time, by paying $203,000 for exclusive rights to sponsor that year's World Series. Gillette has been a sports broadcasting advertiser ever since.

Baseball sponsorship by a single corporation was the general rule in the 1930s and 1940s. This trend extended into broadcasts of Triple-A minor league teams. But this began to change in the 1950s, principally for two reasons: the emergence of regional sports networks and the continuing growth of television. These two factors allowed advertisers to more carefully target their advertising to the audience they were trying to reach.

Those who felt the change in advertising strategy the most were minor league broadcasters. But they adjusted quickly by signing up local sponsors for the local team broadcasts. The smallest teams in the smallest markets always relied on local advertisers. To a large degree, the basic sales and advertising trends developed in the '50s are with us to this day. It's the number of sports broadcasts and dollars that has grown larger.

Strategy

Radio is still sports broadcasting in its purest and most local form. High school and college teams and minor league professional sports can be heard all over the radio dial. In fact, sports to a large degree may have saved AM radio. Today, FM attracts more than three-fourths of all the radio listeners in America. If it were not for sports play-by-play, talk, and other selective programming, AM radio listening levels might have eroded even further. Radio is where a true sports fan can catch the local team in action, home or away. Because radio sells local advertising, its geographic reach does not have to be large to make a profit for its owners.

Television, on the other hand, requires popular sports and sports teams in a large geographic area in order to gain enough viewers to earn a profit. Regional TV networks are now found throughout the country, broadcasting major league teams and many Division I college football and basketball conferences. On the national level, exposure is further limited to the top powerhouses and top twenty-five teams.

At the broadcast network level, which means ABC, CBS, Fox, and NBC, scheduling sports programming is a science. Complete textbooks and college courses are devoted to the subject of programming and program strategy. This is only the briefest outline of what skilled sports programmers must consider in deciding what to cover.

Different camera positions and enhanced audio are all intended to attract the viewer and increase ratings. (Source: From the collection of John R. Catsis)

- *Popularity of the event.* Is there a broadcast history of similar events that shows viewership (rating) information and demographic breakdowns? Ratings are explained elsewhere in this chapter. Demographics is the science of vital and social statistics, such as the study of types of viewers, broken down by sex, age, education, and income levels. Chances are the NFL's Super Bowl will score well in both ratings and demographics, while the world chess championships will come in very low.
- *Popularity of the sport.* Men's college basketball has been a consistent ratings success. It scores high among men, demographically. Women's college basketball, conversely, may score well among women as a percentage of total viewership, but those levels may be too low for a network to successfully earn a profit.
- *Popularity of the event within the sport.* Figure skating, for example, did not receive much attention outside the Olympics or World Championships. But that has changed in recent years. As a result more figure skating events are now being aired by programmers confident of gaining increasing numbers of viewers.
- *Counterprogramming.* This means appealing to a different demographic group than another network or station. Consider a schedule where one network decides to run a boxing match. This probably will score high demographically among men. As a result, a competing network would be wise to find a program appealing to women. If it's sports, women's gymnastics may be called for. A real-life example of the above is found every fall when ABC carries *Monday Night Football*. The other networks attempt to provide counter-programming that will appeal to women. It usually takes the form of non-sports programming, with movies or dramas that are of proven appeal to female viewers.
- *Head-to-head programming.* This involves scheduling events that are similar in appeal to that of the competition. This can be risky, because viewership is diminished, and a third competitor may gain the greatest audience with creative counterprogramming. Some examples of head-to-head sports programming involve several NBA games on different cable networks. The viewer generally picks either: (1) the most significant game of the night, or (2) the game featuring his or her favorite team.
- *Lead-ins.* This is a program that precedes another program. In sports, this can involve a pregame show such as is found during the National Football League season. The programming wisdom is that viewers will select a pregame show they like and stay with that

network and the game that follows it. This, of course, is based on the assumption that the viewer does not have a favorite game to watch that day. Even so, that's the reason networks hire talented hosts and big-name analysts, build lavish sets, and promote heavily.

- *Hammocking.* This is a strategy that is often used in prime-time entertainment programming. To understand this strategy, assume there are three programs—A, B, and C. Shows A and C are consistent ratings winners, and can prosper on their own. Show B, on the other hand, may be a new program or an established show that program executives believe will do well if only more viewers have a chance to sample it. They achieve this by scheduling Show B between A and C. Viewers who love both A and C will probably sit through B, after A is over, knowing that C will come on right after that. This strategy still works, even in the era of the easy channel change brought on by the remote control. It is called

The NCAA college basketball playoffs are ratings winners. (Source: Courtesy of CBS Sports)

"hammocking" because A and C are the supports between which the lower-rated show, B, is suspended.

• *Tentpoling*. This strategy involves only one strong show and two weak ones. The two weak or new programs are scheduled on either side of the stronger show. Hence, the middle show is the support, or tentpole, that holds up the programs on either side. Obviously, this strategy is used when a station or network does not have enough strong programs to effect a "hammocking" schedule.

In sports programming these strategies are not limited to individual programs but to segments within a show as well. For example, an anthology show such as ABC's *Wide World of Sports* has several different segments. The first may be one that creates wide viewer interest because of well-known participants, extensive action, or other factors. Near the end of the show, another popular segment may be scheduled; one that is highly promoted not only in the days before the air date but within the show as well. In the middle of the program one might find segments with reduced appeal.

Audience Measurement

Besides programming strategy, anyone employed in broadcasting must understand ratings. It's just as important in sports broadcasting as any other segment of the industry. There are only five basic terms that one needs to understand in order to have a grasp of audience measurement methods. They are *universe, ratings, HUT levels share,* and *cume.*

Universe

The universe of any station or network is its potential audience, not its actual audience. The actual audience is measured differently and is explained later in this chapter. Not every station or network has the same universe. For example, the audience potential for stations in New York City is much larger than stations in Lubbock, Texas. In 1994, New York City had 6,692,370 TV households. Lubbock had 134,730. Notice that the reference is to "TV" households. Fewer than 2 percent of the households in America still do not have television sets, and as a result, are not included in viewership tabulations.

BROADCAST NETWORKS

There are four established commercial broadcast television networks: ABC, CBS, Fox, and NBC. The noncommercial network is

PBS. Two new commercial networks are in developmental stages: Warner Brothers (WB) and United Paramount (UPN). These networks can be seen on local affiliated stations coast-to-coast. As a practical matter, each of these networks has a universe of 95,400,000 TV households. United Paramount and Warner Brothers have smaller universes, principally because of the shortage of local station affiliate outlets nationwide.

CABLE NETWORKS

Notice that the reference above is to broadcast networks. These are networks whose signal is transmitted from a tower and picked up by an antenna. Except for supplying the antenna, a television set owner incurs no further expense. A cable network, on the other hand, can be received only if the set owner pays for a cable TV service, which includes installation and rental of a transmission line to the set.

While the three established broadcast networks can be said to have the same universe of 95,400,000 TV households, such is not the case for cable networks. This is because local cable systems have the right to select the cable networks they wish to carry. In some localities with limited channel carrying capacity, many cable networks considered popular in other areas may not be available at all. Thus, the universe of each cable network is different.

According to the National Cable Television Association, these are the universes for the ten most popular cable networks in the United States:

TABLE 4.1: Universes for the Ten Most Popular Cable Networks in America, 1992

Network	Subscribers
ESPN*	60,200,000
CNN*	60,000,000
USA*	59,600,000
TBS*	59,000,000
The Discovery Channel	58,000,000
Lifetime	58,000,000
C-Span	57,200,000
TNN (The Nashville Network)*	56,900,000
TNT (Turner Network Television)*	56,200,000
Nick at Nite/Nickelodeon	55,800,000

*These networks carry regularly scheduled sports programming.

DBS

An emerging service that involves most of the so-called "cable networks" is called Direct Broadcast Satellite (DBS). Begun in 1994, DBS delivers its signals from satellites to small dishes mounted on window sills or other convenient locations. DBS will expand the universe of cable networks by making signals available for the first time in areas previously rejected by local cable services because of remoteness or expense. Because of DBS, every place in North America will be able to receive hundreds of television signals. Because of the nature of this technology, all networks carried on DBS should have the same universe.

Ratings

Ratings are the measurements used by sales departments to set advertising rates. Ratings are similarly used by media buyers to help them determine whether to make a purchase of advertising time. In the final analysis, ratings help to accomplish two things: make money and decide whether to continue or cancel programs.

The term "rating" refers to the percentage of potential audience or universe actually watching or listening to a specific program. In radio, rating is a percentage of people. In television measurement, rating is a percentage of TV homes. Each TV home is said to have an average of about 2.5 people in it.

What follows is an explanation of how to determine the rating for a typical television program. In figure 4.1, the universe for this small cable system consists of ten TV households.

Remember that figure 4.1 illustrates homes that have television sets. Homes without TV sets are never considered in ratings calculations. In the first three homes, the first is watching channel 2, the second is watching channel 4, and the third is not watching TV at all, but the third home does have a TV set.

Consider figure 4.1: of all the TV households shown, four or 40 percent are watching channel 2. Thus, the rating for channel 2 for this program is 40.0. Note that this calculation is based on all TV homes, whether all sets are in use or not.

What the 40.0 rating for channel 2 means is that, of all the TV homes in the station's universe, 40 percent have their sets on and tuned to channel 2. Any program manager would drool at the prospect of such a high rating. By today's standards, a respectable rating can be anything approaching 20.0.

FIGURE 4.1: Determining TV Program Ratings and HUT Levels

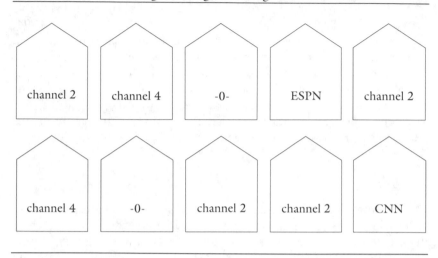

Continuing the example shown above, the rating for channel 4 is 20.0 and 10.0 each for ESPN and CNN.

HUT Levels

Of the ten homes in the universe, as shown in figure 4.1, eight are watching either broadcast or cable networks. Thus, the "Homes Using Television" or HUT levels are 80 percent of the potential TV audience. This number is expressed as 80.0. Note that a digit, which may be a zero, follows a full number when showing HUT levels. This is also true when expressing ratings. Shares, explained next, are written only to the nearest whole number.

Share

Share means "share of the audience." Share is calculated by utilizing only those TV homes that are using television. Thus, in the sample shown above, we include only the eight homes that have TVs operating. To calculate a share, count the homes watching a specific channel and divide by the HUT levels. In the case of channel 2, 4 homes divided by 8 equals 50 percent or 50. The share is 50. Channel 2 thus has a 50 percent share of the audience.

The share for channel 4 is 25 and for ESPN and CNN it is 13 each.

Note that instead of 12.5 for ESPN and CNN, shares are rounded off.

Thus, in many media publications, ratings and shares would be expressed as follows:

channel 2	40.0/50
channel 4	20.0/25
ESPN	10.0/13
CNN	10.0/13

Shares are not taken seriously by sophisticated media buyers. That's because a high share number does not necessarily translate into high viewership. For example, consider a program that airs at 2:00 A.M. At this hour of the morning, only one TV station may be operating and only a few viewers may be watching. The program could have a 1.0 rating and a 100 share, but only because there is no competition from other channels.

Cume

Radio ratings and shares are calculated in a somewhat similar manner to that of television. Additionally, radio uses *cume* as a method of expressing its audience. This is more important to advertisers who buy time throughout the day and week and try to reach as many different listeners as possible. Cume stands for *cumulative audience* and is similar to circulation figures given for newspapers and magazines. Thus, cume is the number of different people who listen for a specific period of time. This measurement can be used by sports talk radio stations to convince potential advertisers that the station reaches many different people during the course of a week.

TV Ratings Leaders

With this understanding of ratings, it is easier to appreciate the outstanding results shown for the top fifteen TV shows of all time.

Of the top fifty TV shows of all time, 40 percent are Super Bowls! Besides the Super Bowl, three other sports shows are among the top fifty. They include two nights of the 1994 Winter Olympic Games from Lillehammer, Norway, and the 1982 NFC Championship Game, in which the 49ers beat the Cowboys, 28–27.

While these programs are the best of the best, the average rating for a good show in the 1990s would be in the mid-teens. For example, during the 1990–1991 season, *Monday Night Football* was the top-ranked

TABLE 4.2: Top Fifteen TV Shows of All Time

Program	Episode/Game	Net	Date	Rating	Share	Households
1 *M*A*S*H*	Final Episode	CBS	2/28/83	60.2	77	50,150,000
2 *Dallas*	"Who Shot JR?"	CBS	11/21/80	53.3	76	41,470,000
3 *Roots*	Part Eight	ABC	1/30/77	51.1	71	36,380,000
4 Super Bowl XVI	SF 26, Cin 21	CBS	1/24/82	49.1	73	40,020,000
5 Super Bowl XVII	DC 27, Mia 17	NBC	1/30/83	48.6	69	40,480,000
6 Winter Olympics	Kerrigan-Harding	CBS	2/23/94	48.5	64	45,690,000
7 Super Bowl XX	Chi 46, NE 10	NBC	1/26/86	48.3	70	41,490,000
8 *Gone With The Wind*	Movie, Pt. 1	NBC	11/7/76	47.7	65	33,960,000
9 *Gone With The Wind*	Movie, Pt. 2	NBC	11/8/76	47.4	64	33,750,000
10 Super Bowl XII	Dal 27, Den 10	CBS	1/15/78	47.2	67	34,410,000
11 Super Bowl XIII	Pit 35, Dal 31	NBC	1/21/79	47.1	74	35,090,000
12 *Bob Hope Special Christmas Show*		NBC	1/15/70	46.6	64	27,260,000
13 Super Bowl XVIII	Oak 38, DC 9	CBS	1/22/84	46.4	71	38,800,000
14 Super Bowl XIX	SF 38, Mia 16	ABC	1/20/85	46.4	63	39,390,000
15 Super Bowl XIV	Pit 31, LA 19	CBS	1/20/80	46.3	67	35,330,000

Source: Statistics courtesy of Nielsen Media Research.

sports series, with a 17.2/30. This ranked it sixth among all shows, led by *Cheers*, which had a 21.6/34.

Cable Ratings Leaders

The rating information shown for the cable programs in table 4.3 are for cable's universe, which is smaller than that of broadcast networks. These totals are from September 1, 1980 through August 31, 1991.

Cable viewing is still quite low, on average. The top ten cable network ratings for a twenty-four-hour period during the last three months of 1994 can be found in table 4.4. Prime-time figures, as might be expected, are higher, as evidenced by results for the top nine cable networks during the same three-month period in 1994 (see table 4.5). Despite these apparently low figures, cable viewership continues to grow, and sports coverage continues to be cable's most watched programming. For example, during the week of September 27 to October 3, 1993, the top nine shows on cable were sports programs. The most popular was an NFL game between the Giants and the Bills, shown on TNT. It was seen in 5,359,000 TV households and earned a cable rating of 8.9. If TNT's universe equaled that of the established broadcast networks, it would have had a national rating of 5.8. The week cited above is fairly representative of the impact of sports on the cable television industry.

TABLE 4.3: Top Cable TV Shows of All Time

	Event	Date	Network	Rating
1	NFL—Chicago at Minnesota	12/6/87	ESPN	17.6
2	NFL—Chicago at Minnesota	12/3/89	ESPN	14.7
3	NFL—Cleveland at San Francisco	11/29/87	ESPN	14.2
4	NFL—Pittsburgh at Houston	12/30/90	ESPN	13.8

Source: Statistics courtesy of ESPN.

TABLE 4.4: Average Cable Network Ratings

Network	Rating
TBS*	1.2
USA*	1.1
TNT*	0.9
Nickelodeon	0.9
A & E	0.8
Cartoon	0.8
ESPN*	0.9
WGN*	0.6
CNN*	0.6
Discovery	0.5

*Cable networks that provide regular sports programming.
Source: Courtesy of *Broadcasting & Cable*.

TABLE 4.5: Prime-Time Cable Network Ratings

Network	Rating	Households
USA*	2.3	1,457,000
TBS*	1.8	1,108,000
TNT*	1.8	1,112,000
ESPN*	2.6	1,649,000
Nickelodeon	1.3	784,000
TNN	0.9	718,000
Discovery	1.0	607,000
A & E	1.1	642,000
Lifetime	1.2	690,000
CNN*	0.9	620,000

*Cable networks that provide regular sports programming.
Source: Courtesy of *Broadcasting & Cable*.

5

The Business of
Sports Broadcasting

S ports is more than a game. Broadcasters and team executives—
both amateur and professional—treat radio and television coverage
of sports events as serious business.

When athletes enter professional sports, they quickly realize it's not
just a game. Where once they played for the fun of it, most now perform
for the high salaries paid in virtually every sport, plus the opportunity to
earn even more through endorsements. They acknowledge it's a business.
Many, like NBA star Dennis Rodman, call themselves "entertainers" as
well as athletes.

Sports broadcasting influences viewers' life-styles, the way the game
is played, and the manner in which broadcast schedules are drawn up.
Here are some examples:

- Soon after television began covering football, basketball, and other
  sports on a regular basis, it became apparent that time-outs had to
  be changed in two ways: (1) scheduling had to be more predictable,
  and (2) the length of each time-out had to be expanded. Teams
  receiving rights fees for coverage did not have to be convinced
  about the financial benefits, even though games took longer to
  complete. Although some sports now study ways to make games

shorter, no one seriously considers eliminating commercials from broadcast coverage as one way of accomplishing that goal.

- The World Series and other sports events became night games, principally to increase viewership during prime time. The Super Bowl is played in the evening, and even weekend NBA and NHL playoff games, once afternoon affairs, are now held at night, for the same reason.

- College football is no longer a Saturday afternoon event. Schools and conferences are playing on Thursday nights under an arrangement with ESPN. College basketball also has teamed up with regional and national networks for special nights, such as ESPN's Big Monday tripleheaders.

- College conference alignments have changed, principally to take advantage of larger rights fees. In recent years, numerous universities have either switched conferences or joined one for the first time.

- The College Football Association, representing most of the largest Division I-A schools in America, was created in 1977 because of a dispute over television rights fees. These large schools objected to the NCAA sharing fees among all seven hundred member schools when only a few of the large universities' games were seen on television.

- In 1994, the CFA was declared dead as individual conferences and networks entered into exclusive contracts. As a result, major conferences became bigger, both in the number of member schools and the income earned from rights fees. Marginal conferences and schools, which once enjoyed some national TV exposure, found themselves with little or none.

- Professional leagues considering expansion place heavy emphasis on the potential television audience in each proposed expansion city. For example, it is claimed that Baltimore lost its bid for an NFL franchise in 1993 largely because Washington, D.C., already had a team just 44 miles away, and Redskins games already were seen in the Baltimore television market. However, Jacksonville and Charlotte, the newest franchises, represent markets where television coverage for the NFL could be increased.

- When punishing universities for athletic violations, the NCAA often imposes television sanctions. By eliminating TV coverage, the NCAA accomplishes two goals: (1) accused schools are denied their share of television rights fees, and (2) a school's recruiting program is seriously affected because of the lack of exposure.

- Ninety-two Chicago-area taverns were sued in federal court in 1992 for signal theft by SportsChannel Chicago, which claimed that the bars illegally intercepted coverage of Stanley Cup playoff games of the Chicago Blackhawks. The National Cable Television Association says signal piracy costs broadcasters $3 billion a year.

- Cable coverage of sports has become a concern of over-the-air broadcasters. The National Association of Broadcasters, the largest organization of radio and television station owners and managers, suggests that legislation may be required to limit the amount of sports that can be carried on cable. Cable reaches more than 60 percent of the television homes in America.

- In response, cable dismisses the NAB recommendation by claiming that the three established over-the-air networks (ABC, CBS, and NBC) increased their sports programming by 19 percent between 1980 and 1992.

- ESPN is leading all cable networks in expanding its coverage of sports by moving into several different areas. In 1993 it began a second sports network called ESPN2, intended to appeal to younger demographics. It also launched ESPN Enterprises, an umbrella subsidiary involved in pay-per-view, home video, and licensing. ESPN previously had launched a radio network and a 900-number telephone service, providing scores and other news.

The National Football League

Two-thirds of the National Football League's income comes from broadcast rights. The other third is from the sale of tickets. In 1994, the twenty-eight teams made $1.08 billion from broadcast rights, and $418 million from ticket sales. Thus, tickets accounted for less than 28 percent of the league's $1.5 billion revenue from these two sources.

TV wasn't always that lucrative. In 1961, NFL teams earned between $150,000 and $500,000 in network TV rights, depending upon each team's market size. Three years later, after Congress allowed the league to bargain with networks as a unit, each team earned more than a million dollars. The upward trend has yet to stop.

The largest single source of broadcast income, of course, is the Super Bowl. It is perennially the most watched event on American television. For the 1994 game, NBC paid $40 million for broadcast rights and expected to make a profit.

A thirty-second commercial during a Super Bowl telecast is the highest-priced spot on television. For the 1995 game, ABC charged $1,025,000 each time a commercial ran during the first half and $975,000 for each spot in the second half of game. With investments like that, it's no wonder many advertisers showcase new products or new commercials during the game. There are two sound business reasons for buying time in a Super Bowl game: (1) viewers will watch at least two-thirds of the spots that are aired, because fans know they probably will see the premiere of an entertaining commercial with high production values; and (2) research has determined that football fans recall a spot run in the Super Bowl at least twice as well as a spot run during a conventional prime-time program.

Local stations carrying the Super Bowl also benefit financially. For spots they get to sell and run as part of the broadcast, network affiliates realize increased revenues. Doubling the standard rate for a thirty-second local commercial is not uncommon. If a local station is in a town represented by one of the teams taking part in the Super Bowl, the spot fee might be significantly higher.

Even networks not carrying the Super Bowl have learned how to benefit from the game. It started in 1992 when Fox ran *In Living Color* during halftime. The program was heavily promoted and was started precisely when halftime began. *In Living Color* earned a 9 percent increase in viewers above the show's normal levels. At the same time, viewership of the Super Bowl halftime show on CBS, featuring singer Gloria Estefan, dropped significantly.

Super Bowl coverage features a number of technical achievements. As explained in chapter seven, record numbers of cameras, tape recorders, and people are used to cover this event. Even the number of blimps flying overhead increased to four in 1993 . . . a Super Bowl record!

For the 1994 game, a so-called "NFL Super Bowl Channel" was created on cable. During the four days leading up to and including the day of the game, forty-one hours of programming was scheduled on two regional cable sports networks. The concept developed from Los Angeles cable channels carrying similar programming for the 1993 game.

While the Super Bowl as a single event makes money, the rest of the season has found TV networks complaining about budget squeezes, mainly caused by high rights fees. Adding to the problem in 1993 was an NFL plan to showcase its regular season during a longer period, with each team playing its sixteen-game schedule over eighteen weeks. The resulting TV viewership was not what was expected, because highly-watched teams or matchups were not on each week's schedule. One weekend in September, for example, eight teams did not play. Viewing levels dropped 18 percent. The league's experiment lasted only one year.

Networks claimed to have lost money on 1993 regular season coverage; the estimate was $250 million for the five networks that carried NFL games. CBS is believed to have lost the most—about $110 million—which probably contributed to Fox winning the bid for 1994

NFC coverage for the first time. Fox is counting on the NFL deal to help increase its exposure and overall viewing levels with the general TV audience as no other single program could. The network realizes that viewership among all stations and cable networks will continue to erode as more and more viewing choices become available, especially with new direct broadcast satellite (DBS) technology, such as Prime Star and DIRECTV, that will give the home viewer up to five hundred channels. Individual shows will most certainly see ratings decline. But Fox believes that there will be no ratings erosion when the NFC is on its network. When it broadcast its first game on August 12, 1994, Fox instantly became a major league network with its major league contract. It also became the first network to regularly carry NFL games in Mexico, when three TV stations along the U.S. border became, in effect, affiliates.

Despite the ratings success of ABC's *Monday Night Football*, the show still can lose money, as evidenced in 1993. Ratings reached new levels and the show made the top ten list of the most popular prime-time programs. Part of the reason given was the lively announcing team of Al Michaels, Frank Gifford, and Dan Dierdorf. Ratings for the first half of the season were the best in seven years.

Radio and the NFL

While television was having its problems with the NFL during the early 1990s, radio was not. Fees paid for rights were either flat or increased slightly. Radio rights ranged from $800,000 a year for Green Bay and Indianapolis to $4.5 million a year for Chicago and $4 million for San Francisco. San Diego carried its games on just two stations. Other teams had network affiliates of from three (New York Jets) to ninety-five (Minnesota). The Dallas Cowboys, with ninety stations, has its coverage extend into Mexico and includes a separate Spanish language network. Miami also has a Spanish network. The Arizona Cardinals broadcast their games in Navajo on some northern Arizona stations.

Stations that serve as "flagships"—that is, home stations that originate broadcasts for the team's network—stand to gain in other ways. For example, research by Arbitron has shown that flagship stations see an increase in the station's overall audience during the football season when compared to the rest of the year. Arbitron determined that in 1991, twenty-four of twenty-nine stations serving as flagships saw their ratings increase by an average of 1.2 percent, while five lost listeners by an average of 0.6 percent. New Orleans station WWL-AM had the biggest increase: 3.3 percent.

TABLE 5.1: The Last Four TV Network Contracts with the NFL

Term	Rights	Average Annual Payment	Year of Ratings Measurement	Ratings					
				ABC	CBS	NBC	ESPN	TNT	Fox
1994–97	$4.39 billion	$1.097.0 billion	1994	17.8	—	12.4	7.0	5.4	12.0
1990–93	$3.65 billion	$912.5 million	1992	16.8	13.0	11.2	5.6	4.3	
1987–89	$1.43 billion	$476.6 million	1989	18.1	13.8	11.0	6.4	—	
1982–86	$2.07 billion	$414.0 million	1986	18.5	15.2	12.3	—	—	

Note: ESPN became a rightsholder in 1987, TNT in 1990. All ratings shown are based on the following broadcast network universes: 1994–95,400,000 TV households; 1992–93,100,000 TV households; 1989–92,100,000 TV households; 1986—87,400,000 TV households.
Source: Ratings information courtesy of Nielsen Media Research, ESPN, and TNT.

NFL Competition

The National Football League faced competition from several areas in the mid-1990s:

1. The established Canadian Football League further expanded into the United States in 1994 after a successful experiment in Sacramento the previous year. The newest teams were located in Baltimore, Las Vegas, and Shreveport, Louisiana.
2. CBS, finding itself without the NFL, attempted to organize a new pro league owned by major advertisers such as beer, automobile, sneaker, and fast food companies. The hope was to utilize a growing number of NFL free agents to stock what's been called "The A League" by 1995.
3. The NFL itself planned to revive the World League for a 1995 season, with a minimum of six teams playing in Europe. Fox agreed to become a financial partner in the venture.

College Football

College football has been a staple of broadcasters almost since the beginning of commercial radio in 1921. Today, hundreds of radio stations air games of major universities, colleges, and junior colleges. Some stations may pay up to $1 million for broadcast rights, which usually include the school's basketball season as well. Other stations may air games of smaller colleges for minimum or nonexistent fees.

Realizing that broadcasters turn a profit, even after rights fees are paid, a few universities are handling broadcasts in house. That means they are performing the role that most radio stations typically employ. This includes signing up a local station to be the originator of the broadcast and creating a network of other stations that will receive the signal of the "flagship" station. The university also hires its own announcers.

Income is earned from each station in the network, including the originating station, which pays a fee for the right to carry the game. Each station is allowed to retain a certain amount of time to sell for its commercial use. Other time periods are retained by the university, which finds its own network sponsors, thereby producing additional income for the school.

Most universities, however, prefer not to get involved in this type of operation because it requires setting up a separate department at an additional expense. However, they usually retain the right to veto a station's selection of announcers for the games. Usually, this is not a problem.

While rights fees, especially those from television, provide a good income for many schools, the bonus of getting to a bowl game can be especially lucrative. The TV rights paid for that one game can exceed an entire season's worth of combined football and basketball rights. For example, most bowls guarantee each participating school at least two-thirds of a million dollars. Each school's conference also receives additional monies to be split among the member schools. For the 1994 Orange Bowl, between #1-ranked Nebraska and #2-ranked Florida State, each school received $4.2 million. Even though this game was for the national championship, the fees paid were less than those of the Rose Bowl, in which each school received $6.5 million for the 1994 game.

When it comes to big money, however, the Rose Bowl is no longer considered the "granddaddy of all bowl games." That's because payoffs escalate in 1996, thanks to the Bowl Alliance, which selected the Orange Bowl in Miami, the Sugar Bowl in New Orleans, and the Fiesta Bowl in Tempe, Arizona as America's premier bowl games. Any participating school can expect to earn $8.5 million for appearing in any of these three bowls. Each of the games will be played on different dates and the expectation is that one of these bowls will feature two top teams battling for the national championship.

Despite these fees, most universities have found it difficult to pay their athletic department bills. An example is the University of Michigan, a school that has a football stadium with 101,701 seats that are sold out for every game. Wolverine teams have enjoyed outstanding success in both football and basketball during the early '90s, marked by appearances in the Rose Bowl and the NCAA basketball championship game. But losses continued. By 1993, Michigan's deficit stood at $5.3 million.

TABLE 5.2: Major College Network Contracts

Year Contract Begins	Conference or Team	Network	Payment	Duration of Contract
1996	Notre Dame	NBC-TV*	$37.5 million	5 years
1996	Big Ten/Pac 10	ABC-TV	$278 million	7 years
1996	Big Twelve	ABC-TV	$57.5 million	5 years
1996	Big Twelve	Liberty	$40 million	5 years
1996	Southeastern	CBS-TV	$100 million	5 years
1996	Big East	CBS-TV	$65 million	6 years
1996	Atlantic Coast	ABC-TV	$70 million	5 years

*Includes basketball

All the while, television coverage and viewership have been increasing. In 1993, 2,133 college games were televised, compared to 676 games just five years before. At the same time, Nielsen ratings were the highest in seven years. For example, Notre Dame's ratings experienced a spurt, mainly due to two exciting games against Boston College and Florida State. The latter was another of the so-called "games of the century." Despite the increased viewership, Notre Dame's season ratings were a modest 6.7 for six games.

Money is at the center of all discussions involving revisions of college athletic programs. For example, the discussion over creation of a college football playoff system became serious when it was apparent more money could be made, both for networks and the schools and conferences involved. Some bowls that historically have featured mediocre matchups may become sites for playoff games, which could suddenly take on added importance. Meanwhile, conference mergers and realignments, coupled with escalating network contracts, were the big newsmakers during the mid-1990s (see table 5.2).

College Basketball

Approximately 85 to 90 percent of the NCAA's total income comes from broadcast rights for basketball. The sport has seen tremendous growth. The Final Four Championship game overshadows opening day in baseball. Viewer interest is so high that Hollywood no longer schedules the Academy Awards in direct competition with the traditional Monday night game. For example, the 1993 championship, pitting Michigan and winner North Carolina, drew a 22.7 rating and 34 share. The game was seen in 20,670,000 TV households by an estimated 32,940,000 viewers.

It not only won the night for CBS, but it also was the highest rated program of any type that week. The 1994 game between Arkansas and Duke had a rating of 21.6, a share of 33, and was watched by 32,730,000 persons.

In TV markets where a team is located, ratings are much higher than the national average. For example, on the Saturday before the Monday championship game of 1992, when North Carolina played Kansas in the semifinals, the Charlotte CBS station had a 38.8 rating. Kansas City had a 31.1. The national average for that game was 12.7.

While not at the same level as the Super Bowl, with its million-dollar fees for a thirty-second commercial, some advertisers have paid up to $300,000 for a spot in the championship game.

In 1991, CBS began covering the entire NCAA tournament under a seven-year, $1 billion contract. In 1994, it renegotiated a $1.725 billion deal that assures CBS exclusivity through 2002. The package includes coverage of track, gymnastics, and the College World Series. When it comes to viewers, college basketball seems to deliver better than the NBA. Of the ten highest-rated basketball telecasts of all time, eight were college games (see table 5.3).

Although the #10-ranked game earned the highest rating of the games in table 5.2, it did not have the greatest number of viewers. The reason is that the number of TV households in 1979 was lower than its present-day level.

While only two universities are represented in the NCAA title game, hundreds of others share in the income from television rights fees for other games during the regular season. For example, ESPN pays $10,000 to $15,000 for the rights to cover a typical college game. Prime, a regional network, may pay $5,000. A university with a strong basketball

TABLE 5.3: Ten Highest-Rated Basketball Telecasts of All Time

Game	Date	Network	Rating	TV Homes
1. NCAA, Duke-Michigan	1992 title game	CBS	22.7	20,900,000
2. NCAA, Arkansas-Duke	1994 title game	CBS	21.6	20,347,000
3. NCAA, Villanova-Georgetown	1985 title game	CBS	23.3	19,800,000
4. NCAA, Michigan-Seton Hall	1989 title game	CBS	21.2	19,300,000
5. NBA, Detroit-L.A. Lakers	1988 finals, game 7	CBS	21.3	18,800,000
6. NCAA, N.C. State-Houston	1983 title game	CBS	22.3	18,600,000
7. NCAA, UNLV-Duke	1990 title game	CBS	20.0	18,400,000
8. NBA, Chicago-L.A. Lakers	1991 finals, game 5	NBC	19.3	18,300,000
9. NCAA, Duke-Kansas	1991 title game	CBS	19.4	18,100,000
10. NCAA, Michigan St.-Indiana St.	1979 title game	NBC	24.1	18,000,000

program that attracts TV coverage for most of its schedule can expect to earn close to $250,000 a year in rights revenue.

Independent sports producers, such as Raycom, often make deals with national networks. For example, ABC contracted with Raycom to pick up coverage of certain Sunday college games over a twenty-six-week season. Since Raycom already had the equipment and technical staff in place for a regional game, all ABC had to do was supply its own announcers, pick up the signal, and distribute it nationally. This form of subcontracting is becoming more and more popular as a means of expanding coverage and saving expenses. It also provides an additional source of income for regional cable networks.

College basketball viewership and profitability continue to increase, along with interest in creating more interesting matchups. For example, before the regular season officially begins, a so-called "Pre-Season NIT" tourney is held, often pitting teams that are expected to do well. There are preseason preview shows as well. Schools also will reschedule games to larger arenas or to different times to gain more ticket buyers, a bigger TV audience, or both. And during the Christmas holiday school break, regional networks will create tournaments involving teams that can create high viewership.

Even in June, when there is no college basketball, television presents the NBA draft, which gives fans of college basketball one last look at their favorites. Viewers now can look forward to the upcoming season knowing with which NBA teams these young men will be playing.

Regular season ratings have shown dramatic growth. CBS averaged a 3.8 rating for the early part of the 1993–94 season, which represented a 45 percent increase over the same period during the previous year.

A new growth area is women's basketball, which is gaining in popularity. Regular season women's games now are being covered on network television, and the field for the women's version of "March Madness" was expanded from forty-eight to sixty-four teams in 1994. ESPN will carry NCAA tournament games beginning in 1996. Income for the tournament has increased from just under $500,000 in 1982 to more than $1,870,170 in 1993. Attendance also has increased fourfold. The 1994 title game had a 3.7 rating and a 12 share, according to Nielsen Media Research.

The NBA

National Basketball Association Commissioner David Stern once said that the NBA can be likened to an enterprise consisting of "27 theme parks." The NBA, like any other sport, amateur or professional, is entertainment. Unlike theater, where the outcome is dictated by the script, athletes attempt to "write their own script."

The NBA has been a success story for NBC and Turner Broadcasting. Both networks have profited from coverage, while networks that carry other sports, most notably major league baseball, were not so fortunate. While the NCAA college championship game enjoys high single-game viewership, regular season NBA contests generally deliver audiences 50 percent greater than regular season college games.

In 1993, NBC and the NBA renewed their contract through the 1997–1998 season. For the first time, a specific dollar amount was not attached to the deal, other than that the network would pay the NBA a minimum of $750 million. That's an increase of 25 percent over the previous contract. Additionally, there was a provision that NBC and the NBA would split profits above a certain amount. This way, both enterprises stood to gain. This unique concept was intended to halt the runaway rights fees that have resulted in network losses. Having rights to certain major league sports may mean prestige for a network, but it may not mean profit. The NBC-NBA deal may mark the beginning of similar deals between other networks and other professional and amateur sports entities. In once instance, it already has. Turner Sports agreed to a similar revenue-sharing extension of its contract with the NBA. Turner and NBC intended to air every playoff game, beginning with the 1994–1995 season.

In terms of local broadcasts, a different situation exists. As of 1992, all but five of the NBA teams were involved in producing their own local broadcasts and selling advertising. At one time, the Boston Celtics even owned a local TV station on which their games were telecast. The reason for these in-house projects was simple: a larger profit. In fact, teams handling production and sales in-house have seen their local broadcast income double. The reader is reminded that local rights fees are in addition to the national rights fees both broadcast and cable networks pay.

The NBA also has recognized the value of prime time. Because of the tremendous viewership generated by the Super Bowl, which is played on Sunday evening, the NBA has scheduled the majority of its playoff games, and its All-Star game as well, for prime time. In some cases, viewership has increased 50 percent. For NBC, the NBA finals in 1993 meant the network had the most prime-time viewers for the week. In fact, three of the games that week were among the top ten most-watched programs. The NBA's TV popularity is not limited to the United States. This has become evident by the league's expansion into Vancouver and Toronto, beginning with the 1995–96 season. Coverage of the NBA playoffs now is seen in seventy countries worldwide. This could, at some future time, lead to a "World Cup" of basketball similar to soccer's event.

The league also has become an innovator in national radio coverage. Starting with the 1992–93 season, the NBA began producing and selling its own radio broadcasts. This is in addition to local coverage of local teams. For example, a station may now find itself as the outlet for both a local team and a national broadcast, as well.

Major League Baseball

Innovation in broadcast rights is not limited to the NBA. Major league baseball attacked its broadcasting problems in a different manner. The innovative approach for the 1994 season came after owners and broadcasters got a "wake up call" following years of declining interest in the so-called national pastime.

From 1985 to 1993, baseball ratings continually declined. Playoff ratings dropped 37 percent during that same period. No network experienced a playoff advertising sellout during those eight years. And from 1990 to 1992, viewership of regular season games dropped 28 percent. One reason given for the apparent lack of interest is that baseball appeals mostly to older viewers, meaning younger viewers are being attracted to other sports.

According to Nielsen Media Research, ratings have declined steadily during the first portion of the 1990s (see table 5.4).

From 1985 to 1992, World Series ratings dropped 30 percent. For the league championship series during the same period, the drop was close to 37 percent. The 1993 All-Star Game had a rating of 15.6, its second-lowest since 1967!

TABLE 5.4: The Decline of Baseball Television Ratings

	CBS			ESPN
	Regular Season	League Championship Series	World Series	Regular Season
1989			16.4[a]	
1990	4.7	11.6	20.8	2.1
1991	4.0	11.9	24.0	2.0
1992	3.4	10.5	20.2	1.5
1993		11.8	17.3[b]	

a. The 1989 World Series between Oakland and San Francisco was marked by an earthquake in the Bay Area.

b. The 1993 World Series between Toronto and Philadelphia was marked by a rain-delayed game 3, which did not end until after 1:00 A.M., Eastern time, resulting in a 15 percent drop in ratings for that game.

After CBS said it lost $500 million during its four-year, $1.057 billion contract with major league baseball (MLB) the network talked of renegotiating a renewal for less money. Team owners worried that a reduced income would fail to cover their payroll commitments. That's when ABC and NBC came to the rescue, proposing a six-year partnership with MLB, starting with the 1994 season. The deal provided the following:

- Formation of a separate entity that includes ABC, NBC, and MLB. The new company, called The Baseball Network (TBN), sells advertising and markets the game.
- Rights fees became a thing of the past. Instead, each of the three parties to the agreement provided $16 million in seed money to get the new entity started.
- During the first year of the six-year contract, MLB was to receive 88 percent of the profits. The two networks would split the balance. The 88 percent figure may seem high to the reader. However, in recent years 90 percent of the expense of televising a game involves payment of rights. For the World Series, rights consume 95 percent of a network's production expenses.
- The leagues were divided into three divisions, resulting in the creation of an additional round of playoffs, with the potential of 20 more postseason games.
- Twelve regional games were scheduled to be aired, none before the All-Star break. The regional concept is similar to the plan utilized by the National Football League with success. Regional games tend to enjoy ratings levels triple those of games receiving national coverage. Additionally, all telecasts were moved to prime time, with games beginning at 7:06 P.M. (EST). During one of the few regular season games played in 1994, a Saturday night game in July had a 6.8 rating and 15 share, double the 1992 season average!
- There were several other changes, including playoff scheduling and rotation of World Series coverage between the two networks.
- Because of the players' strike, only a few weekly games were telecast, before the major leagues canceled the balance of the season.

ESPN was not part of this arrangement. Instead, it renewed a more conventional, six-year contract with MLB that had one notable exception. It gave ESPN the exclusive right to televise the season opener...and on a Sunday night. Traditionally, the season opener had occurred on a Monday afternoon.

It should be pointed out that both these agreements only covered television. CBS Radio had a separate contract with major league baseball.

The ABC-NBC-MLB television venture was a landmark agreement for dealing with escalating rights fees. It may become a common practice in other sports. Proponents argue that television and sports both stand to gain by sharing the risk... and the profits.

Local Baseball Rights

Local television rights were unaffected by the creation of The Baseball Network. Rights fees for local radio and TV coverage totaled $353 million for 1993. That amount was nearly equal to the $400 million CBS and ESPN paid for national coverage. Thus, local rights fees represented nearly half of all the broadcast income for major league teams.

Major league team owners have come to depend on rights fees to help support the ever-escalating salaries they are required to pay players. During 1994, the average player would have earned $1.2 million if the entire season had been played.

The Olympics

The Olympic Games transcend sports. Because of their unique appeal, Olympic telecasts attract male and female viewers equally and dominate upscale markets. Advertisers are attracted to the Olympics for these reasons and broadcasters do their best to provide an attractive package that will generate enough income to at least break even. The Olympics provide more than the potential for profits. For the summer games, TV networks set aside a significant amount of advertising time for themselves. Instead of selling this time to advertisers, the networks advertise their own prime-time entertainment programs. Thus, the network that airs the Summer Olympics uses it as a vehicle to gain viewers for the new prime-time fall entertainment season.

It seems to work. Networks have been employing this strategy for decades. Even during the Winter games, networks promote new, mid-season entertainment show replacements, or attempt to heighten interest in established shows that may be faltering.

During the actual period the Olympics are on the air, the network with the broadcast rights is often the dominant ratings leader. For the 1992 Summer Games, for example, NBC won every night during the first week of coverage, earning an overall 19.2 rating for the week. By comparison, according to Nielsen Media Research, CBS had an 8.2 and ABC a 7.5. While the impact of Olympic coverage can be significant

TABLE 5.5: Rising Rights Fees for Summer Olympic Games Coverage

Year	Network	Location	Fee
1968	ABC	Mexico City	$ 3,000,000
1972	ABC	Munich	13,500,000
1976	ABC	Montreal	25,000,000
1980[a]	NBC	Moscow	80,000,000
1984	ABC	Los Angeles	225,000,000
1988	NBC	Seoul	300,000,000
1992[b]	NBC	Barcelona	401,000,000
1996[c]	NBC	Atlanta	456,000,000
2000	—	Sydney	—

   a. NBC withdrew from coverage of the Moscow games following the Soviet Union's invasion of Afghanistan, and claims to have been refunded most of its deposit.
   b. NBC sold Canadian broadcast rights to CTV for $16.5 million.
   c. NBC sold Canadian broadcast rights to CBC for $20.7 million. NBC also scheduled coverage of U.S. Olympic Trials in June and July of 1996.

during the period the games are aired, critics claim the benefits are not long-lasting and do not carry over to the regular entertainment season that follows They claim a network does not gain an expanded audience but merely "rents" one.

Nevertheless, networks holding rights to Olympic coverage claim that if they can break even, the effort is considered a success, because of the prestige and promotional opportunities the network has received.

Rights fees for the Summer Olympics have escalated over the years. Table 5.5 illustrates these rising fees.

Coverage of the Winter games is nearly as expensive. CBS paid $243 million for the 1992 Albertville games, $295 million for the 1994 Lillehammer games, and $375 million for the 1998 games in Nagano, Japan. Perhaps because it no longer had to worry about losses from major league baseball, CBS was in a better position to outbid the other networks for the 1998 games.

Beginning in 1994, the International Olympic Committee (IOC) decided to hold the Winter and Summer games on alternate even-numbered years. This may benefit broadcasters for several reasons:

- Advertisers can better control budgets, and broadcasters can achieve more consistent sales. More money will be available for spot buys.
- Olympic coverage can be expanded without fear of oversaturating the audience.
- Continuing interest by viewers in Olympic coverage can be maintained.

For the above-stated reasons, and an unexpected one—the attack on figure skater Nancy Kerrigan—CBS enjoyed sales and viewing success for the Lillehammer games. The games from Norway became the most watched event in television history, with at least 92 percent of all American households and 204 million persons watching at least part of the sixteen days and nights of coverage. The overall rating was 27.8, and the share was 42. The Wednesday night figure skating competition, featuring Nancy Kerrigan and Tonya Harding, became the sixth-most-watched single TV show of all time, the third-most-watched sports show of all time, and the highest rated program of any kind ever seen on a Wednesday. With numbers like that, it was no surprise when CBS announced it had made a profit.

One of the techniques employed by network sales departments is to guarantee advertisers a minimum audience and set rates based upon those numbers. For Lillehammer, CBS guaranteed a rating of 18.6. At the time, the estimate was conservative. That's because CBS achieved an 18.7 prime time rating for the Albertville games in 1992.

The 18.6 guarantee was promoted well before the sports world was shocked by the Kerrigan attack and the subsequent investigation that focused on her rival, Tonya Harding. The incident helped spotlight the upcoming Olympic games and especially the women's figure skating competition. Before the games began, some were predicting the ratings might reach 20.

Whether it is Winter or Summer games, a major network provides coverage of only 6 or 7 percent of the total competition. In a notable effort to capitalize on the remaining 93 percent, NBC offered what it called the "Triplecast" on pay cable during the 1992 Seoul Summer Olympics. This was in addition to the 161 hours of free coverage the network provided. For a fee, viewers could select up to 1,080 hours of additional commercial-free coverage. NBC called its pay project a "Triplecast" because viewers had one of three pay-per-view choices, each pegged to a certain amount of coverage. Prices ranged for $29.95 for just one day to approximately $150 for the complete package. The network lost money on the project.

For future Olympics, one major broadcast network may acquire rights and then join forces with superstations and cable networks for additional coverage. Turner Broadcasting already has participated in Olympics coverage in a limited manner, paying CBS for the rights to provide additional coverage of the 1992 and 1994 Winter games.

The Goodwill Games

The Goodwill Games was a creation of Turner Broadcasting Company. It conceived the idea of Olympic-type competition during the even-numbered year between the regular Summer Olympics. The first Goodwill Games were launched in Moscow in 1986, followed by Seattle in 1990 and St. Petersburg, Russia in 1994. Television coverage of the first two games lost money.

Soccer

Although it has received little attention in the United States, soccer is the most popular sport in the world. International viewership exceeds that of the NFL's Super Bowl. The World Cup competition had not involved American broadcasters to any degree until recently, when the United States became the site of the 1994 games. Six months before the competition, only 13 percent of the American people knew that the World Cup games would be held in the United States. This improved after ABC carried eleven Cup games and ESPN carried forty-three. Even so, the audience for the championship game between Brazil and Italy on July 17, carried by ABC, was a modest 9.5 rating and 24 share.

Radio also covered the World Cup. One-On-One Sports Network, an all-sports network with 150 U.S. affiliates, held the English-language radio rights to the games.

The World Cup may have increased awareness and interest in soccer. ESPN, ESPN2, and ABC-TV announced plans to telecast major league soccer in 1995.

The National Hockey League

If the World Cup achieved gains in American TV viewers, part of the credit might go to the size of the soccer ball itself. It's large and easy to follow on television, not unlike a basketball.

One of the major reasons cited for the lack of TV popularity for ice hockey is the size of the puck, barely three inches in diameter. Its smallness makes the puck difficult to follow on television. And play along the near boards also prevents viewing of the puck. Nevertheless, the National Hockey League has expanded, partly because of increased television exposure, most of it on ESPN and ESPN2, which cover the regular season as part of a seven-year, $100 million deal, and ABC-TV, which telecast selected Stanley Cup playoff games.

The league may expand further, thanks to a five-year contract it signed with Fox for $155 million. This was the first time in seven years that the NHL was assured of regular coverage on a broadcast network.

Normally restricted to the colder areas of Canada and the northern United States, the NHL is now expanding to the South and West, recognizing the value of major TV markets such as Los Angeles, Anaheim, San Jose, Dallas, Miami, and Tampa. It is no secret that the league hopes to expand into other larger southern TV markets in the future, such as Houston and Atlanta.

While arena attendance in most towns is good, television viewing is among the lowest of the major sports. For the Stanley Cup playoff games on ABC in 1993, produced by ESPN, ratings were a disappointing 1.7. During the same month, by comparison, the pro bowlers tour had a 3.7. Baseball and seniors golf also outdrew the NHL playoff telecasts. One reason may have been that this was the first national major broadcast network coverage of the National Hockey League since 1980 and viewers simply had not yet discovered it.

In another effort to make the game more compatible with other major sports, and to some degree more understandable, the NHL changed its conference designations from those of people to geographic regions. The Campbell and Wales Conferences were renamed the Western and Eastern Conferences. The Smythe and Norris Divisions are now the Pacific and Central Divisions and are part of the Western Conference. The Adams and Patrick Divisions are now the Northeast and Atlantic Divisions in the Eastern Conference.

The league also produced the 1994 All-Star Game, the first major professional sports league to do so.

Meanwhile, the Anaheim Mighty Ducks, owned by the Walt Disney Company, may be at the forefront of increasing viewer interest in the game. Ducks TV promotion techniques may be adopted by the other teams in the league. For example, the Ducks do not play in a building named an arena. Instead, it is called "The Pond." The Ducks are the reason that the NHL's licensing income has grown faster than any other major league sport. At the same time, the new Florida Panthers team is broadcasting all home games on Spanish-language radio in an effort to attract a brand-new pool of fans.

The NHL must overcome several challenges if it wishes to see increased TV exposure and viewership. The league has experienced difficult years that have seen no national broadcast network exposure, a significant decline in cable viewership, ineffective marketing efforts, and the absence of teams in the South. The smallness of the puck and the necessity for wide TV shots to show developing plays does little to bring the excitement and impact of a truly great sport to the home viewer. In the final analysis, the way the game is designed and played may be its undoing in attempting to draw a larger television audience.

Golf

From a participation standpoint, golf is one of the fastest growing sports in America. As a result, TV golf coverage and viewership is increasing, although it is nowhere near the levels of other major sports. Golf often is perceived to be the sport of middle- to upper-class Americans. After all, it contributes more money to charity than all other sports combined. As a result, advertisers of prestige products flock to buy advertising for these events.

A survey of the Television Bureau of Advertising determined that golf is watched by more voters than any other sport. As a result, it would seem the political advertisers who buy advertising time on golf telecasts are getting more for their money than if they advertise during other sports events. According to the survey, golf delivers 35 percent more voters than an evening network newscast.

Beyond delivering voters, golf also is delivering more viewers. In some cases, the increase has been dramatic. NBC claims its 1993 audience for the Ryder Cup was 52 percent greater than 1991. Still, the 1993 rating of less than 4 was minor compared to the 5.5 rating the PGA Championship received that year on CBS. That was the highest rating for that event in eight years.

Not all golf tournaments have seen viewership increases. Surprisingly, the 1993 Masters on CBS was the lowest-rated ever. Its 6.7 rating represented a 27 percent drop in viewers in four years. Despite this drop, networks are high on the value of golf. For example, in 1995 after twenty-nine years on ABC, NBC was awarded coverage of the U.S. Open for five years with a winning bid of $40 million.

Thanks to cable, golf coverage has expanded to include virtually every weekend of the year, and often all four days of a tournament. ESPN and ABC combine technical efforts for four-day coverage, with the cable network carrying the Thursday and Friday rounds, and ABC—with its own announcers in place—picking up weekend coverage. Other "subcontracting" has seen the USA network acquire cable rights for the 1995 and 1997 Ryder Cup matches from NBC-TV for $1.5 million.

Because golf can provide consistent ratings and deliver an upscale audience, the Skins Game was developed as a "made for TV" event. It was scheduled for a period late in the year when the tournament season had concluded. The Skins Game became so popular that it gave birth to the Senior Skins and the Women's Skins. Further golf coverage began with the creation in 1995 of the twenty-four-hour pay-TV golf cable network. The network has scheduled golf talk and news shows, children's programming, home shopping, instruction, and additional tournaments.

Tennis

While golf enjoys year-round coverage as perhaps no other sport does, tennis has limited television coverage. Even so, rights fees are increasing as significantly as fees paid to cover major sports events. For example, NBC and HBO agreed to pay $140 million to cover Wimbledon from 1995 through 1999. The 45 percent increase was the result of the emergence of the Fox network as a new competitive player. Although Fox actually bid more, the All England Tennis Club apparently decided continuity of coverage was more important than money... this time.

Except for Wimbledon and the U.S. Open, both of which receive extensive coverage, other major events such as the Australian Open receive little exposure beyond a graphic late in a TV sportscast that highlights the efforts of only the top-ranked players.

Curiously, the highest-rated TV tennis match of all time was an exhibition. Dubbed the "Battle of the Sexes," the event was held in the Houston Astrodome on September 20, 1973; Billie Jean King defeated Bobby Riggs.

Auto Racing

Auto racing enjoys nearly year-round coverage, starting with the Daytona 500 in mid-February and continuing until mid-November. In between are thirty other events; one nearly every weekend. Half are covered by ESPN. The balance is shared by Turner Broadcasting and the Nashville Network. Like ESPN, these are cable networks. Of the broadcast networks, CBS airs three races and ABC airs two. But of those two, ABC's coverage includes the world-renowned Indianapolis 500.

TV Promotions

From the standpoint of promotional value to sponsors, the Indy 500 ranks first among all American sports events on TV. In fact, eight of the top ten events are auto races. The other two are the ATP tennis tournament (third) and the Orange Bowl (fourth).

Promotional value is defined as the number of commercial messages seen on TV, with each image given a dollar value based upon time seen on the air. The complete list for 1993 is provided in table 5.6.

Auto racing and television have formed a symbiotic relationship that has proven profitable to both. (Source: Courtesy of CBS Sports)

TABLE 5.6: Promotional Value of Televised Auto Races

Rank	Event	Number of Images	Value
1	Indianapolis 500 (USAC)	307	$72,396,500
2	Daytona 500 (USAC)	174	28,264,025
3	Newsweek Cup (ATP tennis)	70	13,216,445
4	Federal Express Orange Bowl	75	12,490,000
5	Toyota GT Grand Prix	283	7,333,315
6	Chevy Dealers Busch Grand National (NASCAR)	266	6,125,255
7	Mopar Summer Nationals (NHRA)	63	5,395,835
8	Talladega (IROC)	53	4,565,325
9	Motorcraft 500K (ARCA)	532	3,565,135
10	Toyota Grand Prix (SCCA)	354	3,536,420

Source: Courtesy of *Financial World* magazine.

Although other events may have had more images than the Indianapolis 500, the higher rating (8.6 for 1993) contributed to the Indy's higher dollar value.

Promotions are increasingly found everywhere. Inside race cars, we now see advertising that is picked up by on-board cameras. In horse racing, jockeys in New York state wear advertising logos on their boots and clothing. In basketball, signs displayed in front of a scorer's table revolve periodically to show a new advertiser. Minor league and college baseball stadiums display advertising signs on outfield fences. Now, the trend is to add these signs to the backstop. This way, a camera positioned in center field would be able to see the advertiser's message on every pitch. Major league teams are expected to raise from $750,000 to $2 million a year in added revenue. In college football, the bowl sponsor's logo is sewn on to every player's jersey. These various promotional devices are now competing with the more traditional method of presenting an advertising message during a break in the action. And it also means the radio or TV sales person is competing more fiercely with billboard operators and others for the advertising dollar.

Other Sports

Not all sports generate consistently high viewership. Yet, even some sports considered "minor" can attract large audiences for major events or championships. For example, the Kentucky Derby horse race of 1992 had a rating of 8.9, which outdrew the combined audiences that day of pro basketball and major league baseball. When America had a team in the Little League World Series in 1993, the game drew an audience of 6.6: the highest since 1985. Again, this single event for that day outdrew viewership of major league baseball.

Sports anthology programs such as ABC-TV's *Wide World of Sports* have enjoyed loyal viewership over the years. The pro bowlers tour, also on ABC-TV, is becoming middle-aged, with more than thirty-four years of coverage. No sport is too small for the small screen. For example, a dog show can outdraw college basketball. That happened in February 1993 when the Westminster Kennel Club show averaged a 3.6 for two nights on USA. College basketball on ESPN normally earns less than a 2.

One of the newest trends is the movement into television by the magazine industry. While *Sports Illustrated* has gone into special programs and videos, a major step was taken by Times Mirror Magazines. In mid-1994 it announced the creation of the *Outdoor Life* cable channel, which could draw together the corporation's publications dealing with hunting, fishing, camping, skiing, and yachting.

Pay-per-View

Pay-per-view, or PPV as it is most often called, has been utilized with great success by boxing promoters. Title fights are most often seen on PPV, which allows the bout itself to be held in a relatively small arena. Non-heavyweight title fights are now attracting PPV audiences of more than 1 million homes. At prices approaching $40 for rental of a descrambler, the income potential is enormous.

Americans accustomed to seeing most other sports on free television are concerned about losing what they believe is their "right" to free TV. So far, the fear has not been realized. The growth of PPV has involved events that networks have elected not to cover because of low viewer interest. As stated earlier in this chapter, additional events of the 1992 Olympics were covered by NBC on its Triplecast. These often included the less popular sports or preliminary events that had not normally been part of Olympics coverage. College football and basketball games are often on PPV, along with a few professional games as well. All of these games are considered to be of secondary interest, even to a regional TV audience. ABC-TV began experimenting with pay-per-view in 1992. Customers received two to four PPV college football games per week. For this, viewers had the choice of purchasing one week or an entire season, at rates ranging from $9 to $60.

The NFL is a partner in "Sunday Ticket," a satellite service that provides games for dish owners. During 1994, 70,000 subscribers signed up for the season's coverage, at $99 each.

Other PPV games can generate sufficient income to cover production expenses and result in a profit for their producers. The colleges and universities also benefit. A local rivalry can be especially profitable. For example, Oklahoma State University earned $70,000 from pay-per-view coverage of its football game with the University of Oklahoma in 1991.

Pay-per-view has been called an unregulated arm of a highly regulated industry. Because few rules restrict the business, PPV has experienced tremendous growth. Sales during the seven-year period ending in the year 2000 were expected to jump from $200 million per year to more than $1 billion. This includes all forms of programming, including non-sports offerings such as movies.

The Future

It is clear that sports on television—and radio—will continue to grow. Television is creating events to fit scheduling niches or to ensure continued coverage. Examples include beach volleyball, celebrity golf, three-on-three basketball, and roller hockey. If a network owns a sport or a league, it does not have to worry about escalating rights fees or having another network take the event away, leaving a scheduling void, such as the loss of NFC football by CBS. For example, CBS quickly introduced a new sports anthology show, *Eye on Sports*. ESPN launched what it called *The Extreme Games*, featuring activities such as bungee jumping, in-line skating, sky surfing, skate boarding, windsurfing, and street luging. Meanwhile, other sports, such as track and field, have been working to get national television exposure.

Interactive Sports

Interactive television involves the viewer more personally than ever before, because the viewer is able to send a signal back to the broadcaster. For example, the Interactive Network, which started operations in San Francisco in 1993, charges viewers $15 a month to forecast plays while watching NFL or MLB games. Like a pinball machine, viewers get to compare their scores with those of other viewers.

The Creek Nation announced plans in 1994 to telecast its bingo games. Viewers could buy a bingo card and watch a proxy play it for them. The same year the Maryland Racing Commission tested a method of wagering on horse races using a viewer's home television set, a special cable box, and a credit card.

The future of sports broadcasting means more than interactive television. It also includes programs to sell sports merchandise. For example, ABC-TV has offered specially made gear such as *American Sportsman* hiking boots and *Monday Night Football* slippers as part of its merchandising "club." ESPN announced that it would offer video games produced by Sony. WGN-TV in Chicago was one of the first local stations to jump in with a home shopping club, offering Cubs memorabilia in an hour-long telecast. "NewsSport," a sports news cable network partly owned by NBC, began operations in 1994.

Sports trivia game shows are now starting up and may be offered nationally. Awards shows are blossoming. ESPN now has the *Espy*. Others have been started and may enjoy yearly success.

Broadcasters are recognizing that Spanish is America's second, unofficial national language. As a result, more is being done to accommodate this rapidly growing segment of the population. A Spanish-language regional all-sports TV network was announced in 1993. A national Spanish-language all-sports network may not be far behind. This might feature sports most non-Spanish Americans may not be familiar with, such as soccer, jai alai, and bullfighting.

In radio, more and more professional teams are adding Spanish-language play-by-play on their regional networks. Nationally, the CBS Hispanic Radio Network launched a daily sports show.

A sports/talk radio network was starting in 1994. By the end of its first year, SportsFan Radio Network was heard on sixty stations, and in twenty-two of the top thirty markets.

Even while flying, travelers now have the choice of two in-flight sports radio services. *USA Today* Sky Radio and FlightLink On-The-Air both provide extensive sports programming, including play-by-play broadcasts.

As we approach the twenty-first century, the venerable telephone has adapted and become an even more important partner in broadcast sports. While still providing the vital link that brings a high school basketball game to its home market many miles away, other phone services are being offered by local stations providing scores and highlights. ESPN, for example, gives scores over a 900 number, costing 95 cents a minute.

The phone is not limited just to scores. Two Ohio companies provide play-by-play of virtually every local sports team in America, pro or amateur. For fees beginning at $30 an hour, fans can dial up any game in the country from their own telephone.

Two broadcasting giants, TCI and Westinghouse, have started broadcast representative firms that deal exclusively with sports programming. These rep firms, as they are known, work for individual stations or networks and generate advertising orders, known as "spot" buys, from advertisers and ad agencies.

It's not just a game, anymore.

The MVP for This Chapter

Anne K. Elliot, Director of Communications for Nielsen Media Research, provided and checked many of the figures in this chapter, and portions of the previous chapter as well. Her assistance is appreciated.

6 Radio Technology

F or much of the twentieth century, broadcasts of most sports events involved the use of the telephone. To a large degree, especially for radio, they still do. The technology then—and now—was simple. A radio station would order a telephone line a couple of weeks in advance of the event, and the phone company would string a line into the stadium or arena where the event would take place.

From that point, an announcer would simply attach a telephone and use its handset to deliver the play-by-play. The other hand was conveniently free to jot notes and statistics. That's exactly how some of the early sports events were broadcast. But the quality was often tinny because of the early telephone's tendency to reproduce mostly high frequencies. Compounding the problem was the difficulty of providing coverage from long distance. Many lines were poorly amplified, resulting in signals that were difficult to hear at best.

So-called dedicated phone lines solved these problems, but at a much higher expense. One reason was that AT&T had a monopoly over these circuits. That monopoly was challenged in 1967 by an invention of Thomas Carter. His device, which he called the Carterphone, would patch ordinary telephone conversations into radio equipment and allow for the connection of mobile radio telephones into AT&T's land line network. AT&T claimed it alone had the right to control connection of any accessory equipment to its cables. When the corporation refused to allow Carter to sell his invention, he filed an antitrust suit against AT&T. The FCC ended up deciding the case, and it ruled that the connection of such devices was not harmful to the system and therefore AT&T could not unreasonably prohibit the connection of equipment manufactured by Carter or any other competitor. The FCC ruling cleared the way for the development of other types of devices that could be used with AT&T equipment, including broadcast equipment.

As a result, apparently to minimize competition, AT&T developed its own device known as the "QKT Voice Coupler" in 1968. This enabled ordinary broadcast lines to be used as broadcast circuits. The coupler allowed radio equipment to be hooked up to those lines, called "business lines" by the phone company, at a fraction of the cost of dedicated circuits. The coupler was available on a rental basis from the phone company.

This example of cost savings is based on a 200-mile remote broadcast within the state of Missouri. Installation of a dedicated line cost a minimum of $263, plus a monthly rate of between $288 and $1,742, depending upon the quality of the line. With the development of the coupler, however, installation was reduced to $115, with a monthly fee of $40. In either case, the actual cost of each call (for each game) was an additional amount that was charged to the phone bill. In other states, rates were even cheaper. In Kansas, installation was $5 and the monthly rental fee was 50 cents.

The voice coupler still had a problem of creating a less than realistic or tinny sound. This imperfection was corrected in 1978 with the invention of the "low frequency extender." As its name implied, the ability to retransmit bass and baritone sounds greatly improved the fidelity of remote broadcasts.

During the last half of the twentieth century, reliable mixers were developed that made radio coverage of sports and other remote broadcasts easy to handle. These mixers allowed up to four microphones to be plugged into the back of the small unit, which was not much larger than a big phone book. Each microphone had its own volume control on the mixer, with a master control that handled all mikes at one time. Units such as the Shure™ mixer became popular because of their small size and ease of operation. This unit, plus microphones and earphones, plus an available telephone line, were all that was needed to bring sports play-by-play into America's homes. Many sports broadcasters got their starts with a Shure mixer, a microphone, and a telephone packed in a battered suitcase. They were the staples of the radio remote industry.

Now, radio has become more sophisticated. Even the terminology has changed. A remote is no longer called a remote. It is called a NEMO, which is an acronym for Not Emanating Main Organization. Additionally, wireless methods of sending a program back to a station for retransmission have been developed and refined, resulting in reception quality equal to the standard of FM radio.

The Marti

The best known portable remote unit is the Marti™, a transmitting device that was developed when vacuum tubes powered all broadcast equipment. Now smaller and lighter thanks to solid state electronics, it is lightweight and small enough to fit in a briefcase. A Marti comes complete with a battery pack, thus eliminating the need for an external power source. Depending upon the model power output, the range is around 20 miles or more, depending upon local terrain and antenna position. This makes the Marti ideal for broadcasting local games to a local station. Beyond 20 miles, a broadcaster still must depend upon a telephone connection or a cellular system.

Because of its price, which is less than $2,500, even small stations can afford a unit. The money spent is generally recouped by savings in telephone charges. Even with a Marti or similar system, a sports broadcaster still needs a mixer and microphones.

The Cellcast

With the advent of cellular telephone communications, the radio broadcast industry now has a new device called a Cellcast™. Somewhat similar to the Marti, it boasts two added advantages:

1. There is no range limitation. The Cellcast can be taken anywhere in North America where cellular telephone service is available (usually anywhere that there are enough people to support a local sports team). This makes it ideal for out-of-town broadcasts.
2. A mixer is built into the 16-pound unit, thus requiring only the addition of up to four microphone-headsets, which it can accommodate.

A Cellcast or similar system requires payment of a cellular telephone fee. However, the cellular phone system is somewhat different in its billing methods from a normal telephone service; a local call is any that occurs within an area code. Thus, in twenty-three states where there is only one area code, a cellular call from one end of the state to the other is considered local and long distance charges do not apply.

The Mobile Unit

Devices such as the Marti or Cellcast normally are carried from event to event in a mobile unit. Although a vehicle generally is not needed for such compact equipment, a mobile unit is valued as a promotional device by stations. Usually emblazoned with the station's call letters and dial location, a mobile unit serves as a traveling billboard. It is a continual reminder of the station's service to the community. Even when a mobile unit is not needed to cover a remote, it often is assigned to other station personnel so it can spend as much time as possible in front of the public. The story is told about a mobile unit belonging to a station in New England that was ordered to be continually driven on major highways, seven days a week, and allowed to stop only for gas, maintenance, or remotes. Such is the importance attached to station promotion.

A mobile unit can be any kind of vehicle, including a compact car, van, or four-wheel-drive utility truck. In addition to the remote gear, the mobile unit normally contains police scanners for use by the station's news department, a communications system such as a cellular telephone or two-way radio linking the vehicle to the station, a tape recorder or two, assorted maintenance equipment, and emergency clothing and supplies.

The economics of radio sports broadcasting are such that stations can make handsome profits covering games of even modest interest. Now that equipment and telephone costs have become reasonable, the only other major expense involves personnel. The bulk of most radio sports programming by most stations involves only two persons; the individual at the studio who plays the commercials during time-outs, and the person actually handling the play-by-play. Because of equipment reliability and simplicity, one person can be trained quickly and easily to cover a typical game.

For more ambitious projects, such as a statewide radio network of a college basketball team, a broadcast manager might employ a play-by-play announcer, color analyst, and an engineer. The engineer may string extra crowd microphones to add greater realism to the broadcast, or extend another line to a locker room where postgame interviews are to take place.

For college football games, a sideline announcer may be added, along with a producer to handle the added complexities of the broadcast, a spotter, and a statistician. It is not unusual to have seven or more persons working a football broadcast.

Radio stations can make a handsome profit covering games. This is because sports radio broadcasts can be accomplished with very little equipment. (Source: From the collection of John R. Catsis)

Microphone Placement

Radio depends upon the imagination of its audience for its success. To enhance that imagination, radio engineers and technicians seek new ways to add realism. The most significant way to do this is by the proper use of microphones. Not all microphones are created equal. Knowledge of the different types of mikes and what they can do are of utmost importance to the sports broadcast technician. By selecting the right kinds of mikes and placing them in the proper position at the correct volume, a broadcast is brought to life. It can mean the difference between an exciting broadcast and an ordinary one.

Technicians attempt to provide three essential aural elements to a sports broadcast.

1. *The announcer or announcers.* Mikes for play-by-play and color announcers are now attached to earphones. The completed headset allows for a dependable signal while permitting the announcer almost total freedom of movement.
2. *Crowd noise.* While the headset mikes of announcers can pick up crowd noises, it's usually not enough to add realism to the broadcast. This can be corrected by dedicating a third microphone exclusively

to the crowd. At a football or baseball stadium, these are often suspended from the press box over the seats below. At smaller stadiums or in gyms, the mike can be mounted on a stand and pointed toward the stands.

3. *Game action.* Coaches yelling, squeaky shoes, and basketballs "swishing" through the nets are examples of sounds picked up by microphones dedicated to these jobs. In some instances, wireless microphones are used. Usually, these require the cooperation of a coach or whoever is asked to wear the mike and tiny belt-mounted transmitter. There is a major hazard to using a wireless mike. Because it is generally mounted so that the speech of an individual can be clearly heard, it raises the prospect of profanity accidentally getting on the air. Producers and technicians must exercise caution in their use.

Summary

The advantage of radio sports is that it requires little equipment, the equipment it does require is easy to use, only a few individuals are necessary, events can be broadcast with little advance notice, and the expense is modest. There are now greater opportunities for a station to earn a profit and permit additional sports broadcast opportunities for its personnel.

The MVP for This Chapter

Bill Hodges, the chief technician for the School of Journalism and Broadcasting at Oklahoma State University, is recognized for reviewing and correcting this chapter. He is especially appreciated because of his ability to take a complicated engineering principle and make it easy for the novice to understand.

7 Television Technology

Television coverage techniques and complexities vary with the sport. A sports broadcaster should know what the responsibilities, abilities, and limitations of the TV engineering staff are in order to provide the best possible broadcast.

Know Your Equipment

Engineers insist that broadcasters know what the limitations of the equipment are. Often, when a producer is told something "can't be done," it's not because the engineering staff doesn't want to satisfy the request. More likely, the equipment is not capable of achieving the desired result. If that is the case, the producer should know this well in advance of any telecast, not minutes before airtime. Of course, malfunctions do occur at the last moment and equipment may experience a sporadic problem that cannot be repaired immediately. In those cases, adjustments are made so the telecast may continue.

Producers and on-air talent should make it a point to learn as much as possible about the equipment that is covering their sport. It certainly will help these individuals do a smoother and better job. A by-product of

During inclement weather, cameras are protected by rain covers. Notice the microphone attached to the left of the lens. (Source: Courtesy of CBS Sports)

this knowledge is the ability to suggest new ways of utilizing cameras, character generators, switchers, and audio equipment.

By knowing the equipment, you will also gain the respect of engineers, whose biggest complaint about those who are not members of a station's or network's engineering staff is that they lack equipment knowledge. Engineers will go out of their way to explain equipment to persons who display a sincere effort to learn more about the television sports business.

Union and Nonunion Engineers

During your professional career you will probably work in both union and nonunion shops. Each has advantages and drawbacks for both the engineer and the broadcaster. In a nonunion operation, the engineer may be expected to perform many functions. A person normally assigned to operate a videotape machine, for example, may be called upon to perform maintenance on that machine. Or she may be pressed into service installing cables in a press box.

The advantage of a nonunion shop extends to the nonengineer employee as well. You may have the opportunity to operate some of the equipment used in sports coverage, such as cameras, videotape recorders, switchers, audio mixers, and character generators. Although you already may have had some experience with these in school, chances are your skills will be upgraded by working with state-of-the-art equipment under professional guidance. These skills will help you progress up the professional ladder, even if you never touch another piece of equipment.

Two of the biggest unions are NABET, the National Association of Broadcast Engineers and Technicians, and IBEW, the International Brotherhood of Electrical Workers. At a union shop, unless you are a member of that union, you are prohibited from operating, and in some cases even touching, electronic equipment. Engineers in these operations normally are specialists who have had many years of experience in their assigned area. They can provide invaluable assistance, and are often delighted to show any interested person how they do their job and how the equipment works. The big difference, of course, is that you will not be allowed to operate the equipment.

Whatever kind of shop they work in, union or nonunion, engineers and technicians are professionals. Like you, they probably have chosen to work sports events because they like the excitement, the travel, good pay, and most of all, because they like sports. Like you, they are away from their families on weekends, working long hours as well. In fact, they normally spend more time at the site of a sports event than most producers or on-air talent.

Pregame Preparations

Traditionally, coverage of an out-of-town event such as a college basketball game usually saw a remote truck arrive at the site thirty-six to forty-eight hours before game time. More recently, however, this has been reduced significantly. In some cases, remote production trucks now arrive twelve to twenty-four hours before the scheduled event. There are two reasons for this reduction in pregame preparations:

1. To save money. Network sports production costs have increased dramatically, and one way to save is by reducing the costs that involve transporting, housing, and feeding crew members.
2. Many arenas, stadiums, and even some golf courses now have permanent audio and video cables in place. Because there are no cables to string, numerous work hours are saved.

When they arrive, engineering crew members immediately begin work by setting up cables not already in place, installing cameras, and sometimes even installing lights. While this is going on, announcers and production personnel spend most of their time conducting interviews and shooting individual player head shots for graphics use. These functions will be dealt with in greater detail in chapter 8.

It is probable that a member of the engineering staff and a producer visited the arena weeks before to determine if any unusual problems existed or if any special equipment or accessories might be required. For example, an old arena that never had a game televised there before might have inadequate electrical power. An engineer would quickly discover this. The production manager or technical manager would then make arrangements to rent supplementary power such as auxiliary generators. Most remote production trucks do not carry generators.

Arena Lights and Cables

Arena operators experienced with live television coverage have upgraded their power needs, assuring technicians that an adequate amount of electrical power will be available for their broadcast needs. Other arena operators have even installed permanent power and camera cables. This makes the job of setting up for a game easier and faster.

The benefits to the operator are twofold: First, disturbance to the arena's facilities is minimized. Holes that needed to be drilled, for example, have already been drilled to the arena's specifications. Golf courses are especially subject to visual damage because cables must be buried or covered for safety reasons. These precautions result in unsightly areas, usually where cables cross cart paths or lead from camera towers to greens. As a result, the Augusta National Golf Course in Augusta, Georgia, site of the annual Master's Tournament, and Pebble Beach in California, where numerous prestigious tournaments are held, have permanently buried TV audio, video, and power cables. Augusta has already installed special equipment for the day when new technology called high definition television (explained at the end of this chapter) becomes operational. Second, the operator can charge rent for the use of its pre-installed cables, resulting in an additional source of income. The broadcaster does not object to this, because it means the crew can save a day or two of set-up time.

Early Setup

When the remote truck arrives on the scene before the event, the routine is nearly the same at every venue. The engineer in charge locates the power box. Hopefully, this is close to where the truck is assigned to park.

Once in place, other spots inside the basketball arena are located. One is the press area where the announcers sit. In a few arenas, this is not necessarily on the floor. And even where the announcers are on the floor, it may not be on the same side as the official scorer's table.

Engineers, along with the production department, also must determine camera locations. Although there is a standard pattern for camera placement, and a specified coverage role for each camera, adjustments often need to be made, depending upon the arena. For example, if an action camera is located above midcourt, it may serve double duty by getting a close-up of the possession arrow. But if that arrow is not located on the opposite side of the court from the camera, this would be impossible. The generally accepted solution is to assign this to one of the two floor cameras located under each basket. The producer and director must be aware of these peculiarities of coverage.

Basketball

Camera Assignments

Five cameras are normally used to cover a basketball game (see illustration 7.1). Two are located at or near midcourt, and are elevated to duplicate the viewing angle of a fan seated in the middle of the stands.

ILLUSTRATION 7.1: *Standard Five Camera Setup for Basketball*

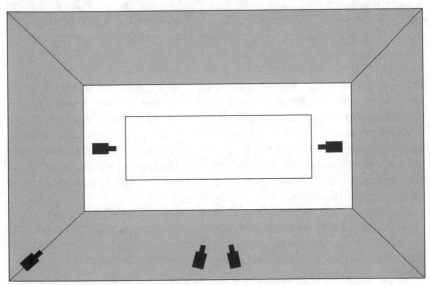

One camera in a basketball telecast is located in a high corner of the arena, and provides background for graphics. (Source: From the collection of John R. Catsis)

Camera one is the principal game camera. Its job is to provide a medium-wide shot of the action. Camera two concentrates on providing close-up action of the ball handler. A director may select camera two when it's clear a player is uncontested for a shot; say, a three-point attempt when the player is loosely guarded, or during a breakaway. Camera two is frequently utilized as a replay camera to capture the individual action. During time-outs, each of these cameras often takes a shot of each bench, photographing the players huddled around the coach.

The third camera also is placed in an elevated position, usually the highest possible location in one corner of the arena. This is often referred to as the transition camera. With the zoom lens placed at its widest setting, it is used to provide an action background into and out of commercial breaks, and to provide a background for character generator data—usually the score.

These three cameras are always tripod-mounted to provide the most stable picture possible for the home viewer. A tripod is especially important because of the cameras' distance from the action and the magnification their lenses are often expected to provide. As with any camera, the combination of distance and magnification can result in a very shaky picture unless a firm support such as a tripod is provided.

The final two cameras do not fall into this category. In fact, their role is just the opposite of the first three. The cameras are hand held and the lenses are often set for wide-angle shots. They are placed right next to most of the action, directly under each basket. The closeness and wide-angle lens settings allow for hand-held photography, which results in a minimum of camera jiggle. And because the cameras are so close to the action, the camera operator does a lot of panning and tilting.

These two cameras are often used in taped replays, but their best-known purpose is to provide intimate close-ups of players during the stoppage of play such as when a foul is called and a player is at the free throw line. The camera operator's principal responsibility is to cover the action that occurs under his or her assigned basket. These camera operators often have the build of athletes. Some even wear knee pads. They must be quick to get into position for the best shots and to get out of the way when necessary.

During pregame, halftime, and postgame segments, these two camera operators serve double duty by photographing the announcers and those they interview. In these cases, the cameras are tripod-mounted. Often, portable supplementary lighting, each on its own tripod mount, is supplied to provide more natural lighting. Arena lights generally are mounted in the ceiling, and point straight down. While ideal for the sport, this form of lighting does not compliment an individual. Without supplementary lights, harsh shadows combined with flat lighting can be the result.

Basketball coverage includes photographers stationed under each basket. (Source: From the collection of John R. Catsis)

Before a game or at halftime, the photographer mounts his or her camera on a tripod, providing a steady platform for interviews with announcers, players, and coaches. (Source: From the collection of John R. Catsis)

A recent development in basketball coverage is to attach small, unattended cameras directly above the center of each backboard. With a wide-angle lens, this provides a unique perspective for replays and free throws. If these cameras are equipped with remote control motors, they also can provide an end-zone look at both offensive and defensive formations at the opposite end of the court.

Microphone Assignments

As with any sports telecast, audio is a critical part of the total broadcast. This is quickly appreciated whenever audio is lost during a game. Good audio is more than just hearing the announcers describe the action. Good audio has become an art, and unique ways of enhancing audio have made sports telecasts even more exciting to watch.

Crowd noise is an important aspect of any broadcast. In basketball, this is usually accomplished by utilizing microphones that are part of cameras one and two, which are the elevated cameras assigned to covering the principal action, plus cameras four and five, which are the two hand-held cameras under each basket. Additionally, there are microphones mounted on each backboard to capture the unique "swish" a ball makes when it goes through the net.

Often, an additional microphone or two is hand held at courtside to capture the squeaking sound of the players' shoes. Including the two announcer microphones, basketball audio can consist of nine or more microphones. Fortunately for the audio engineer, riding gain (keeping the levels constant) is not as difficult as it might seem. Once set up, only minor adjustments are required during the course of a game to keep audio at proper volumes.

Ice Hockey

Camera Assignments

Ice hockey coverage is virtually identical to the camera configuration used for basketball with one exception. The two hand-held cameras, numbers four and five, move to opposite corners of the ice, behind the glass partitions (see illustration 7.2). These capture dramatic close-ups of both action and audio. When a goal is scored, the video from these cameras is often used for slow-motion replay

ILLUSTRATION 7.2: *Typical Camera and Microphone Installation for Ice Hockey Telecasts*

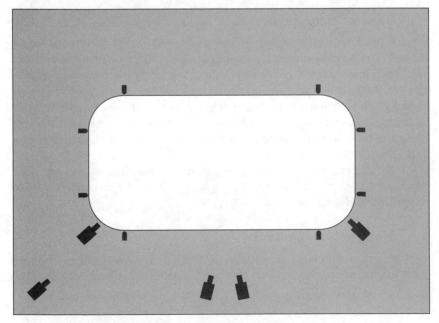

Two recent developments are the installation of cameras in or just behind the goal judge's box, or inside the goal itself. These shots provide a unique perspective of play around the goal and can often illustrate more clearly how a goal may have been scored.

An operational distinction in hockey relates to the way the camera operator views the action from either camera one or two. Under most circumstances, the fast back-and-forth action across the ice is captured while looking through the viewfinder. But that's not the best procedure to follow when the puck is hidden from view by the near boards. Experience has proven that it is better to determine exactly where the puck is located by using the naked eye. To do this, the camera operator looks over the top of the camera. When the puck reappears, he or she returns to using the viewfinder.

Microphone Assignments

As in basketball, microphones are attached to all cameras and pick up the crowd and action noise. Additionally, for some games, especially playoffs, microphones are attached at the top of the glass protective partitions to pick up the sound of skates on ice. Adequate audio coverage can be achieved by installing four mikes on each side of the rink.

Volleyball

Camera Assignments

Camera placements for volleyball are similar to those utilized in basketball. Cameras one and two are placed in the same relative locations with the same assignments. Camera three is located in an elevated area in the end zone, thus minimizing camera or lens movement. The technique is similar to that used in covering tennis. Some volleyball events require additional cameras such as two hand-held cameras located on each end of the court to capture floor-level closeups, time-out conferences, interviews, and crowd reactions.

A final camera, which is unattended, is mounted at the net. It is often used in replay situations, for closeups of blocks and spikes, and to determine if the net was touched.

Microphone Assignments

All cameras used in traditional volleyball coverage are equipped with microphones. For special coverage, such as the Olympic games, up to twenty-one additional microphones are used. Of these, eight are aimed at the audience to pick up crowd noise. Four are located at the outside corners of the playing court to pick up floor sounds, two are mounted on the posts at each end of the net, two are located near each bench, one at the scorer's table, one at the interview area, and two for the announcers. A final microphone, mounted in a parabola (a 24-inch plastic dish), picks up action at the ball.

Tennis

Camera Assignments

A typical tennis match is covered with five cameras. Two cover game action. Both are located at either end of the court, one higher than the other. This is probably the biggest distinction, because of the rapidity with which play alternates from court to court. Can you imagine how dizzy a viewer would become if the cameras were located in the stands directly behind the referee!

There also are two hand-held cameras. But unlike basketball, where the camera operator is free to roam almost as far as the cable will permit, these individuals are required to stay put, seated in a chair at a location assigned to them. This can be in either of two locations: on the sidelines or in the corners. Whenever possible, hand-held cameras are located behind the serving lines to obtain close-ups of the players.

At some events, a fifth camera, remotely operated, is mounted at the net and used for close-in action during replays. The popularity of this camera among producers is diminishing; as a result, it is being utilized less frequently.

Microphone Assignments

Up to fourteen microphones are used to cover the typical tennis match. One is assigned to each of the five cameras. Four others are placed at or near court level directly behind the service area. Another is on or near the net, and two shotgun (highly directional) mikes are mounted near the net, pointing to the center of each player's court area to pick up the sound of shoes and the ball. Finally, the referee is equipped with two mikes mounted on either side of his or her chair. That's so the referee will be heard closely no matter which direction he or she faces. These two microphones also serve as part of the public address system.

Football

Camera Assignments

Television camera coverage of football games is based on some of the principles explained earlier, but there are some variations. For one thing, more cameras are used. A typical network football telecast will see eight cameras employed (see illustration 7.3). For a Super Bowl game, up to seventeen cameras have been used. For a regular season game, there are three cameras assigned to cover the principal action, all at or near press box level. One is located on the 50 yard line and the other two are near each 30 yard marker. Thus, as the action moves across the field, the camera closest to the ball becomes the primary action camera. The other two then isolate (provide a closeup of) players other than ends for replay purposes.

A fourth camera is also on the 50 yard line, often above the other three. If it is possible to locate the camera on the roof of the press box, that's where it often goes. It provides a wide-angle view of the playing field and is principally used for instant replay purposes. One such

ILLUSTRATION 7.3: *Typical Camera Configuration for Televising a Football Game*

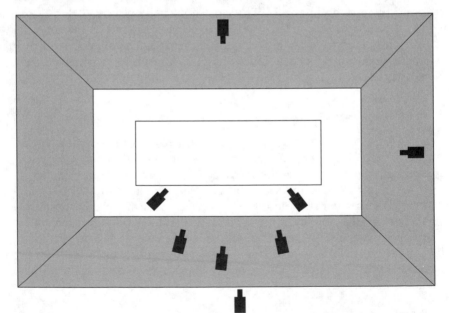

A camera placed in the end zone of the football field covers field goal attempts at both ends of the field, plus closeup shots. (Source: Courtesy of CBS Sports)

example is the Telestrator™, a piece of equipment that allows the color commentator to appear to draw lines and other marks directly on the TV screen.

CHROMA KEY

If one or more of the cameras is located near the announcers, these cameras also serve double duty by photographing the announcers before or during a game. When there is time and space to prepare adequately, one of the walls of the press area is painted in a specific shade of either green or blue. Some stadiums already have walls painted one of these colors. For cases where a colored background is needed quickly, production trucks now carry a green or blue cloth. In most cases, green is preferred.

While the announcers are photographed in front of the colored wall or cloth backdrop, a second camera takes a wide-angle shot of the field. This image is electronically superimposed on the colored wall. While the wall remains blank, the viewer at home sees the announcers with

The wall behind football announcers Robert Allen and John Walls is painted blue, allowing for the blending of a separate image behind them in a process known as chroma key. (Source: From the collection of John R. Catsis)

the playing field behind them; the result of two electronically blended camera images. This is called a chroma key process, or simply "key."

REVERSE-ANGLE CAMERA

In the past few years, a fifth game-action camera has come into use. It is known as the "reverse-angle" camera because it is located on the side of the field opposite from the other four cameras. CBS has been known to use up to three reverse-angle cameras. Whether one or three, the reverse-angle shot is principally used for replay purposes. That's because the reverse-angle camera, with its lens set at a magnification greater than the action camera, often spots detailed action that was not visible to the other cameras. Whenever a reverse camera is employed, announcers are quick to point it out, because the team with the ball that had been moving from left to right across the field, for example, is now moving in the opposite direction. Unless the viewer is warned, both visually and aurally, this can become confusing.

OTHER CAMERAS

A sixth camera is normally elevated above the playing field. This is located behind one of the end zones. Its principal job is to shoot field goal and extra point attempts at both ends of the field. The rest of the time it is used for replay purposes, generally isolating on the ends, and at other times on the sideline coaching action.

On the playing field, two additional cameras are used for various ground-level shots. These cameras are often mounted on a movable platform. Each camera is then able to move between its goal line and the 50 yard line. The camera on the side of the field where the action is occurring is usually located five yards ahead of the play. Its principal responsibility is to provide a close-up image of the quarterback. The other camera may cover both players and coaches on the sidelines. Where permitted, a third ground-level camera is placed on the opposite side of the field. Hand held, it also provides close-up shots of coaches and players on the sidelines.

SPECIALTY CAMERAS

For major college bowl games and the NFL playoffs, additional cameras are used to provide even more close-up or replay possibilities. It should be noted that for every camera assigned replay duties, there is a videotape recorder and VTR operator. Therefore, the number of cameras used in any coverage is dictated in large part by the number of videotape machines available in the remote truck or trucks. In a few cases, such as the Super Bowl, where NBC used up to seventeen cameras and fourteen tape machines in 1993, several remote trucks are required for videotape and graphics support. For some games, cameras have been installed on the crossbar of each goal post. Remotely controlled, they are able to tilt and pan and follow place kicks and other action. Other cameras are installed atop one or more of the uprights.

CBS developed a robotically-controlled camera that it mounted over the sideline; it was able to zoom in for tight shots. At the New Orleans Superdome, a system of cables stretched over the playing field allowed for a movable "Sky Cam" that seemed to fly over the action.

Microphone Assignments

A minimum of five microphones are used for football coverage. The play-by-play and color announcers each have a mike. Even though most announcers are stationed in open-air booths and their mikes are capable of picking up crowd noise, this is usually not as good as dedicating a separate microphone for this purpose. As a result, a third mike is usually located just outside the booth, and its volume can be adjusted separately from those of the announcers.

All cameras assigned to the playing level are equipped with

microphones. In addition, two to four individuals, with split assignments on opposite sides of the field, hold parabolic microphones. These are wireless mikes mounted inside an acrylic dish about two feet in diameter. From a position five yards ahead of the play, the dish gathers and helps magnify sounds from the middle of the playing field, thus providing a greater sense of realism to the game. That's how the great hits are often heard.

In 1994, Fox introduced Dolby™ Surround technology to its NFL coverage. Viewers with stereo sets could, with additional speakers, receive up to four channels of audio. This became possible by the use of a series of parabolic microphones placed around the playing field.

Soccer

Camera Assignments

Interest in soccer in the United States has been heightened by coverage of the World Cup matches, held in the United States in 1994. At least eighteen cameras, plus a nineteenth in a blimp hovering overhead, were used in the semifinal and championship matches at the Rose Bowl in Pasadena, California.

There is a similarity between football and soccer in terms of camera placement. Two cameras are located at the announce booth area in the high center of the stadium. These provide the main action shots, plus occasional close-ups of the announcers. A third is located above the announce booth, providing wide-angle shots of the field. Two others are midway down the seating area, and 20 yards on either side of the center line. These provide additional game action shots. Two more cameras are at field level, along the sideline, or in the end zones, either hand held or mounted on lowboys. Once in position, these cameras do not move. They are used for tight close-ups of action and players' faces. Finally, two other cameras are mounted above and behind each goal line to provide a different perspective of the action. Most often these "end zone" shots are used for replays. Each of these nine cameras is equipped with an extremely long telephoto lens.

Taking a tip from pro football, two additional cameras with standard-length telephoto lenses are placed on opposite sides of the field. These cameras provide reverse-angle shots that are mainly utilized for replay situations.

Five hand-held cameras are another part of soccer coverage. Two are equipped with long cables that permit the operators to roam the sideline from the center line to behind the goal line. These two cameras provide ground-level action close-ups. Two more cameras concentrate on

Camera Information, 1994 World Cup Soccer Coverage

LOCATION: PASADENA					MOBILE UNIT		
CAM #	CAMERA INFO		LENS INFO		MOUNT	LOCATION	CABLE INFO	
	TYPE	MODEL	TYPE	FOCAL LENGTH			TYPE	LENGTH
1				55 X 1	TRIPOD	LEVEL 3 TELEVISION BOOTH	TRIAX	
						BOOTH 315		
2				55 X 1	TRIPOD	LEVEL 3 TELEVISION BOOTH	TRIAX	
						LEFT OF CAMERA 1		
3				55 X 1	TRIPOD	LEFT SIDE SEC 17 ON PLATFORM	TRIAX	
						IN VOMITORY		
4				55 X 1	TRIPOD	RIGHT SIDE SEC 20 ON PLATFORM	TRIAX	
						IN VOMITORY		
5				55 X 1	LOW BOY	LEFT SIDE LINE FIELD LEVEL	TRIAX	
6				55 X 1	LOW BOY	RIGHT SIDE LINE FIELD LEVEL	TRIAX	
7				55 X 1	TRIPOD	LEFT END ZONE UNDER SCOREBOARD	TRIAX	
						DO NOT BLOCK SCOREBOARD		
8				55 X 1	TRIPOD	RIGHT END ZONE UNDER SCOREBOARD	TRIAX	
						DO NOT BLOCK SCOREBOARD		
9				18 X 1	HAND HELD	LEFT END ZONE FIELD LEVEL CABLE	TRIAX	
						DROP TO CENTER FIELD POSITION	RF	
10				18 X 1	HAND HELD	RIGHT END ZONE FIELD LEVEL CABLE	TRIAX	
						DROP TO CENTER FIELD POSITION	RF	
11				55 X 1	TRIPOD	ON ROOF ANNOUNCE POSITION	TRIAX	
					WHEELS	ALSO FOR BEAUTY SHOTS		
12				18 X 1	HAND HELD	FLASH AREA FAR RIGHT END ZONE	TRIAX	
						AT TUNNEL		
13			POV	WIDE ANGLE	ON NET	LEFT GOAL NET REMOTE PAN & TILT	RF	
14			POV	WIDE ANGLE	ON NET	RIGHT GOAL NET REMOTE PAN & TILT	RF	
15				18 X 1	HAND HELD	LEFT BENCH AREA	TRIAX	
						FOR SEMI & FINAL GAMES ONLY		
16				18 X 1	HAND HELD	RIGHT BENCH AREA	TRIAX	
						FOR SEMI & FINAL GAMES ONLY		
17				55 X 1	TRIPOD	REV ANGLE LEFT SIDE ACROSS FROM	TRIAX	
						CAMERA 3 ON PLATFORM VOMITORY 7		
18				55 X 1	TRIPOD	REV ANGLE RIGHT SIDE ACROSS FROM	TRIAX	
						CAMERA 4 ON PLATFORM VOMITORY 2		
19				55 X 1	BLIMP	FUJI BLIMP	RF	
20						NOTE: 2 HAND HELDS GO TO STUDIO		
						FOLLOWING GAME		
						CABLE TOTAL		0

Source: Courtesy of EBU International

each team's bench area, providing close-ups of the coaches and reserve players. A fifth camera is located near the passageway where the teams enter and leave the playing field. This allows for quick interviews during halftime and at the end of the game.

Remote-control cameras are attached to each goal. These tiny cameras are able to tilt and pan, providing a vantage point that closely resembles the action a goalie might see. These two cameras are mostly used in replay situations.

Microphone Assignments

Six of the cameras assigned to the semifinals and finals were equipped with microphones intended to pick up crowd noises. Twelve other mikes encircled the Rose Bowl at playing level to provide audio from the players. Four of these twelve were mounted on parabolas. Officials had three wireless mikes, the announce booth had two wired mikes, and the ground-level interview area near the exit to the field also had two. Additional microphones were utilized in a studio area. World Cup soccer audio was broadcast in stereo, but most viewers with stereo TV sets were unaware of this. That's because the satellites that carried the games were equipped only for mono broadcasts.

Baseball

Camera Assignments

Baseball television coverage provides some of the biggest challenges in sports because there is often action in two areas of the field at the same time. For example, an outfielder may be chasing down a base hit to the wall, while a runner is rounding third base and heading for home. For the fan at the ballpark, seeing both events is not very difficult. However, television coverage requires expert camera work and a talented director and production team. That's why ESPN, for example, has one crew that works only baseball games. They know each other and baseball so well that they rarely say much to one another during a game. Talented teams are not limited to the playing field.

Generally, seven cameras are used to cover a typical baseball game (see illustration 7.4). In a few instances, up to nine have been employed. The most significant camera is the one located in center field. With a powerful telephoto lens, it provides a close-up view of the pitcher delivering the ball to the batter. This shot effectively shows the "action"

TIME-OUT 7.2

Audio Equipment, 1994 World Cup Soccer Coverage

No.	Microphone Type	Area	Mount	Cable Length
1 2 3 4		NEAR SIDE LINE FAR SIDE LINE	RF PARAB RF PARAB	
5 6 7 8	SENN 816	LEFT END ZONE BEHIND NET RIGHT END ZONE BEHIND NET	ON STAND OR WALL MOUNT	
9 10 11 12	SENN 416	LEFT CORNER FLAG RIGHT CORNER FLAG	GROUND MOUNT GROUND MOUNT	
13 TO 18	ME - 80	CAMERAS 3, 4, 5, 6, 9, 10	CAMERA MOUNT	
19 - 20 21	WRT - 27 ECM - 50	REFEREE AND LINESMAN	RF WIRELESS	
22 - 23	RE - 50	ANNOUNCE POSITION	HAND HELD	
24 - 25	EV 635	FLASH AREA	HAND HELD	
26 TO 33	EC 635 OR ECM - 50	STUDIO AREA MIGHT NEED UP TO EIGHT MIKES	LAVALIER OR HAND HELD	
34 - 35		CENTER CHANNEL MIKE FOR STEREO		
		MICS FOR CROWD NOISE TBD AT EACH VENUE		

Remarks:

ALL AUDIO TO BE BROADCAST IN STEREO

LINESMAN AND REFEREE WIRELESS TO BE USED IN ¼, SEMI, AND FINAL GAMES ONLY

Program Title	Event	Prod. Date

Source: Courtesy of EBU International

TIME-OUT 7.3

Camera Coverage Outline, Sunday Night Baseball

CAMERA	LOCATION	RESPONSIBILILITIES
Camera 1	Low 3rd	Right-handed pitchers -- left-handed batters -- both dugouts -- lead runner until he reaches 3rd base.
Camera 2	High Home	Play by Play -- follow the ball at all times -- cover all appeals to 1st and 3rd base umpires.
Camera 3	High 1st	Shag infield and outfield -- backup on right-handed batters, left-handed pitcher, and umpire appeals at 1st and 3rd bases -- 3rd base dugout -- lead runner when he reaches 3rd base.
Camera 4	Center-Field	Pitcher, batter, catcher, umpire shot -- go with the ball on passed balls, wild pitches, pop-ups behind the plate, and steals of second -- after tally goes out, go with the ball at all other times.
Camera 5	Low 1st	Right-handed batters -- left-handed pitchers -- both dugouts.
Camera 6	Low-Home	Tight pitcher -- pitcher, batter, catcher, umpire shot -- depending on stadium, plays in foul territory behind the plate -- when tally goes out, go with the ball at all other times.
Camera 7	Left-Center Field	Left-handed batter, catcher, umpire -- right-handed batter, shortstop and third baseman -- lead runner -- pivot at 2nd base and throw to 1st for double play -- outfield shag.
Camera 8	High 3rd	Shag infield and outfield -- backup on left-handed batters and right handed pitchers -- 1st base dugout -- pick off shot at 1st base with pitcher and runner.
Camera 9	Down 3rd Base Line*	Batter and right half of infield -- depending on the stadium, include pitcher in shot.
Camera 10	Handheld	Booth and various additional locations.

* - Where Available.

This camera numbering system will be standard on all ESPN telecasts. While they may differ from what you are accustomed to, (particularly 4 and 5), we must adhere to them.

Individual stadiums will often dictate where we put our cameras and what our cameras can see. Situations will determine many responsibilities. Shot of bullpens, crowd, etc., will depend on who can see them. Every stadium is different, so our approach will vary from city to city. We will take what the stadium gives us. Also, additional isolation responsibilities will be determined by the producer.

Source: Courtesy of ESPN

of the ball. Both the announcers and the fans are able to identify the type of pitch employed and the ball's location upon crossing the plate. This camera is equipped with a 55-1 or larger lens, meaning it is able to get fifty-five times closer than a normal wide shot. From a center field position 410 feet from home plate, a shot at full magnification translates to taking the picture from a distance of seven and a half feet away from the batter!

The reverse of this camera angle is one that is placed at ground level directly behind home plate. This camera is called the "low home" camera. In major league parks it is placed behind shatterproof glass. New parks constructed in recent years have provided custom-made booths for this camera plus a "jugs gun," which is the device that measures the speed of a pitch. This booth is just one of many special accommodations baseball has made to enhance television coverage.

ILLUSTRATION 7.4: *Normal Camera Locations for Baseball*

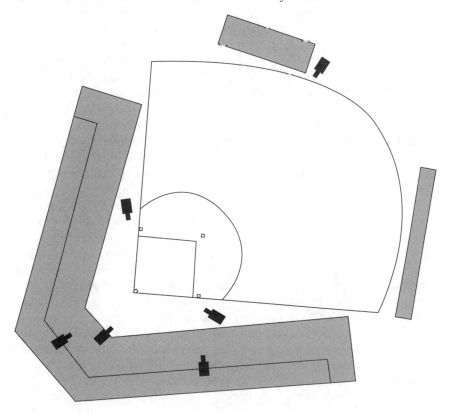

In the 1950s and 1960s the camera was placed in the front row of seating and as close as possible to the chain link fence. By doing so, the lens was able to see "through" the wire fence—the lens was focused sharply on action 30 or more feet away, resulting in a close-up blur that was so extreme, the fence became "invisible." This technique can still be employed successfully in college and minor league baseball stadiums. The most frequent practitioners of this technique today are videographers who capture a few minutes of taped highlights for the local evening news. The blur is hardly noticed by most viewers.

Above the low home camera is the "high home" camera. This camera is located above the net that is extended to catch foul balls hit behind home plate. From this position it is able to provide a traditional view of the infield. When a ball is hit this camera always follows the ball.

Two other cameras are employed in elevated positions behind first and third base. These cameras are known as "high first" and "high third." Both cameras cover action occurring in center field. The first base camera also catches action in left field, while the third base camera's responsibility is right field. There's logic to this apparent discrepancy. In some ballparks, it would be impossible for a camera to pick up action on its side of the field. For example, in Chicago's Wrigley Field, a hit in the left field corner is hidden by a wall. The high third camera would not be able to capture any of the action of the outfielder chasing down the ball. But a "high first" camera shot would have an unobstructed view. The same is true for Wrigley Field's right field corner.

The high position cameras also provide close-ups of the two dugouts. If located in the announce booth, the cameras are used for occasional shots of the announcers.

The final two cameras are called "low first" and "low third." These are placed at or near field level and provide shots of the batter and the opposing dugout. Like the center field camera, these also are often equipped with 44-1 or 55-1 lenses, which is the reason we often see very tight head shots of players and managers. These cameras are capable of zooming in so tightly, viewers can read the printed lineup on the dugout wall. They also pick up shots of the pitcher or of the manager walking to the mound. Some engineers refer to these as "junk" cameras. It's not a derogatory term. It simply means these cameras pick up video scraps, additional shots or angles not available to other cameras. It's up to the creative camera operator to find unique action for the director to call up.

Finally, two additional cameras are sometimes utilized, especially for significant games such as the playoffs and the World Series. These are unattended cameras that point directly down each foul line. Their usefulness in determining how closely a ball was hit fair or foul can easily be appreciated. Finally, there is a growing trend to employ hand-held cameras to provide shots from the fan's perspective, whether it is in the last row of the upper deck or out in the bleachers.

Producers have experimented with cameras mounted on bases and in umpires' helmets. These have yet to capture the imagination of the viewing public.

Microphone Assignments

Setting up audio for most baseball games is a relatively easy job. For one thing, all cameras have microphones. These pick up ambient crowd noises. Additionally, one or two other microphones are located behind and on either side of home plate to pick up sounds of the ball hitting the catcher's mitt or the umpire calling balls and strikes. The faithfulness with which these sounds are reproduced depends upon the acoustic qualities of the ballpark and the distance the mike is placed from the plate.

Beyond that, the audio engineer need only provide microphones for the announcers in the broadcast booth. For special games like the World Series, extra microphones are placed along the outfield wall to catch the sound of an outfielder crashing against the wall as he attempts to catch a fly ball.

Golf

The most time-consuming and difficult of all sports events to cover, from an engineering standpoint, is golf. And that's just the reason why some engineers and technicians enjoy working on golf tournaments—they like the challenge. Unlike other sports, where playing surfaces are essentially identical, golf courses are designed to be different from each other. This offers the technician new layout obstacles to overcome with each tournament assignment. These are challenges Arnold Palmer and Jack Nicklaus never encountered. To gain an appreciation of what's involved, consider what is utilized for a typical golf tourney: fourteen cameras, seven camera towers, eleven video recorders, thirty-five separate microphones, 100,000 feet of audio cable, and 120,000 feet of video cable. And virtually all of the cable must be buried for safety reasons.

Installing video and audio cable has become a science. The key is a special machine called a sod cutter, which resembles a power mower. The blade underneath cuts into the soil at a 45 degree angle, the cable is dropped into this slit about three inches below the surface, and the sod is then tapped down. This prevents spectators and others from tripping

After technicians spend days of laying audio and video cable, announcers make it look easy, as shown in this interview of golfer Lee Trevino by reporter Andy North. (Source: Courtesy of ESPN/Jerry Pinkus)

over exposed wiring. It also prevents the possibility of electrical shock. When a tournament is over, workers grab one end of the cable and simply pull it out of the ground as they walk along the slit.

As explained earlier, golf courses that are frequent tournament sites have begun to install their own cables so there is a minimum of disturbance to the landscaping. Even without this chore, getting ready for a golf tournament is still a lot of work. Often, preparations begin six months in advance, especially if a course is the site of a televised event for the first time. Producers and engineers visit the course to see, first hand, where to run cables and place elevated platforms and cables. From this visit, they are able to determine what special equipment will be needed.

For a typical tournament, members of a network's engineering crew arrive at the golf course five to six days before the tournament is to begin; usually the Saturday before a Thursday start. In some cases they only have four days to set up, because all equipment must be in place in time for a Wednesday pro-am tournament.

Camera Assignments

Golf coverage normally requires several elevated camera positions, and towers and 120 foot tall "cherry pickers" are used. The networks do not own these towers or cranes. They are rented, instead; locally if possible. In the case of the larger, scaffold-type towers on which cameras and sometimes announcers are located, two companies now specialize in renting this equipment nationwide.

Elevated camera positions are useful for two reasons. First, they provide ideal perspectives, especially at the greens. Second, an elevated camera can cover more than just one green or fairway. As a result, fewer cameras and operators are needed. Even so, fourteen cameras and two remote trucks linked together are often used to cover a golf tournament.

The reader should keep in mind that the equipment cited above is sufficient only for seven holes of golf. A typical tournament is covered only from the twelfth to eighteenth holes. For the major tourneys such as the U.S. Open, coverage may include all eighteen holes, in which case more equipment and more cable are required. Twenty or more cameras, for example, are needed if all eighteen holes of a tournament are to be covered.

Because of careful planning, these twenty cameras are able to cover eighteen tee boxes, eighteen fairways, eighteen greens, and the press area. That's because all eighteen holes do not have to be covered at the same time. By Saturday, when a broadcast network typically picks up coverage on the third day of the event, the tourney leaders are known. From these leaders, the eventual winner normally emerges. Therefore, it is not necessary to show every golfer on the course. Those who run these tournaments schedule the leaders to be the last to tee off to heighten excitement for both the gallery and the TV audience. Since the eight or ten leading golfers are grouped together in twosomes, seldom are more than four holes covered at one time by camera crews.

If a tourney ends in a tie, there is sometimes an immediate playoff that often begins on the sixteenth hole. However, there is no requirement that playoff holes be scheduled in any particular order. Even so, tournament organizers are careful to allow for complete television coverage when planning possible playoff holes. Engineers and producers are aware of which holes will be designated playoff holes before the start of the final round.

In any case, with no more than four holes of a typical tournament covered at one time, it's easy to see how fourteen cameras can provide complete coverage. It's done by leapfrogging. For example, if coverage begins on the twelfth, thirteenth, and fourteenth holes, featuring the six leading scorers, then cameras and crews are in place on these holes, plus the fifteenth. As play moves out of the twelfth hole, three camera crews from that hole move over to the sixteenth hole. In some cases, because of tower placements, not all crews will have to move. That's because the towers are often in positions that oversee more than one green or

Golf is the most complex of all sports, technically, to cover. (Source: Courtesy of CBS Sports)

fairway. But reassignment is generally mandated by cameras located at ground level, such as tee boxes. This leapfrogging technique continues until the tournament reaches the last four holes, unless a playoff is required, in which case the procedure begins anew.

Certain camera operating techniques are also unique to golf. This is especially true when showing a ball in flight. Two types of shots are used for this. The most popular involves a camera stationed behind the green. It photographs the ball as it heads toward the camera. Another shot, using an elevated camera, follows the ball as it moves laterally. This is a dramatic shot that requires a high degree of skill on the part of the camera operator.

Even so, computers are now playing a larger part in keeping the ball centered on the viewing screen. Until recently, three other techniques were used to keep the tiny ball in the viewfinder. One method—used principally in the days of black and white television—was to reverse the polarity in the viewfinder. The resulting image would resemble a black and white photographic negative, in which light shades are dark and dark shades are white. When color TV came along, operators would turn on only the green adjustment to the black and white monitor. This would cause the ball to appear darker against the sky. A third method was to rely on a pair of binoculars, which were mounted atop the viewfinder.

SKINS GAME CAMERA COVERAGE

In 1984, sports producer Don Ohlmeyer developed an idea for a different kind of golf event that would feature four prominent golfers playing for thousands of dollars on each hole. The tourney was initially intended to fill a TV golf coverage void during what was then known as the off season, a short period late in the year. Ohlmeyer also wanted TV coverage to be more intimate, and to use wireless mikes to pick up conversations by the golfers.

Before he could develop his idea into a concrete plan, he had to make sure the technology could match his dream. He called in engineers Joe Commare and Horace Ruiz, and for two days the three men walked the Desert Highlands course in Scottsdale, Arizona. In the end, they had agreed that most of what Ohlmeyer wanted could be achieved. As Commare put it, "Don always said that as long as we agreed and he went ahead and made all his arrangements, the only thing that made him go through the wall was when engineering at the last minute said it couldn't be done."

As the very successful Skins game has proven, it could be done.

Since those early beginnings the show has become so successful that it is no longer relegated to the "end of the golf season." And now there are three Skins games—for women, men, and seniors.

One of the innovations of the Skins game was to use cameras that were uncabled, battery-powered, and hand held. Freed of cable restraints, the camera was able to follow the ball and the golfer more closely than in a conventional tournament. Close-ups are what help to make the Skins coverage special.

Unlike a typical golf tournament requiring fourteen cameras and scores of microphones and other equipment, Skins coverage can be achieved with far less. Eight cameras are used. Four are tripod-mounted or "hard" cameras that usually cover greens or fairways. These are moved in the same leapfrogging manner as in a conventional tourney. The four remaining cameras are all hand held, uncabled, and battery powered. These cameras are assigned to follow and stay close to the golfers at all times.

Getting a picture on the air from one of these unwired cameras requires a bit of ingenuity. Basically, the signal can get back to the remote truck by one of two methods.

1. The most widely used method involves a short video cable from the camera connected to equipment held by a second individual standing just a few feet behind the camera operator. He or she has a pole on top of which a small dish is mounted. This dish, which is connected to a small transmitter, sends the TV picture to a tall tower, on which a receiving antenna is located. From there, the signal is relayed to the remote truck by either a conventional cable or another wireless link or "hop" utilizing the same electronic equipment; but in this case, the signal path is locked in. In other words, neither the transmitting nor receiving dish on the tower needs to move.

2. ABC-TV sometimes utilizes a different system for getting the signal back to the remote truck. Instead of a tower, it uses a small tethered blimp as its relay point.

Whatever system is employed, a clean and steady signal is mandatory if the viewer is to see a sharp picture. To accomplish this, the individual behind the camera operator must constantly and accurately point the transmitting dish toward the tower. Additionally, the tower operator must point the receiving dish toward the sender. If either person does not do his or her job, the result is either signal breakup or complete loss of picture. Because of the high degree of skill, experience, and professionalism exhibited by technicians, these problems rarely occur.

Microphone Assignments

The ultimate challenge for an audio engineer is preparing for a golf tournament. That's because the typical tourney requires anywhere from seventy to 150 separate audio lines! They are laid out in three systems: on-air microphones, intercoms for spotters, and intercoms for scorers.

On-air microphone requirements are the least complicated. Each ground-level camera has a microphone mounted on it to pick up the natural sound of the action near its lens. Cameras mounted on towers are not equipped with mikes because they are too far from the action. Each tee box has a mike mounted on a six-inch-high stand. The mike is aimed at where the players will tee their balls. This mike picks up the sound of the "swoosh" made by the golf club as it swings through the air, the "click" of the club striking the ball, and the crowd noise immediately following.

At the greens, all ground-level cameras, including hand-held ones, are equipped with mikes. Until a few years ago, a special microphone, developed exclusively for golf, was used by NBC-TV at major tournaments. It picked up the sound of the ball as it fell into the cup. A regulation cup had been modified to hold a microphone at the bottom, along with a mini-transmitter. The transmitting antenna was wound around the cup and the entire assembly replaced the standard cup. Visually and legally, there was no difference between the two cups. But for the audience back home, it added to the drama.

The balance of the on-air microphones are those used by the announcers. A ground-level microphone with a long cable is used at the eighteenth green so the announcer can interview the winner of the tourney and at the award presentation, while another microphone is situated in a tent or wherever other golfers are interviewed while the tournament is still in progress.

ESPN utilizes a different set-up for its announcers. Instead of being located at a site overlooking the eighteenth green, the announcers work next to one of the remote trucks. From there, they are able to see the tournament develop, almost as a viewer at home might. The exception is that the announcers are able to see action on more than one hole because they are equipped with several monitors.

The second audio system involves intercoms and spotters. There are usually ten to twenty persons, and more for major tournaments. They are assigned to each tee, fairway, and green where play among the leaders is taking place. They use a closed-circuit audio system that does not go on the air. They communicate by means of walkie-talkies or a traditional wired system. These spotters inform the producer of what each golfer is about to do. "Nicklaus about to tee off." "Trevino ready for second shot." These spotters are the reason the at-home viewer can see quick-paced action on several holes in any given minute or two. Beside sending messages back to the producer, these spotters are also tied in to the official scorer, either through a standard cable called a "hard wire" or by walkie-talkie.

The third system of audio, and the second closed-circuit system, involves scorers who are employed by both the tourney operators and the television production company handling the telecast. At the end of each hole, they call the score of each golfer back to a central scorekeeper, who posts the updated scores on the leader board, which is seen by other golfers and the gallery. At the same time, the scorers also notify the TV graphics operator who is back at the main TV production compound. The graphics operator enters the scores on the character generator for TV viewers at home.

Bicycle Races

Some of the coverage techniques used in golf, especially those from the Skins games, are utilized in bicycle road races. These races are most frequently seen during Olympic coverage and can involve unduplicated highway coverage over many miles.

The picture is picked up by a camera mounted on a vehicle that travels along with the bicyclists. The vehicle is equipped with an antenna that has 360-degree coverage. This means that unlike golf, it is not necessary to point the transmitting antenna toward a receiving target. Because the vehicle is moving at a brisk rate, this would result in frequent signal loss. As a result, a special antenna was developed that sends the signal out in all directions. All that is required is for the signal to be received.

This is accomplished by a helicopter flying overhead. With its receiving antenna it takes the signal and relays it through a transmitting antenna to a fixed location, which could be several miles away. The distance between the helicopter and the stationary receiving point is limited by what is known as "line of sight." Since television signals travel in a straight line, line of sight across flat terrain is close to 50 miles. With the aid of a helicopter, which is able to ascend hundreds or even thousands of feet above the ground, transmission distances far in excess of 50 miles are possible. In this case, the distance is most frequently limited by the power of the transmitting equipment located aboard the helicopter.

Auto Racing

Auto racing often involves utilizing tiny cameras that are mounted on several race cars. Owners and drivers must agree to allow the cameras to be installed, and more are doing just that. One reason is that some camera angles, such as a view through the windshield, allow for a new location for printed advertising—the dash just below it. The car owner earns additional advertising income by allowing TV cameras to come along for the ride!

These interior cameras often include motors that allow them to be remotely controlled. The camera can tilt and pan, allowing views not only through the windshield but also out the rear. A third shot shows the driver shifting gears during sharp turns and other occasions. Some drivers object to moving cameras or those that point at their helmeted

Auto racing attracts a loyal audience, and can provide opportunities for announcers seeking additional sports to cover. Here, Gary Lee and Larry Rice cover a race for ESPN. (Source: Courtesy of ESPN/Tom Strattman)

faces. They consider them a distraction. Others believe that the weight of the equipment, averaging fourteen pounds, may affect race performance. But as the equipment continues to get smaller, the objections by car owners and drivers are becoming fewer. However, that's not necessarily the case among advertisers. A show sponsor has seen a competitor's logo displayed inside more than one race car. Solving this dilemma gets the sales department involved.

As a whole, however, the auto racing fraternity is probably more cooperative with broadcasters that any other sport. One reason is the opportunity for additional advertising revenue from displays inside the race car. Another is the excitement the interior views bring to the viewer. This added coverage may be a factor in auto racing's growing TV audience.

Another popular place to mount a TV camera is on the outside of the car, usually on the right-hand side, so as to get a more dramatic shot of the race car as it travels closely toward an outside retaining wall. (In the United States, races on oval tracks are conducted counterclockwise.) One of the problems with this camera is that it can accumulate dirt on the lens. This problem was solved by installing a plastic protector in front of the lens, which unwinds from a clean supply roll every few seconds.

For the 1993 Daytona 500 stock car race, fifteen car cameras were used, including one placed underneath the car driven by Geoff Bodine. Pointing toward a front tire, the idea was to dramatically show how shock absorbers worked and perhaps even to capture tire wear.

Special Techniques

As cameras become smaller and lighter, they are being put to more and better use. One of the memorable first uses for the tiny new breed was the "helmet cam," which made its debut in the United States Football League. This camera was mounted as part of the total helmet design worn by a team's quarterback. With the cooperation of the league, usage of the helmet cam was widespread, and for the first time provided a unique view of the action from a player's perspective.

Since then, tiny cameras have been placed in other locations. ESPN, for example, has converted an infrared camera that was developed originally for use in U.S. spy satellites. Instead of tracking enemy missiles, this camera, mounted in a blimp, is capable of following race cars at night during such events as the twenty-four hours of LeMans, France, or the twelve-hour IMSA race in Sebring, Florida. Because the cameras track heat, they are able to spot cars that are braking even better than a standard camera can during daylight coverage.

Another development is the jockey cam, used for the first time by ESPN during the 1992 horse racing season. This tiny, 20-ounce camera was mounted on the outside of a jockey's helmet and wired to a transmitter attached to the jockey's belt. This equipment counts as part of his or her tack.

Unlike a quarterback's helmet cam, which provides a jerky picture due to the rough-and-tumble action on the football field, the jockey cam is much smoother, thanks to the jockey's skill and the horse's grace. Producers quickly learned that the jockey cam is especially dramatic and exciting if used with a horse that runs well back of the pack and then closes quickly near the finish. Like cameras mounted outside race cars, the jockey cam also suffers from the risk of dirt splatters on the lens.

Hockey is seeking new ways of covering the sport, which is problematic because the puck is so small and often difficult to follow. One technique used during the 1993 National Hockey League all-star game involved a camera mounted on the helmet of Montreal goalie Patrick Roy. Similar to football's helmet cam, this camera was always pointed at the player with the puck and provided a dramatic new perspective to the sport.

During the 1987 Little League Baseball World Series, another camera similar to football's helmet cam was used for the first time, mounted on the umpire's helmet. Appropriately dubbed the "ump cam," this new vantage point showed the pitches as batter, catcher, and umpire might see them. The experiment was such a success that ABC hoped to expand its usage to major league baseball.

Super Bowl telecasts are known for, among other things, premiering new commercials for sponsors willing to pay fees now exceeding a million dollars for thirty seconds of airtime. The Olympics, on the other hand, are known for introducing new technologies.

American networks covering the Olympics, both Winter or Summer games, buy all-new equipment for the two-week events. That means state-of-the-art cameras, recorders, and other devices. The latest in gadgetry gets a real workout at the Olympic games. Those that succeed enjoy a bright future at other networks and TV stations around the country. Producers interested in learning about the latest equipment and techniques should read the trade publications such as *Broadcasting & Cable* and *TV Technology*.

HDTV

By the beginning of the next century, a new system of television should be prevalent throughout much of America. It is called "high definition television" or HDTV. It has two significant features. The first is apparent when you see the TV set. The screen is longer than conventional sets. This will accommodate wide-screen movies better. It will also mean that more of a playing field or track will be visible to a sports fan at home. The size of this new screen, called the aspect ratio, is 16 units long by 9 units high. A conventional TV screen, by comparison, is 16 units long by 12 units high.

The second most significant development will be increased sharpness. Today's American television sets have a limit of 625 scanning lines per screen. HDTV will have about 1100 lines per screen. This will result in pictures approaching the sharpness of those found in movie theaters.

The conversion to HDTV means that virtually all the television equipment in use today will become obsolete for both consumers and broadcasters. It is predicted that the average television station will have to be reequipped at costs ranging from $7 million to $12 million. These costs may come down as a result of anticipated developments in HDTV technology. In any case, HDTV will become reality, because the Federal Communications Commission, which approves and finalizes all broadcast technical specifications, has stated that HDTV is now U.S. broadcast policy.

HDTV is sure to improve sports coverage in many ways that cannot be imagined today. It may prove to be especially beneficial to certain sports, such as ice hockey, where the small puck is difficult to see. HDTV could make a big difference.

Conclusion

The uses of existing and future TV technology are limited only by the imagination of producers and technicians, who are continually striving to provide exciting and innovative perspectives to the sports they cover. However, care must always be taken to prevent the gimmickry and gadgetry from getting in the way of covering an event. It is easy for a broadcaster, especially one with limited experience, to get caught up in the new "toys." One should question whether the new camera angle or new technique will help or hinder the telecast. Will it add or detract from the event? Will it clarify or confuse coverage for the viewer? Will it have long-lasting value to the sport? New technological developments should be welcomed and examined for use in sports coverage. Some, yet to be envisioned or invented, may just take sports television to a new level of excitement.

The MVP for This Chapter

Mr. Joe Commare is acknowledged as one of America's premier sports broadcast engineers. He has headed up technical coverage of hundreds of events for ABC-TV and ESPN. At the time this chapter was written, he was organizing worldwide television coverage of the World Cup soccer tournament. This chapter would not have been possible without his help and dedication.

8 Producing

E ngineers are sometimes heard to say, with a smile, that without them to provide a signal, broadcasting would not exist. Those who work in programming would argue that if there were nothing to put on the air, engineers would not exist. Sales people would join in the discussion by arguing that without them to generate income, there would be no need for either an engineer to turn on the power or a programmer to fill the airwaves. Rather than start the argument anew, the point being made here is that broadcasting, whether it includes sports or something else, requires teamwork and cooperation from everyone to make it succeed.

Every team has a leader, someone who runs the show. While a quarterback might be compared to a director, someone who calls each play or each shot, a coach might be compared to the individual responsible for the entire program. In broadcasting, that person is the producer.

Viewers and listeners are vaguely aware of the role of the producer. They suspect that someone other than the announcer is actually running the show. However, the only mention of a producer is a brief credit at the end of the broadcast, identifying that person to the audience as someone who played some undefined, behind-the-scenes role in the program.

Professional broadcasters know how important a producer is. Whether at the network level or at a medium-market television station, producers wield tremendous power. The novice may not recognize this until after entering the job market. The new employee quickly learns that the producer is the boss. Some are very well paid. Terry O'Neill, NBC Sports Executive Producer, earned a yearly salary of $800,000 in 1993.

There are three basic types of producers, although they are known by more than three names or titles. In large, highly-structured organizations— usually networks—the job functions are more tightly defined, resulting in the need for additional producers. For this text, however, we will explain the three common types.

The Executive Producer

At the top is the executive producer. A station or network may employ more than one. One executive producer may be in charge of sports and a

TIME-OUT 8.1

Chopping Up the Nation

One of the demanding and exciting functions of producers and other sports executives is deciding what games to air. When league schedules are published well in advance of the actual season, there is adequate time to come up with creative schedules that will interest the greatest number of fans. In the case of some broadcasts, such as NFL games, different parts of the country will see games featuring teams from the local area.

This is also the case when it comes to the first two weeks of the NCAA basketball playoffs. It may be called "March Madness" because network sports executives have only days to decide what parts of America will see what games. The first weekend has thirty-two games played over the first two days— sixteen games a day!

CBS met the challenge in 1993 by scheduling coverage of all sixteen games each day. The following list shows the percentage of the nation that saw each game scheduled for the first day of the tournament:

Percentage	Game
72%	Duke-Southern Illinois
61	St. John's-Georgia Tech
42	Holy Cross-Arkansas
37	Illinois-Long Beach State
34	North Carolina-East Carolina

second may oversee news. At a local station, the executive producer, or EP, answers to the news director and is directly under him or her. At the network level, an EP normally has a division president as the boss.

The main function of an executive producer is to coordinate all the programs under his or her authority. This entails several responsibilities.

Budgeting

An effective EP recognizes that his or her division must make money. Covering sports in exotic places may be fun, but if the show and the entire season's efforts don't make a profit, a station or network may quickly be looking for another executive producer. The EP is normally given a budget by the news director or division president. The budget is created following consultation with the EP and others, and is generally realistic. The sports EP is expected to live within that budget. Unlike

34	California-Louisiana State
22	Florida State-Evansville
19	Arizona-Santa Clara
19	Seton Hall-Tennessee State
17	Kansas-Ball State
13	Temple-Missouri
11	Southern Methodist-Brigham Young
9	Kansas State-Tulane
5	Rhode Island-Purdue
4	Western Kentucky-Memphis State
1	Vanderbilt-Boise State

Scheduling decisions were based on three major factors: (1) the national ranking of each team, (2) major population centers that have teams in the tourney, (3) great rivalries.

Duke was seen across most of America because of its number one national ranking. St. John's received a large exposure because of the school's location in the New York City television market. North Carolina-East Carolina was a natural matchup that would interest much of the populated east-central states. Probably few outside of Nashville or Idaho were able to see the Vanderbilt-Boise State game, because it met none of the three major parameters.

news, where major events can occur without warning and cause expenses far in excess of budget forecasts, sports is far more predictable. For the most part, sports involves coverage of scheduled events, where the parameters are known and predictable months in advance. Near the end of the season however, when important games become more predictable, coverage schedules are sometimes changed up to three days prior to a game.

Negotiating Rights

The EP often finds herself in the middle of establishing or extending broadcast rights contracts with professional or collegiate teams or leagues. Here, lawyers hired by the network or station are called in to assist in actually developing the contracts. However, the nuts-and-bolts analysis and negotiation often rests with the executive producer and a small team that often involves the news director or division president. The cost of rights is the single biggest expense item in covering sports. That's why negotiations—property handled—are critical to a broadcast operation's financial success.

Scheduling Events

Once the broadcast network or station knows what events it has the opportunity to cover during the next twelve months or more, it is up to the EP to devise a schedule that will attract the biggest possible audience. This scheduling function is performed in consultation with others, including programming and sales executives, the news director, and a division president. Sometimes, a rights fee contract allows the broadcaster the opportunity to play an important part in the actual scheduling of events for the widest possible audience. This is especially true at the network level. ESPN has been especially effective at this, creating doubleheader and tripleheader basketball nights featuring different college conferences. It has also established Thursday night for college football and Sunday night for the NFL. Just a few years ago, college football was not a regular Thursday night feature on any network. Neither was pro football on Sunday night. Television changed all that.

Scheduling Personnel

As part of the budgeting process, the executive producer must know how many people it will take to cover various sports events over the course of the season or year. The EP normally deals with numbers of

TIME-OUT 8.2

On-Site Production Schedule, Sunday Night Baseball

FRIDAY

| 12:00 NOON | Mobile Unit Park and Power |
| 5:00P | Stadium Walk-through |

SATURDAY

3:30P	Engineering Set-Up
4:30P	VTR Bytes
5:30P	Beauty Shot
7:00 - 7:30P	Edit Fax
7:30 - 8:30P	Break/VTR Game
8:30 - 11:30P	ESU Continued/Pre-Production
11:30P - 1:00A	Engineering Fax Check

SUNDAY

2:00P - 3:00P	Camera Meeting
3:00P - 4:00P	Fax Check
4:00P - 5:00P	Break
5:00P - 6:00P	Voice-overs
6:00P - 7:00P	Satellite Stereo Line Check
7:00P - 8:00P	Rehearse On Camera/Baseball Tonight Cut-in
8:00P - 11:00P	Live Air
11:00P - 12:00Mid	Post Feed/Build ESR

Source: Courtesy of ESPN

people, not specific individuals. The specifics are left to other producers, and will be explained later. The executive producer works closely with the person in charge of engineering, who recommends a minimum number of technicians for each type of sports broadcast.

Other staffing formulas are determined following consultation with producers who are assigned to specific sports. As the reader can appreciate, more persons are required to handle a football broadcast than a basketball game. This is true of both radio and television broadcasts.

Establishing Policy

A station or network must have uniformity in the way it approaches all of its broadcasts. This is called policy. Often, this consists of a written memo that may be a few paragraphs long or the size of a pamphlet. Policy memos may address the following issues: (1) chain of command within the broadcast operation, (2) clothing, jewelry, and hair styles, (3) production values, (4) journalistic ethics, and (5) philosophy.

Creating an Image

A sports division or sports department should have a unified look no matter what is broadcast. The look helps to identify the station or network in the mind of the audience. Visual logos, colors, and audio effects are selected and aired for the purpose of imparting a feeling of quality coverage. In effect, a station or network tries to tell its audience two things:

1. "We cover sports better than anyone else." Elaborate production opens of radio or television sportscasts, called "opening billboards," are an attempt to convey the image of quality. There seems to be no end to the sophistication that is now possible on TV, thanks to remarkable new equipment that allows intricate opens to be created.

    Additionally—and this often involves individual show producers—the network or station tries to create new ways of covering sports events. This can include unusual camera angles or intricate graphics.

2. "We cover the best or most important events." Promotional advertising on a station or network is used to convey this message. This takes the form of 30-second or one-minute promos that tell of upcoming big games or events. At a local radio station this promo might say, "We're your station for exciting Bruins high school football, basketball, and baseball action throughout the year." A TV network may

TIME-OUT 8.3

1991–92 College Basketball Philosophy

ESPN productions, no matter what the sport, have achieved a high
level of consistency, accuracy and creativity. Based on recent
success, the viewing public expects us to be the network of record
in college and professional sports. Based on our volume of events,
we should also expect that of ourselves.

Your involvement in this project is not by accident. You've either
demonstrated your ability through past performance on this and/or
other sports, or you've demonstrated that you have the desire and
knowledge to help improve our product. Now that our team is
selected, our first objective should be to improve upon the success
demonstrated in the past. This can be acheived by paying close
attention to the following performance goals.

1) <u>**ACCURACY**</u> - Our #1 goal is to be informationally correct. We
    must be informative, never compromising our level of accuracy.

2) <u>**FAIRNESS**</u> - Be fair in your reporting. Get both sides of the
    issues. Be objective.

3) <u>**ANALYSIS**</u> - Present the facts in a manner that gives impact to
    the events. Tell why and how things happened. Lend perspective
    to the events as they unfold.

4) <u>**DOCUMENTATION**</u> - Capture the event, including the color,
    pageantry and excitement. Help the viewer experience the event.
    Innovate to improve audio (see last page of this section) and
    show events from a new perspective.

5) <u>**CREATIVITY**</u> - Develop story lines. Take the viewer beyond the
    obvious. Entertain and inform with graphics, vignettes and
    elements our viewers haven't seen before. Update these
    storylines when appropriate.

6) <u>**CONSISTENCY**</u> - Maintain your level of ambition throughout the
    season. Each game is another opportunity to succeed, but you
    must motivate yourself and those around you. Do not become
    complacent or allow your performance to slip.

7) <u>**FLEXIBILITY**</u> - Follow established formats, but treat every game
    as a new event. Don't fall victim to patterns that may diminish
    creativity.

Obviously, it's easier to state these goals than to achieve them.
The task is enormous considering the volume of events and the
aspirations we hold. But the satisfaction and recognition is
fulfilling after a job well done. I urge you to challenge
yourselves and your crew members. You have the ability to achieve
these goals and outperform the competition. I'll provide the
opportunity and together we'll demonstrate just who the leader is in
televising College Basketball.

Source: Courtesy of ESPN

TIME-OUT 8.4

Promotion

The promotion of our baseball coverage, and the entire network for that matter, is second in importance only to the actual production of the games. We must have a thoughtful, and yes, relentless use of every promotional tool if we are going to be successful in our ratings goal. Production teams will be judged not only in their approach to game coverage, but in their consistent carrying out of our promotional goals and objectives.

PHILOSOPHY

Our plan this season is to heavily promote the current stars of Major League Baseball. We have determined that the way in which we have the greatest opportunity to achieve greater viewership is by "selling" the players... "Bo", "Rhyno", "The Rocket", "Straw", "Rickey", "Nolan", etc., etc., etc.

Baseball has been traditionally a local sport, and thus it is difficult to suggest to those in Southern California, for example, that the Detroit Tigers versus the Kansas City Royals is a better game for them to watch than the Dodgers versus the Mets. However, if we sell this as a great opportunity to see the feats of Cecil Fielder, Bo Jackson and George Brett, then we clearly have the chance at garnering additional viewers.

In short, it will take awhile for baseball to take on the national character that the 49ers have, or that the Boston Celtics have. But Joe Montana and Larry Bird "sold" years ago... and so will "The Thrill" and "The Rocket" this season.

There will be a specific "thematic approach" to each game. This approach will be determined seven days in advance of each telecast. We fully intend to unify our promotional campaign, incorporating all forms of print, visual and radio promotional vehicles.

PRODUCTION

The visual promo format closely resembles the other production elements. It incorporates specific frames and areas for the usage of headshots. The promo will certainly mention the team match-up, but the emphasis will be on the players.

The promo format will be comprised of three types of visual promos:

- Animated, with front end logo fly

- Animated, seat position

- Still Frame

The compilation of all promos for each week will be done in a production session on Monday mornings. Reels will be distributed via Federal Express for delivery every Tuesday.

Source: Courtesy of ESPN

promote an important professional or college matchup or remind viewers that it is the network of the upcoming Olympic games.

Creating Effective Advertising and Public Relations

This goes hand-in-hand with creating an image. However, there is a difference. Image creation is an area that involves a promotion manager who is responsible for the on-air look or promotional sound of the broadcast station or network. For advertising and public relations, another promotion manager is usually charged with print promotion. This involves newspaper and magazine advertising, brochures, and public relations handouts. Some of the material for this textbook was obtained from these sources. Broadcasters rely upon newspaper and magazine columnists to spread the word on special coverage and other aspects of the business. Even other networks and shows, such as *Entertainment Tonight,* depend upon broadcast promotion departments as news sources.

Not all of the news, however, is positive. Negative stories involving a station or network cannot be ignored. Broadcasters cannot wish them to go away. That's why a good public relations or promotion department is so important. The best approach is to deal with the problem head on, with honesty and brevity. To ignore, delay, or lie is to perpetuate negative coverage. Negative news then tends to become even more damaging and more difficult from which to recover.

Creating Special Shows

The executive producer may seek to expand sports coverage without always paying expensive rights fees. This can include pregame and postgame shows such as *The NFL Today,* year-end retrospectives, championship preview specials, or anthology programs such as ABC's *Wide World of Sports.* While the concept of the program may have originated with the executive producer, it is then up to the individual show producer to carry it out. His or her role will be explained later in this chapter.

The Operations Producer

This individual is also known as the production manager or assistant manager. This position is common in television at the network level, where sports broadcasts tend to be more frequent and coverage more complicated.

The role of the operations producer, or OP, is to prepare for a telecast up until airtime. Although this does not include the production of graphics that are used in a telecast, it does mean making sure staff and equipment encounter no unexpected problems when they arrive at the scene of a telecast and prepare for the broadcast. If the network has previously covered events from a particular site, arrangements by the OP can be completed by telephone over a period of a few hours. If the venue is new to the network, then an on-site inspection or survey is required. Finalizing these arrangements may take two days.

The operations producer has three basic functions: (1) coordinating camera positions, (2) coordinating transmission information, and (3) coordinating crew.

Coordinating Camera Positions

This involves working with the venue's promotion people and stadium supervisors to determine the best places to locate cameras. Although each sport requires certain camera positions for the best possible coverage as explained previously, their precise locations must be worked out. At some sites, scaffolds must be rented. In other instances, seats are covered by specially constructed camera platforms. In these cases, the production company buys the seats since they can no longer be sold to fans.

Cable routings between each camera and the remote truck must be determined. In some cases, this may involve additional construction or even punching holes in buildings. Of course, none of these modifications would be made without the approval of the stadium operator.

Adequate stadium lighting for cameras is required. Where the lighting may be deficient, additional lights may be rented. If the stadium or arena is expected to be the site of future television coverage, it may be more economical to install permanent additional lighting. Although major stadiums and arenas don't have this problem, minor league parks and most high schools do not have the level of lighting necessary for satisfactory coverage.

The operations producer must also make sure that there is sufficient electrical power to meet the heavy demands of the cameras, remote truck, and other equipment. A detailed plan is then drawn up and provided to the person in charge of coordinating the engineering. In some situations, the engineering coordinator and the operations producer are the same individual.

Coordinating Transmission Information

It is clear that the operations producer must have a strong familiarity with the technical aspects of sports coverage. For example, a production truck parked next to a stadium may be fully capable of obtaining complete coverage of an event. But if the truck has no means of sending the picture to a satellite, the broadcast will go nowhere. Many remote production trucks have no means of transmitting a signal, while others

Remote control cameras sometimes are used to solve difficult production problems. This camera, for example, is mounted under a suspended platform to provide a normal perspective that is not otherwise possible in this basketball arena. (Source: From the collection of John R. Catsis)

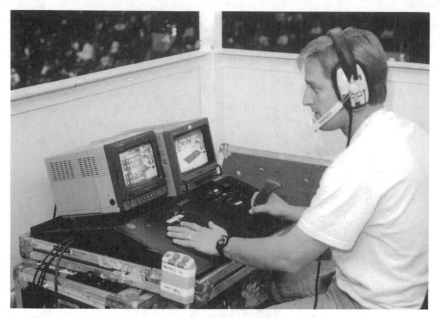

*A remote control camera can be operated from nearly any location, and the lens
can be made to pan, tilt, and zoom. Here, the monitor on the right
tells the operator what the camera sees. The monitor on the left shows what is
on the air. (Source: From the collection of John R. Catsis)*

do. Knowing the difference is critically important. If a remote truck has
no delivery capability, the operations producer must either rent a satellite
truck or microwave the signal to a permanent satellite uplink location.

Additionally, the operations producer must reserve satellite and
transponder time for the day and period the event will be held. Once
these are known, he or she will issue a transmission order, notifying the
engineer in charge of the broadcast.

Coordinating Crew

This is not as difficult as it may seem. Networks like ESPN that
cover many events involving a single sport may have several crews that
specialize in the sport. They not only understand the game but also know
what's involved in covering the game. A crew often stays together as a
team, traveling from site to site. However, vacations and illnesses do
occur and when they do, those jobs must be filled by others. Additionally,
some crew members, such as spotters or cable pullers, are hired at the

TIME-OUT 8.5

On-Site Production Requirements, Sunday Night Baseball

SUNDAY NIGHT

PERSONNEL

PRODUCTION	**TECHNICAL**	**FREELANCE**
Producer	Operations Producer	Technical Director
Director	Technical Manager	Audio Mixer
ISO Producer	Engineer In Charge	Audio Assist (2)
Associate Producer	Maintenance Engineer	1 Travel/1 Local
Associate Director	Maintenance Engineer	Cameras (10)
Stage Manager	Utility Driver	7 Travel/3 Local
Jugs Operator	Operations Runner	Videotape (6)
Stats (3)		4 Travel/2 Local
1 Travel/ 2 Local		Super Slo-mo Maintenance
Production Runner		Sr. Video
		Video Assist
		Chyron

Production will hire all statisticians and spotters.

EQUIPMENT SPECIFICATIONS

CAMERAS

8 Hard
1 Handheld (Booth on camera)
1 Handheld (Rover)
1 Super Slo-mo

VIDEOTAPE MACHINES

4 1" Playbacks
1 1" Super Slo-mo
2 1/2" Playbacks with controllers
1 3/4" Playback (Line)
2 VHS Record Machines

GRAPHICS

Chyron 4200 EXB with hard disk-motion

EFFECTS

A-53D DVE
A-42 Stillstorer

EDITING

Sony 900 Editing System

Telestrator

Jugs Gun

CAMERA LOCATION

Camera One: Low Third
Camera Two: High Home
Camera Three: High First
Camera Four: Center Field
Camera Five: Low First
Camera Six: Low Home
Camera Seven: Left Center
Camera Eight: High Third
Camera Nine: Down the 3B Line
Camera Ten: Handheld; booth-roving

Source: Courtesy of ESPN

TIME-OUT 8.6

NFL on TNT

Not all engineering surveys are beautifully drawn, but they are accurate and informative.

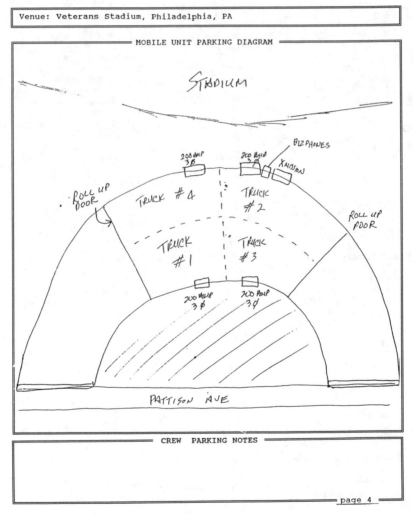

Source: Courtesy of Turner Network Television

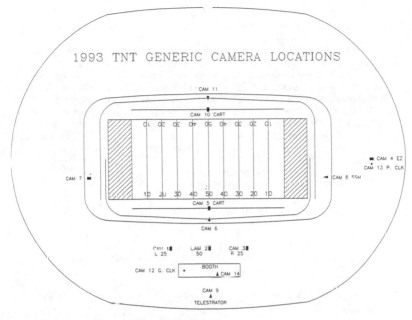

1993 TNT GENERIC CAMERA LOCATIONS

Source: Courtesy of Turner Network Television

site of an event to work a single broadcast. It is the job of the operations producer to find and hire qualified individuals for these jobs.

Each of the major networks has a staff of operations producers who are kept busy throughout the year. There also are several dozen freelancers as well. Many of these freelancers have found that they can earn a living as operations producers. Usually, they have had extensive experience in television, often with exposure to the technical aspects of the business, and have achieved a reputation for reliability.

The Show Producer

Once the remote truck arrives at the site of an event, the show producer becomes the person in charge of the telecast. Everything that happens in that program must be approved by him or her. However, it should be

TIME-OUT 8.7

College Basketball Audio

I.   OUR OBJECTIVE:

"One of the factors that makes college basketball such an exciting event is also one of the prime reasons that we have trouble picking up audio effects......the game takes place in an environment that is audio-hostile. The basketball floor, walls and ceilings are composed of hard, reflective surfaces that bounce sound waves right back into the room. This crowd noise amplified by a brass band with percussion makes it extremely difficult to hear isolated game effects....it bleeds into all mics on the court and into headset mics." One of our objects at ESPN this season is to hear more individual sounds without disturbing the crowd/announce mix. Here are some examples:

- sneaker sounds
- ball-bouncing
- hitting the rim
- hitting the backboard
- swish of the net
- band
- coach chatter
- pushing, shoving, grunts under the boards
- players calling out plays

If you listen carefully, there is much more than crowd cheering to be heard.

II.   HOW TO ACCOMPLISH OUR OBJECTIVE:

EQUIPMENT:
- Noise cancelling headset mics
- Less use of crowd mics
- Use of directional shotgun mics (Sennheiser 816 or equivalent)
- Lavalier-type mics embedded in the rubber underneath the net (ECM-50 or equivalent)

PERSONNEL:
- Two shotgun microphone holders (corner court/foul lines)

MIXING TECHNIQUE:
- Less emphasis on crowd noise
- Discreet use of effects mics

FEEDBACK:
- Careful listening in truck and in Bristol
- Feedback to audio technicians on location

Source: Courtesy of ESPN

made clear that the show producer is expected to follow the policy guidelines laid down by the executive producer or other superior.

The major responsibility of the show producer is to coordinate the entire telecast. This entails working with the engineering crew and other technical individuals such as the director, technical director, and audio and character generator operators. The producer is also responsible for the announcers and how they do their jobs.

Segment Producers

Often on major network broadcasts, halftime and postgame shows that originate from a stadium have an additional producer assigned just for these programs. This producer, often called a segment producer, also has his or her own crew. Some of these crew members will be assigned only to the show overseen by the segment producer. Others, such as camera operators, may work both the play-by-play and the segment. The functions and responsibilities of a segment producer are similar to any producer: to be in charge of the production of an assigned program.

Producer Functions

One of the first major functions of a producer preparing for a telecast is to create a series of graphics. This can involve hours of work, and in many cases is performed the day before the event. Graphics can entail the following elements:

- *Starting lineups.* Quickly done, lineups often involve little more than listing a player's name and other information on the character generator and placing this data in memory. Then, it can be recalled almost instantaneously during the broadcast.
- *Individual performers.* This takes time, and the cooperation of both teams. Members of each team are photographed and recorded on videotape. From there, the producer selects the best pose or expression, which is then retained in a device called a still store. This image plus character generator information are combined into a single graphic and placed back into computer memory. For a typical football game, several dozen individual graphics may be produced featuring key players on both teams. However, not all of them may be used during a telecast.
- *Statistics.* This is an area that has literally exploded over the past decade or so, largely because of the computer. Prior to 1980, most statistics were created manually, with little more than an adding

Producers and technicians work closely together to create graphics that are both eye-catching and easy to understand. (Source: Courtesy of CBS Sports)

machine or pocket calculator for support. Now, thanks to computers, sophisticated software, and skilled operators, we can quickly determine which left-handed pitcher with a losing season last year is now outperforming others on artificial turf in night games played in Canada on a Saturday night!

- *Interviews.* Another pregame function is to arrange interviews with coaches and/or key players. This requires setting up cameras and scheduling announcers and guests. Key parts of the interviews are then edited and saved on videotape to be played at an appropriate time during the telecast. It is important for the producer to note the content of each interview and, with the help of the announcers, determine at what point to run them during the telecast.

- *Meetings.* Even though a producer may have worked with the same technical persons and announcers for many events, a pre-telecast meeting is scheduled, because each game or event is different. A game is not just another of many confrontations between two long-standing rivals. There are always differences in players, player health, coaching techniques, strategies, pregame hype, standings, game site, and weather.

    At a meeting with camera operators and the director, the producer may discuss changing assignments from those considered normal. It may be because one team has an outstanding player on whom a single camera will isolate throughout the game. Or perhaps the producer wishes to utilize a new technique in coverage.

- *Telecast duties.* If the producer and the crew have done their jobs and communicated their responsibilities well, the telecast should air with little difficulty. An observer may be amazed by the quiet professionalism exhibited inside the control room of a remote truck. Commands are brief and usually spoken in a normal voice with little emotion. The producer normally sits either next to or near the director. The director calls out individual camera shots for

TIME-OUT 8.8

Producers and Graphics

Graphics don't magically appear on the screen during a telecast. They are conceived and created hours or days in advance by the producer assigned to the telecast. Following a pregame meeting with announcers and production assistants, the producer will create special graphics that are not normally seen on other shows.

The September 4, 1993 ESPN telecast of a college football game between Colorado and Texas is a good example. For this game, the producer developed a series of graphics that could be used in the later stages of the telecast. With Colorado holding a lopsided 34–14 lead in the fourth quarter, sideline reporter Adrian Karsten talked about a weight program that helped Colorado players. As he discussed this, a graphic appeared supporting Karsten's discussion.

A little later, Mike Gottfried, the color analyst in the booth, discussed the affect of high altitude on players not accustomed to it. He compared Texas' fourth-quarter problems to John Elway's ability to stage fourth-quarter comebacks against opponents in Denver, just 30 miles south of Boulder, where the Colorado-Texas game was being played. Again, a graphic appeared.

A short time later, play-by-play announcer Ron Franklin discussed the results of games played by the Longhorns in the heat and humidity of their home stadium in Austin, Texas. A graphic appeared.

These graphics were the result of planning from the day before the game, involving persons with reporting skills who were able to obtain this unusual information. With the help of the producer, this research was transformed into three informative features that were displayed at a time when viewer interest in the game might be waning.

In the business, these features are often referred to as "blow out packages," and every smart producer tries to create several of them but hopes they are never used.

Sportscasters hear the producer through an earphone device called an IFB. Note that the wire hanging from the announcer's neck connects the producer to only one of the two headphones. The other ear hears only broadcast audio. (Source: From the collection of John R. Catsis)

the technical director to punch up on the switcher. The producer instructs the director when to include special graphics, replays, interviews, or breaks for commercials.

At the same time, the producer must be keenly aware of what the announcers are saying. He or she listens through a speaker located in the control room of the remote truck. The producer is able to speak to each announcer during the telecast using a special intercom called an IFB, which stands for "interrupted feedback." The announcers wear headsets with a microphone attached. In one ear they hear the telecast audio. In the other ear they can hear the producer and other nonbroadcast audio such as a spotter, statistician, or even the network during a commercial break.

Professional announcers are able to read copy or perform play-by-play functions and still pay attention to producer instructions through their headphones. Even though they have this skill, it is still important for a producer to issue instructions in as few words as possible. A producer may alert announcers that a replay or the second part of an interview is about to be shown, or that it may be time to go to commercial. The instructions for these three events might be disclosed to the announcers as follows: "Rebound replay," "Smith interview two," "Break."

Talking and listening are not as easy as they may seem.

Commercial Formats

Every broadcast runs commercials. Entertainment programs and other shows originating from a studio depend upon a "station log." Remote broadcasts such as sports events rely upon a format sheet that details when all spots should be run and how long each break should be.

Effective Date: ___3/91___

E * S * P * N

Commercial Format

TITLE : ___MAJOR LEAGUE BASEBALL___   LENGTH : ___3 HOURS___   SEGMENT TIME: ___2:25:45___
            SUNDAY

<table>
<tr><td colspan="2" align="center">Commercial Breakdown</td><td colspan="3" align="center">Billboard Breakdown</td></tr>
<tr><td></td><td></td><td></td><td>#</td><td>Length</td></tr>
<tr><td align="right">National:</td><td>:25:30</td><td>Open</td><td>4</td><td>:20</td></tr>
<tr><td align="right">Local:</td><td>:06:00</td><td>Middle</td><td>2</td><td>:10</td></tr>
<tr><td align="right">ESPN Promo:</td><td>:01:45</td><td>Middle</td><td>2</td><td>:10</td></tr>
<tr><td align="right">Other:</td><td>:01:00 MLB</td><td>Close</td><td>4</td><td>:20</td></tr>
<tr><td align="right">Total:</td><td>:34:15</td><td></td><td></td><td></td></tr>
</table>

****

Opening BB's (4)

	1. 2:00
	Starting Line-Up
Top of First	2. 1:15
	Starting Line-Up
Bottom of First	3. 2:00 (:90L/:30net.promo)
Top of Second	4. 1:45
Bottom of Second	5. 2:00 (:90N/:30MLB)
Top of Third	6. 2:15 (2:00N/:15net.promo)
Bottom of Third	7. 2:00
Top of Fourth	8. 1:30 Local
	Middle BB's (2) out of break 8
Bottom of Fourth	9. 2:00
Top of Fifth	10. 2:15 (2:00N/:15net.promo)
Bottom of Fifth	11. 2:00
Top of Sixth	12. 2:00
Bottom of Sixth	13. 1:30 Local
	Middle BB's (2) out of break 13
Top of Seventh	14. 2:00 (:90N/:30MLB)
Bottom of Seventh	15. 2:00 (:90N/:30net.promo)
Top of Eighth	16. 1:30 Local
	Last Set BB's (4) out of break 16
Bottom of Eighth	17. 2:00
Top of Ninth	18. 2:15 (2:00N/:15net.promo)

****If pitching change occurs, breaks would move up and be backed filled
with network promos, "if necessary" spots and host cut-ins****

United Airline tags will run at the end of the game

Source: Courtesy of ESPN

Kareem Abdul-Jabbar experienced this on January 14, 1993, when he joined ESPN as a basketball color analyst. He said later that his only problems were looking at the camera and listening to people talking in his ear.

- *Signs.* Fans love to make and display signs at sports events. Producers love to show them. Before or during a game, a producer may jot some notes on significant signs and when they can best be shown.
- *Commercials.* One of the most vital functions of the producer is to make sure all the commercials scheduled for that telecast are aired. It's no secret that television has created time-outs that are in addition to those provided by the rules of most games. These time-outs provide for insertion of commercials. Producers do not count on teams using all of their time-outs. That's why in some

TIME-OUT 8.10

Producers and Geography

Good producers don't believe that they are the only ones who understand a sport or how to cover it. They get advice not only from colleagues but also from fans and friends.

One of the exciting aspects of producing is that there are no limits to creativity. As new equipment is developed, new ways of covering a game will evolve.

Despite the gadgetry and wizardry, a producer must remember that a sports broadcast—whether on radio or television—contains only two vital elements: information and entertainment. Information includes giving the score and time remaining and describing and/or showing the action. It includes ancillary information that helps to make the broadcast more meaningful. Entertainment certainly includes the above aspects, plus the ability of the announcers to impart excitement to the game.

Sometimes, information is lacking. Geography seems to be a recurring problem. Producers (and announcers, too) are advised to study atlases that pinpoint town locations. For example, during the early '90s, Bryant "Big Country" Reeves played basketball for Oklahoma State University. Every announcer who covered the games told the audience that Reeves came from "tiny Gans, Oklahoma." Other than adding a little color to the broadcast, it did little to inform the audience. Just where is Gans? What part of the state? Is it in the prairie-like panhandle or the verdant eastern hills? Is it near a big town? Is it a suburb? What is its population? A more accurate description might have situations, when a team has called its last allowable time-out, the announcers will say: "we're staying right here." The reason is not because the announcers wish to provide a public service for the viewer at home. It's because the producer has managed to run all of the scheduled commercials.

• *Debriefing*. At the conclusion of the program, the producer again meets with key members of the crew to discuss problems with the telecast and how to correct them. He or she may also be required to complete a discrepancy report, which is turned in later to the executive producer for review and possible action. These reports generally are not intended to lay blame on individuals who may have performed their job poorly, but rather to suggest solutions to problems.

---

been: "Gans is a community of 346 persons located in the rolling hills of east-central Oklahoma, just 15 miles from the Arkansas state line." Or: "The closest big town is Tulsa, 75 miles to the northwest."

Often, announcers say a player is from Conroe or Tomball, Texas, for example. Texas is a big state. Are these country boys or do they have some big-city sophistication? In this instance, both Conroe and Tomball are just north of Houston. In fact, downtown Conroe is closer to Houston's international airport than downtown Houston is.

While covering college games, announcers quite frequently disclose a player's hometown. In the pro game, for some reason, this is rarely the case. Instead, announcers tell the audience where the player attended college. Often, a player's university has no relationship to his or her hometown, especially today, when colleges and universities recruit athletes from all over the country.

Knowing a player's hometown, in addition to his or her college, may create additional interest for some listeners. And don't forget junior colleges. Illustrating this point is another Oklahoma State University player, a cornerback for the football team. Delvin Myles was originally from Mobile, Alabama, but his parents moved to Alaska, where Delvin went to high school. From Anchorage, he attended College of the Desert in Palm Desert, California, before competing at Oklahoma State. In a national telecast, referring to Myles' three residences before attending OSU would add interest to the telecast.

The Radio Producer

The job of the radio producer is quite similar to that of the television producer. While graphics are not required, information still is. This can take the form of compiling statistics and preparing them in a form the announcers can quickly comprehend and utilize. Additionally, the producer may also obtain interviews and set up special pregame, halftime, and postgame locker room shows.

During the broadcast, the producer sits near the announcers and is linked to them with the same IFB system television uses. The announcers can hear themselves in one ear and all the nonbroadcast audio, including the producer, in the other.

A producer located near the announcers may keep a stack of 3"x5" or 4"x6" cards on which promotional announcements or other information is contained. At the appropriate time, the producer will hand a card to an announcer to read. This minimizes conversation and helps announcers avoid ad-libbing errors.

Non-network sports broadcasts often find the producer serving double duty as engineer. He or she is expected to set up the equipment prior to the game, establish an audio connection with the station or network, control the volume of announcer microphones during the game, play interview tapes, and in some rare instances, run commercials as well.

In smaller operations, the color analyst may also be the producer; and in the most economical situations, one person may wear four hats: producer, engineer, play-by-play announcer, and color analyst. Many big-name professionals got their start in small radio markets. The experience they gained was invaluable in understanding what is required to put on a quality sports broadcast.

The MVP for This Chapter

Mr. Bruce Stevens is an operations producer for ESPN. He contributed significantly to the success of this chapter by providing valuable information and reviewing a draft manuscript.

9 Sportscasts

M ost radio and television sports broadcasters are hired to write and deliver daily radio or TV sportscasts. Only a small percentage devote any significant amount of time to play-by-play or color duties. In fact, most play-by-play or color announcers probably got their start by delivering sportscasts at local radio or television stations, thereby gaining valuable broadcast experience while broadening their knowledge of sports.

Sportscast preparation and delivery helps the novice learn more about each of the many sports in which athletes participate, as perhaps few other activities can. It also helps the experienced play-by-play or color broadcaster keep abreast of daily developments, especially during the off-season.

In recent years, the number and quality of sportscasts has increased on both radio and TV. The number of radio and television outlets has grown dramatically as well, as evidenced by the development of all-sports radio stations and networks, plus regional and national television cable networks. These new sources provide increased employment opportunities for individuals who are skilled in sports talk, sportscasts, play-by-play, color, or any of these combinations.

Preparation of sportscasts can be easy or complicated depending upon the station or network. As a general rule, sportscasts on small, local radio stations are the easiest to prepare and deliver, requiring little more than reading Associated Press (AP) or United Press International (UPI) wire copy, with perhaps a reporter-written item or two about a local event. At medium- to large-market radio stations, greater emphasis is placed upon local sports news and interviews, both of which require good writing skills. At a large TV station or network, a number of individuals may work as a team to provide a sportscast that will include video, graphics, and other elements. In the final analysis, whether the station or network is small or large, it is the responsibility of the sportscaster to select the stories that will have the greatest impact on his or her audience. Understanding what makes a story newsworthy is obviously vital.

Local Impact

One of the most common mistakes newcomers to the profession make is to ignore local sports activity. This includes not only the local college or university but also area high schools and junior high schools. Just as important, sportscasters should be aware that parents comprise a significant part of the audience, and they are interested in the activities of Little League, the latest from the local bowling tournament, and who scored the latest hole-in-one at the municipal golf course. The professional sportscaster is also aware that no broadcast is complete without coverage of girls' and women's events.

The student who watches a nightly sportscast on CNN or ESPN should not be lulled into believing that the most important story of the day involves the Dallas Cowboys or Phoenix Suns or San Francisco Giants. CNN and ESPN are national programs and cannot hope to provide the sports information that viewers and listeners in your hometown are most interested in; namely, how the local college fared in its game with a cross-state rival, or if a local swimmer set a new city record for the 100 yard freestyle.

The achievements of Emmitt Smith, Charles Barkley, and Barry Bonds may be bigger than life, but the woman who just won the seniors tennis tournament in your hometown can be more exciting news, especially if she's your next-door neighbor.

Experienced sportscasters have a policy of leading a show with local news whenever possible. This is good advice. Rarely should you lead with a national story. If you do, it usually means one of two things:

1. Nothing has occurred or is about to occur on the local sports scene. In reality, this is probably not the case. What this normally

means is you did not dig enough to find out what was happening locally, and took the lazy way out by leading with a national story.

2. A national event was of such importance, interest, or timeliness that it clearly surpassed all local sports stories. These occasions should occur only in rare instances. Local sports news, after all, is what makes your station unique, and separates it from all the other regional and network voices.

Local Angles

A modified form of a local story can be one involving a former local athlete who now plays for another team in a distant area. For example, let's say you are working for a radio station in Mankato, Minnesota, and a former local high school field goal kicker is now attending the University of New Mexico. Normally, the activities of this school would not be of high interest to your local audience. However, if the athlete kicked the winning field goal to clinch an important victory for UNM, it would be of interest to your audience, and the story should become part of your sportscast.

All nationally prominent athletes come from cities and towns all over North America. Some are from your region, or perhaps they attended school in your immediate area. By referring to their achievements, you remind your audience that these persons are local figures. You also provide additional interest to what might otherwise be an ordinary sports event.

Sources of Information

Obtaining information about local sports events and sports figures is not difficult, but it takes time, organization, and persistence. If you are new to a community or area, the easiest way to learn about the local sports scene and gain a broad overview is by reading area newspapers. Subscribe to the papers that cover the communities where your station's signal is well received. These newspapers will provide a quick education, but that's all they should do. You should not rely upon them to supply the information that you include in your sportscasts. There are four reasons for this:

1. Broadcasting is supposed to be more immediate. If the story you are reporting on the air is already in the local paper, why would anyone want to listen to your sportscast? A sports fan wants news, not history.

2. By relying upon a newspaper as your news source, you develop bad work habits that are difficult to overcome. Unfortunately, all-too-many sports—and news—broadcasters count on newspapers to do their reporting for them. Newspapers should be a source of background information only.

3. The information might be wrong. Newspaper reporters and typesetters are human, and they can—and do—make mistakes. By repeating inaccurate information, you jeopardize your integrity and that of your station.

4. Reading stories that come from a newspaper without first checking facts and rewriting the story is against the law. You and your station could be sued and you could be fired. You should obtain your stories utilizing your own initiative. Using your own skills is professional, not difficult, and most important, satisfying.

Local Contacts

The first thing you need to do is to contact as many sports information directors, coaches, and others as possible. It's best to do this in person, but if time and distance prevent personal visits to everyone, then use the phone. Let them know you are new at the station and that it is your goal to make your sportscast the best in the area. Ask for current schedules and media guides, and request to be placed on a regular mailing list. Be sure to learn if the coaches hold regularly scheduled media days or set aside certain times to receive calls from reporters. Ask about practice sessions. When are they held and are they open to the media? Obtain office phone numbers, preferably those that bypass switchboard operators and secretaries. Ask for home phone numbers and find out the best times to call. Some coaches will refuse to divulge home phone numbers, and you should be sensitive to their need for privacy. All information should be placed on a telephone card file, such as the Rolodex™ method. Have a card for each coach or official, not just a single card for a school. This way, you can keep your file current and provide room for additional information on each individual. Don't forget to include the managers of the public golf course, country club, YMCA, and karate and gymnastics schools. Remind them to call with results of local matches or competitions. Golf course managers should be encouraged to call whenever anyone scores a hole-in-one.

Follow up your visit or phone call with a written letter reiterating your key points. This can be a letter created on a word processor, basically identical in its wording to all coaches or officials, but individually prepared and printed with that person's name at the top. In computer talk, this is often referred to as "mail merge."

TIME-OUT 9.1

Sample Letter

This letter to coaches, sports information directors, and others should follow a phone call or personal visit. It should be written on station letterhead. Be sure to enclose a business card that shows both your work and home telephone numbers and FAX numbers.

Coach Sam Jones
Bismark Junior College
Midtown, Michigan

Dear Coach Jones,

    I enjoyed talking with you the other day, and look forward to more meetings in the future, to discuss your team's activities
    As I mentioned, although I'm new to this station, I have enthusiasm and the goal to make our daily sportscasts the best in the Midtown radio market. I intend to do this by concentrating on local teams and local athletes, which is what I believe our listeners want.
    With this goal in mind, I plan to be contacting you frequently. Some visits, either in person or on the phone, will be for information gathering. Others may include interviews that I will use on the air. All contacts will be brief and to the point, so I don't waste valuable time.
    If news happens before I should call, please don't hesitate to contact me anytime at the telephone or fax numbers shown on the enclosed business card.
    I look forward to working closely with you and your staff this season.

Sincerely,

Rick Dawson

Rick Dawson
Sports Director

Enc.

Although this may seem like a lot of work, it is relatively easy and accomplishes two major goals: (1) it establishes you as a professional who is serious about doing a good job, and (2) it provides a handy reference to the coach or official who may want to get in touch with you for a story. Enclose a business card with both your work and home phone numbers. This way, they can put the card in *their* files.

The sports you will cover include team events, and the methods of obtaining information are well established, as described above. Other sports, such as professional golf or tennis, track and field, skiing and skating, may take a little more time. That's because you will have to establish relationships with individual athletes. Some of them participate in tournaments or events that do not receive the attention of the AP or UPI. But you can ask these athletes to call you with results of their matches.

Getting Scores

The telephone is also used to obtain scores of high school and junior high school games and matches. Before each season begins, contact area coaches and let them know that you will give the score and highlights of all home and away games your station is not covering live if they will simply call you soon after the game is over. Ask them to designate a responsible individual to call the station. Make it clear that they may call collect if they are out of town. If you are fearful of prank calls, provide a code word for your contact to use to confirm a legitimate call. While some coaches may select a student trainer to make the calls, they often will do it themselves. If this is the case, and you have the opportunity, you can provide expanded coverage by recording an interview with the coach. If you are working on a radio sportscast, it is a simple matter to edit and air a portion of that interview. For TV, you can transcribe pertinent quotes.

Besides the opportunity for interviews, getting scores by phone has the added advantage of getting them sooner than if you rely on the wire services. It can mean the difference between having or not having the result of a key game on your sportscast. Some wire services experience delays of forty-five minutes or more before they are able to transmit the score to individual stations.

Wire Services

The Associated Press (AP) and United Press International (UPI) are the two major national and international news gathering organizations that serve North American broadcasters. Both provide scores of regional and national sports events, plus written summaries and stories of the more important games and matches of the day.

Both the AP and UPI operate two basic information sources for sports. One is called the "newspaper wire" and the other is the "radio wire." The newspaper wire has a service that provides only sports on its own dedicated system. The newspaper sports wire, as it is known, provides expanded stories of major sports events, and updates them a couple of times a day, or whenever new information surfaces. If you want to know every possible detail, the newspaper wire will contain it.

The radio wire provides the same information, but packages it differently for radio and TV stations. In fact, sports news on the radio wire shares space with regular news, weather, and business information. Even so, scores are provided while games are in progress as well as at the conclusion. Summaries are short and are frequently rewritten.

Most radio and TV stations subscribe only to a radio wire service— either AP or UPI—because it is easier to work with and provides faster results. Networks and a few large stations subscribe to both radio and newspaper wires from both the AP and UPI. The advantages include obtaining expanded coverage of an event not available on the radio wire, and gleaning additional quotes or information the other service did not provide. For the typical medium- or small-market station, however, keeping costs down is always of prime importance. And usually, the radio wire of either AP or UPI serves the average station quite well.

Until recently, stations received wire copy on printers that operated unattended in the station's newsroom. This frequently resulted in problems such as a mechanical jam up, running out of paper, or an aging ribbon that became tangled up. Even if the equipment operated flawlessly, a pile of paper would soon accumulate behind the printer, much of it unwanted news. However, all of it had to be cleared and examined so that a valuable story would not be missed. Considerable time was required to cut and sort the information.

Today, thanks to computers, the system has been improved. A reporter now can sit down at a terminal, review a displayed summary, and print out only the stories he or she is interested in. The ability to call up selected stories results in four significant benefits:

1. There is no danger of missing any information because of an inoperative printer.
2. Because of the computer's memory, scores or stories that were transmitted up to twenty-four hours earlier can be called up.
3. Paper can be saved. A large percentage of the information that is

TIME-OUT 9.2

Associated Press Wire Copy

Twenty-four hours a day, wire services provide continual updates on scores and sports stories. The code at the bottom of each transmission identifies the date and time sent. For example, this AP scorecard was filed from New

```
v3325 la1--
r q., AP-Scorecard    03-20 0237
AP-Scorecard

      Here is the latest from today's major sports action:

      N-C-A-A Tournament - Second Round

         EAST REGIONAL - U-S Air Arena - Landover, Maryland
      Final      Indiana       67  Temple        58

      In 2nd    Boston College 64  North Carolina  60

         SOUTHEAST REGIONAL - Thunderdome - St. Petersburg
      In 2nd    Marquette      62  Kentucky      55

      Michigan State (20-11) vs. Duke (24-5), 30 minutes following

         MIDWEST REGIONAL - The Myriad - Oklahoma City
      In 2nd    Tulsa          82  Oklahoma State  78

      Arkansas (26-3) vs. Georgetown (19-11), 30 minutes following

         WEST REGIONAL - ARCO Arena - Sacramento
      In 2nd    Arizona        45  Virginia      41

      Louisville (27-5) vs. Minnesota (21-11), 30 minutes following

         N-B-A
      Final      Atlanta      101  Boston        80
      Final      Seattle      124  Charlotte     115

      In 3rd    Philadelphia  69  Milwaukee     69
      Half      Chicago       50  Minnesota     38

      Washington  at   Denver, 9 p.m.
      Portland    at   L.A. Clippers, 9 p.m.
      Orlando     at   L.A. Lakers, 10 p.m.

         N-H-L
      In 3rd    Calgary       5  Toronto       3
      In 3rd    Washington 3     Tampa Bay     0
      After 2   Buffalo       4  Ottawa        2
      In 2nd    Chicago       2  St. Louis     0

      Los Angeles  at   San Jose, 5:05 p.m.
      Philadelphia at   Florida, 6:05 p.m.
      Pittsburgh   at   N-Y Islanders, 7:05 p.m.
      Edmonton     at   Quebec, 7:35 p.m.
      Vancouver    at   Dallas, 8:05 p.m.

         AP-NY-03-20-94 1611EST
```

York (NY) on March 20, 1994 (03-20-94) at 4:11 P.M., Eastern time (1611 EST). Note that military time is used. The complete code is AP-NY-03-20-94 1611 EST.

```
v4017 Ook-n
r s. . AP--BKC--NCAA-Georgetown-       03-20 0226
AP-BKC--NCAA-Georgetown-Arkansas Ejection


                    --------------------
                    ! Oklahoma Sports !

-----------------------------------------------------------------------
Georgetown, Arkansas Players Ejected
-----------------------------------------------------------------------

    (Oklahoma City) -- Don Reid of Georgetown and Scotty Thurman of
Arkansas were ejected late in the first half of a very physical
second-round game in the N-C-A-A Midwest Regional today.
    Both players were thrown out for leaving the bench to join a
skirmish that broke out after Georgetown's Robert Churchwell and
Clint McDaniel of Arkansas tangled and fell to the floor.
    The incident occurred with just over three minutes remaining in
the half. After McDaniel stole an entry pass under the Georgetown
basket, Churchwell bear-hugged him from behind and both players fell
to the floor.
    McDaniel then elbowed Churchwell in the head and Churchwell hit
McDaniel with his left arm. McDaniel kicked Churchwell as the two got
off the floor.
    Several players tangled briefly but order was quickly restored.
    A personal foul was called on Churchwell and a technical on
McDaniel.
    McDaniel made both free throws and Georgetown made the one
technical foul shot, making the score 36-to-34.
    AP-NY-03-20-94 1951EST




o0771 Ook--
r q,. BC-BBC--OklaScores Writethru     03-20   0066
BC-BBC--Okla Scores, Writethru
Eds: Adds scores
By The Associated Press

    Oklahoma State 10, Missouri 8
    Kansas 14, Oklahoma 4
    Central Oklahoma 9, Fort Hays State 7
    Central Oklahoma 8, Fort Hays State 7
    Southwestern Oklahoma 11, Oklahoma Christian 10
    Oklahoma Christian 13, Southwestern Oklahoma 6
    Kearney 8, Cameron 5
    Oral Roberts 4, Centenary 2

    AP-NY-03-20-94 0159EST
```

(continued next page)

TIME-OUT 9.2

Continued

Regional Wire Service Updates

Wire services have two kinds of transmissions. One provides news for the entire nation. The other provides news of regional interest only. This is accomplished by dividing the country up for predetermined periods each hour, not unlike regional telecasts of NFL games. In wire service jargon, this is called a "split," when the local news bureau splits off from the home office and sends information that is usually pertinent to only one state. The illustrations show two examples filed by the Oklahoma City bureau of the Associated Press. The basketball story would be retransmitted on the national wire immediately because of its national importance. The area scores do not have such a priority.

Source: Courtesy of Associated Press

provided by the API and UPI during a typical broadcast day is never used. The experienced broadcaster quickly recognizes what is useful for a particular program. In the past, this excess information was printed, even if unnecessary, only to be discarded. Now, only necessary information is printed, thanks to the computer.

4. Multiple copies of the same story can be printed out without relying on photocopiers or messy carbon paper.

Both domestic wire services produce stylebooks that can be useful to the sports broadcaster. The Associated Press, for example, has a section devoted exclusively to sports, and contains useful information not available elsewhere. These stylebooks can be found in many college book stores.

Preparing the Radio Sportscast

Experienced broadcasters quickly establish a regular routine for preparing a radio sportscast. It includes the following seven basic elements:

1. *Read the local newspaper(s).* As stressed earlier, this is important for obtaining background information. In many newsrooms, writers and reporters read the local papers before learning what news the station may have obtained on its own. Also, by reading local

Wire Service Stylebook

Both the Associated Press and United Press International publish stylebooks that deal with grammar, spelling, and usage problems, which are often confusing to writers. Additionally, both stylebooks offer sections exclusively dealing with sports.

246

---

hit and run (v.) **hit-and-run** (n. and adj.) *The coach told him to hit and run. He scored on a hit-and-run. She was struck by a hit-and-run driver.*

hockey The spellings of some frequently used words:

blue line	play off (v.)
crease	playoff (n., adj.)
face off (v.)	power play
faceoff (n., adj.)	power-play goal
goalie	red line
goal line	short-handed
goal post	slap shot
goaltender	two-on-one break
penalty box	

The term *hat trick* applies when a player has scored three goals in a game. Use it sparingly, however.

LEAGUE: *National Hockey League* or *NHL.*
For NHL subdivisions: *the Patrick Division of the Campbell Conference, the division, the conference,* etc.

SUMMARIES: The visiting team always is listed first in the score by periods.
Note that each goal is numbered according to its sequence in the game.
The figure after the name of a scoring player shows his total goals for the season.
Names in parentheses are players credited with an assist on a goal.
The final figure in the listing of each goal is the number of minutes elapsed in the period when the goal was scored.

Philadelphia	3 0 0—3
Edmonton	2 2 1—5

First period—1, Philadelphia, Rick Sutter 1 (Ron Sutter, Smith), :46. 2, Edmonton, Coffey 10 (Huddy, Kurri), 4:22 (pp). 3, Philadelphia, Bergen 4 (Zezel, Crossman), 6:38 (pp). 4, Philadelphia, Craven 4 (Smith, Marsh), 11:32 (sh). 5, Edmonton, Huddy 3 (Coffey, Kurri), 18:23 (pp). Penalties—Poulin, Phi (high-sticking), 3:31; Hughes, Edm (high-sticking), 5:17; Messier, Edm (slashing), 5:59; Crossman, Phi, double minor (holding-unsportsmanlike conduct), 8:32; Hospodar, Phi (slashing), 16:38.
Second period—6, Edmonton, Anderson 10, :21. 7, Edmonton, Gretzky 15 (Coffey, Huddy), 12:53 (pp). Penalties—Tocchet, Phi (roughing), : 48; Fogolin, Edm (roughing), :48; Paterson, Phi (hooking), 12:11; Allison, Phi (slashing), 17:39; Hunter, Edm (roughing),17:39; Lowe, Edm (holding), 18:02; Crossman, Phi (holding), 19:07; Hunter, Edm (holding), 20:00.

Third Period—8, Edmonton, Gretzky 16 (Messier, Anderson), 3:42 (pp). Penalties—Hospodar, Phi (hooking), 2:46; Hunter, Edm (kneeing), 7:58.
Shots on goal—Philadelphia, 10-6-7 23. Edmonton 10-10-13 32.
Penalty shots—Ron Sutter, Phi, 8:47 1st (missed).
Goalies—Philadelphioa, Lindbergh at 8:56 2nd; re-entered at start of 3rd, (10-9) Edmonton, Fuhr (23-20).
A—17,498. Referee—Kerry Fraser.

STANDINGS: The form:
Campbell Conference
Patrick Division

	W	L	T	Pts.	GF	GA
Philadelphia	47	10	14	108	314	184
NY Islanders	45	17	9	99	310	192
Etc.						

horse races Capitalize their formal names: *Kentucky Derby, Preakness, Belmont Stakes,* etc.

horse racing Some frequently used terms and their definitions:

colt A male horse 4 years old and under.

horse A male horse over 4 years old.

gelding A castrated male horse.

filly A female horse 2 to 5 years old.

mare A female horse 5 years and older.

stallion A male horse used for breeding.

broodmare A female horse used for breeding.

furlong One-eighth of a mile. Race distances are given in furlongs up through seven furlongs, after that in miles, as in *one-mile, 1 1-16 miles.*

entry Two or more horses owned by same owner running as a single betting interest. In some states two or more horses trained by same person but having different owners also are coupled in betting.

mutuel field Not *mutual field.* Two or more horses, long shots, that have different owners and trainers. They are coupled as a single betting interest to

---

Source: Courtesy of Associated Press

papers, you'll have a feel for the sports stories the newspapers believe are important. You'll also know that if you are reporting on the same event, you will need a fresh angle that the newspapers did not include. Finally, you will know what the papers did not cover. This is especially important in selecting the stories that will be on your show.

2. *Collect wire copy.* It's a simple matter to print out the stories you believe will be of interest to your listeners. As described above, today's computers make this process especially easy. Start with the most current news and work backwards. It's a good idea to reach back to the time you aired the last sportscast, even if it was twenty-four hours ago. By limiting yourself to the most current update of any sports story, you will not create an excess of paper. And by the time you go back twenty-four hours, there will probably be little to print out, which will confirm that you have all the news that AP and UPI has provided.

3. *Check the mail.* Most of what is mailed to a radio or TV station is never used on the air. But you should check all mail carefully because you never know when a good story might come your way. Today, "mail" also includes delivery by facsimile or "fax," and computer correspondence services such as "E Mail." Stories that have potential should be placed in your futures file, sometimes referred to as a tickler file. This also includes wire stories you have called up that are better suited to a future broadcast.

4. *Search your futures file.* If you have established a strong futures file, you should have a fistful of material involving local sports activities. For example, this may be the day an area high school team leaves for the state championship tournament. A story that includes an interview with the coach is called for. Another note tells of a local tennis tournament getting under way. A call to the organizers might be a good idea. Or this may be the last day for signing high school players to letters of intent. That's your clue to call the local college.

   If the current day's futures file is skimpy, check the file for the next day or even the next week for promising stories of upcoming events. These are called "advance" stories. Perhaps the NBA draft will be held next week and a local college player has a chance of being selected. This might be a good time to interview him for a feature. The interview would be both interesting and timely, even a week before the actual draft.

5. *Call your local contacts.* Now that you know most of what's happening locally, you can make the calls that result in notes, additional

TIME-OUT 9.4

Building a Futures File

A futures file, sometimes called a tickler file, is an important part of any newsroom. It should become a part of your life even if the station you work for has its own futures file. By establishing your own file, you will be in better control of the stories and ideas you put in it, and where you file them. The project is easy.

First, you will need a file cabinet or box and at least thirty-one pieces of paper, cardboard dividers, or file folders. File folders are best. Number each from 1 to 31. These numbers represent each day of the present month. For other months, you will need twelve more files, marked January through December.

As you come across stories or ideas that are best developed weeks or months from now, simply insert that document in the proper file. Let's say today is April 12. If you find a story idea that's good for April 20, put the document or reminder note in the file marked "20." If the idea is for May 20, put it in the May file. When May finally arrives, pull out the May file and refile the items in the folders marked from 1 to 31.

That's all there is to it. Now you have a file that's useful every day of the week. Some reporters are further organized by having additional files for next year or the year after. This way they can be reminded of important sports anniversaries. For example, if you work in San Francisco, you might want to note the anniversary of the earthquake that struck the city and disrupted the World Series on October 17, 1989. Elsewhere, you might want to recognize the anniversary of a local high school's state championship. Or it might be a story about an athlete's dramatic comeback following a life-threatening accident the year before.

It's important to look beyond the current day's file. This way, you can see what stories for tomorrow or next week you might need to begin working on today. One way of not getting trapped is to put a note into a file days or weeks before a major event as a reminder. It might say: "Coach Smith marks 25th year at junior college." Now you have time to prepare a complete story in advance instead of rushing around on the day of the anniversary trying to put a report together in a hurry.

information, or interviews, such as to the player described above. Another series of calls should become rather routine. These are calls to coaches and officials. During the off-season, a call every week or two is a good idea. You never know what you might learn. A coach may have just hired an assistant and you're the first to find out, or the school board may be considering a petition not to renew the coach's contract. These are but a few examples.

When a sport is in season, daily calls will provide updated information on practices, injuries, and eligibility matters. These calls should be short, so as not to waste the coach's time or yours. Get to the point quickly, and move on to the next call. Your sources will appreciate the professionalism.

6. *Organize your notes and wire copy.* This is done by creating a series of piles, in one of several manners: (a) by sport, (b) by school, or (c) by region. The system you use one day may not be the same the next, because of the changing nature of news. Then determine your lead and the order your stories will take.

7. *Write your stories.* Start with the local stories that must be written and concentrate on these. If you have time, review the wire stories and rewrite those that can be localized or made more timely. The best way to develop your writing skills is to utilize the following system: (a) Read the wire copy or your notes thoroughly so that you understand the story. (b) Put this material down and begin writing, using your memory. (c) Emphasize the latest development, whenever possible, in your lead. (d) Refer to the notes or wire copy only to verify important quotes or scores. (e) Write in a conversational style that you feel comfortable with. (f) After completing all your stories, go back and edit them. This includes correcting errors and improving grammar. One smart person once said, "There is no such thing as good writing, there is only good rewriting." Good writers know this. (g) As you reread what you have written, do it out loud. You may feel self-conscious at first, but remember that professionals do this all the time and think nothing of it. By reading out loud, you will catch three types of errors that are not readily apparent by sight reading. These are writing mistakes (grammar and spelling errors that often cause embarrassing slip ups), errors of fact, and tongue twisters.

For example, one broadcaster learned early in his career that it was difficult to say the phrase "in an attempt" without stumbling. By changing the phrase to "in an effort," he was able to permanently overcome the difficulty without changing the meaning of what was being said.

Radio Scripting

The form for writing radio scripts is easy. By following a few simple rules, you will assure yourself of copy that will be easy for you or others to read. First, some basic points to keep in mind:

1. Slug each story. A slug is a one-word description that is placed on the top-left corner of the page. For example, the story of a heavyweight championship fight might be slugged "bout." The story of the local football team might be slugged "Tigers."
2. Double or triple space. Never single space. Double- or triple-spacing makes for ease of reading and also provides room for making handwritten corrections.
3. Indent each sentence for additional reading ease.
4. Write your copy in upper and lower case. This is easier to read for most persons than writing in all caps.
5. Never run a sentence on to another page. Sentences must always end on the same page on which they begin. This will result in smoother reading and reduce paper-shuffling noises on the air.
6. If a story continues on to another page, write "more" at the bottom and circle it. The circled mark means you are not to read the word on the air.
7. After all the scripts are written, organize them and write page numbers in the top right corner.

By following these tips, you'll have a story that looks like this:

BUCS

    The Tampa Bay Buccaneers head into this Sunday's Super Bowl,

optimistic of repeating as N-F-L champions.

    Las Vegas oddsmakers agree, making the Bucs 14-point favorites

over the Buffalo Bills.

    Tampa Bay finished the regular season 16 and oh, and stormed

through the playoffs, easily beating the San Francisco 49ers and the

Dallas Cowboys.

(continued next page)

TIME-OUT 9.5

Continued

```
BUC - 2                                                    (4)


    Coach Jimmy Johnson predicted victory for his team.


                        ---30---
```

Note that the Bucs story is the third page of the sportscast. The extra page of the story is slugged "BUCS - 2." The "—30—" is a frequently-used designation placed at the end of a story. The numeral 30 was a telegrapher's code that signaled the end of a transmission. Its use has been carried over to the present era by many writers. Another frequently used symbol is "#."

Interviews

The process of writing a lead-in to a tape recorded interview should follow three essential steps:

1. Once you have decided the portion you wish to use, do not repeat what your guest says on tape. Paraphrase, as in the example below.
2. Always write a tag of a sentence or two. This helps to reidentify the person to the listener and provides a smoother transition to the story that follows. Failing to use a tag can confuse the listener, often resulting in the inability to determine when one story ends and another begins.
3. Write out the in and out cues, plus the running time of the tape.

   The following example illustrates these points:

For some individuals new to the business, writing may be the most difficult part of the job of preparing a broadcast. Writing involves three skills that must be learned:

1. Basic to writing is the development of touch-typing skills. Although it's still called "typing," most of what presently is scripted is prepared with a computer and a word processing program. The

```
HORNETS


    Central High girls basketball coach Pat Baker is predicting a

tough battle tonight, as the Lady Hornets take on the Ashland

Bulldogs in a battle for first place in Division 5-C.

    Baker says the Bulldogs utilize an aggressive offense.


                TAPE : "They use the fast break. . . .

                0:17   ". . . we'll have to out-rebound them."


    Coach Baker also says her Hornets will have to overcome a height

disadvantage if they hope to win.

    Tip-off is set for 7 P-M at Jarvis Gym.


                              #
```

Note that the audio information provides a lead-in, total running time (TRT), and the outcue. The outcue should be a minimum of three words. Five or more is better. This allows the announcer to be better prepared to read the tag, thus minimizing dead air.

result is copy that's both easier to edit and easier to read.
2. Since computers are now used in virtually all broadcast sports departments, it's important to learn how to use a computer.
3. In order to become faster and more skilled at writing sportscasts, one must practice writing. There is no easy way to learn to write. One must write. Writing courses and writing textbooks can help accelerate the learning process.

Preparing a Television Sportscast

So far, all of the material discussed in this chapter applies equally to both radio and television sportscasts. For a TV sportscast, one must also consider the visual aspects of the medium in order to provide a show that will be interesting to the viewer.

Videotape

Video used on sportscasts comes from four sources: station photographers, freelancers, sports news sources, and networks.

STATION PHOTOGRAPHERS

Station photographers are assigned by the sports director to cover a story either by themselves or with a reporter. The manner of coverage is based on the importance of the event. If the intention is to show a number of high school football game highlights on a Friday night, for example, the photographer may be asked to shoot several games, attending each for only a quarter or less. It also is his or her responsibility to take notes of game action so a script can be written later.

If one of the games is for the league championship, the photographer may be teamed with a reporter who will prepare an expanded story called a package, complete with one or more interviews. In this situation, the reporter will take all the notes since she is the one who will be writing the script.

Whatever the type of video obtained, the photographer returns to the station and edits the tape. If it is highlight video, the photographer tells the producer or writer what he has, and following the discussion a script is written. The photographer then edits the video to match the script. If the resulting product is to be a reporter-prepared package, the reporter first selects the interview segments she will use. These are called sound bites or SOT, which stands for "sound on tape." Once these are chosen, the script is written and narrated by the reporter.

FREELANCERS

Photography by freelancers appears to be a growing trend in the television business for three reasons. First, more persons now own quality video cameras, especially Hi8, which, while relatively inexpensive, can provide a top quality image. Second, freelancers are a way of covering more sports events than would otherwise be possible with a

After a game, a station photographer often covers a news conference before returning to the studio or feeding video by microwave or satellite. Big games mean big coverage, and getting a good vantage point can be a challenge; there's more room for print reporters than camera operators. (Source: From the collection of John R. Catsis)

station's staff. For example, large market stations will assign freelancers to cover dozens of high school football games on a Friday night. The video, complete with notes, is picked up by the station's helicopter for airing either during the regular sportscast or on a special high school football program later in the evening. Third, station operating expenses can be trimmed or controlled through the use of freelancers. The trend by television stations is to do more with less, and one of the methods is to use freelancers. This way, the station only pays for what it decides to use on the air. Additionally, a station does not incur expenses that would be required in the case of a regular employee. These include Social Security taxes, medical plans, paid sick leave, vacation time, and other benefits such as a company car. Many photographers at most TV stations are assigned a news car to drive, either twenty-four hours a day or during their shift.

SPORTS NEWS SOURCES

Sports news sources generally offer highlight videos of national events, with perhaps some regional action as well. The advent of satellite transmission has made this a growth industry. These sports news sources will monitor games from across the country and prepare edited highlights. Scripts are sent by computer modem to the subscribing station.

The sports news video companies obtain permission from each team, station, and/or network to record their games and prepare short edited highlights, usually of one minute or less. Often, permission is granted only if the highlights are not used by subscribing stations until the game or event is over. This prohibition is not universal, so you will see highlights of some games that are still in progress.

Many stations find this service to be beneficial for two reasons: (1) it provides the station with video highlights it otherwise would be unable to obtain, and (2) it saves time and money because the station does not have to employ an individual to record and edit what could amount to dozens of events per day.

Stations pay for this service in one of three ways: (1) a cash fee, (2) barter, in which the station pays no money, but does provide free advertising time to the sports news service. The service will later provide commercials it has sold and the station is obliged to run them at times both parties agree to, and (3) a combination of cash and barter.

NETWORKS

Networks provide a service similar to a sports news service, but network service is more limited because of three factors: First, a network is often limited in the times it can transmit closed-circuit material to affiliates. Thus, a station may not receive the highlight it needs when it needs it. Second, sports highlights are included in a transmission that includes regular news. A closed-circuit feed regularly has national and world news stories sent first, with sports transmitted near the end of the feed. Third, a network often fails to obtain highlights of a regional game played on another network that is of interest to a particular station. For example, Texas Rangers baseball is of interest to many fans in Oklahoma and is often covered by HSE, a regional TV sports cable network. A broadcast network (ABC, CBS, or NBC) may not provide regular highlights, but a sports news video service will, because it would have an ongoing relationship with HSE and other regional cable sports networks.

Editing

As mentioned earlier, video shot by a station's photographer or freelancer must be scripted and edited into highlight form at the station before it can be aired. Video from sports news services or networks come ready to use, complete with scripts Whatever the method used, each game highlight is recorded on a separate tape called a cassette. Thus, a typical sportscast can entail the creation of a dozen or more cassettes containing highlights. Each is labeled to correspond to the name or "slug" contained in the rundown.

Stills

Still pictures are often used in TV sportscasts. They are created in one of three ways.

1. Almost since the beginning of television, 35mm slides have been used either full screen or as a background graphic seen over the shoulder of the sportscaster. These slides, also known as transparencies, are usually created by companies that offer their services on a subscription basis. At the beginning of each professional sports season, for example, the service will ship slides of rookies plus updated versions of other athletes. As often as once a week, the service will supply a dozen or so updated slides, some of which artistically relate to a current story. Examples might include: "Jordan Retires," "MLB Strike," "Expansion Sites," "Conferences Merge," and so on.
2. Similar slides occasionally are created by the TV station's sports or production department, and usually consist of local sports stadiums,

events, and personalities. However, this second method is not very popular because stations find it difficult to justify the expense and time to purchase 35mm camera equipment and pay a photographer. The delay in processing, even if only an hour or so, is also an inconvenience.

3. For local photos, a different method is employed utilizing the station's video equipment. When a sports story is shot, a single image of the videotape (called a frame) can be used instead of a slide. The image is placed in an electronic piece of equipment known as a still store. The still store creates a computer reproduction of any picture it sees, either from a videotape player in the freeze frame mode, or from a slide projector. Once the image is in computer memory, the original videotape or slide is no longer required. Each picture in still store is given a number. Then, during a sportscast, it is a simple matter for an operator in the control room to call up any needed photograph, which the director then puts on the air.

Rundown

The rundown is the outline of how the sports show will be aired, and what elements are to be used for each story. Without a rundown, along with accompanying scripts, no TV sportscast can hope to air with any hope of professionalism. Rundowns can be prepared manually, but most stations now utilize a computer. That's because the computer provides the flexibility for last minute changes and also calculates backtimes, which are vital to the smooth success of any program. Backtime is the time remaining until the end of the show or segment.

The sports anchor generally prepares the rundown based upon the stories he or she intends to use. The rundown lists the order each story will be aired, along with additional information such as video usage, slides, or on-screen printed information that is called by several names, including CG, Chyron™, character generator, or super. If there is no visual support, the story is known as a reader, and it is also noted on the rundown.

Preparing Scores

A predictable factor in sports coverage is knowing what events or games are scheduled for a given day. The wire services provide this information on a daily basis. As a result, a sports broadcaster can prepare a schedule of the games he or she wishes to report to the audience by

TIME-OUT 9.6

TV Show Rundown

```
                        TV SHOW RUNDOWN

Page    Slug                Type    Time    CG              BkTime

301     Title Game - Brooks  PKG    1:40    Eagles Soar     21:20

302         Coach of Year    RDR     :10    Davis           23:00

303     Swim Meet            VO      :30    New Record      23:10

304     Course Opens       W-VO/SOT  :40     - - -          23:40

305         Course Tag       RDR     :05     - - -          24:20

306     Bulls-Rockets        VO      :20    NBA Playoffs    24:25

307     MLB Scores           CG      :35     - - -          24:25

308         Title Fight      RDR     :10     - - -          25:00

AAA ***    SPOT BREAK  *** ***       2:10                   25:10
```

A TV show rundown tells announcers and technical personnel what elements will be included in a show or segment. In this example, page 301 tells us that one minute and forty seconds is devoted to a package on a title game, by a reporter named Brooks. There will be an over-the-shoulder graphic (or box), which will probably be a photo of the team's namesake. Added to it will be the words, "Eagles Soar." This story is to begin twenty-one minutes and twenty seconds into the show, and end at 23:00.

Some stories, such as 304, do not require a box. This is because the video is played immediately following the previous story. And since there is no video with 305, it is indented so it can easily be identified.

The viewer will not see the anchor between pages 303 and 304 because of the W-VO/SOT symbol. "W" means "wipe," which is a form of electronic transition. VO means the anchor will narrate video and the SOT stands for "sound on tape," which signifies that there is an interview.

The entire sports segment runs from 21:20 to 25:10, when the commercials are to air, for a total running time (TRT) of 3:50.

TV Scripting

A typical TV script is divided into halves. The left side contains all of the video instructions, and the right side contains all of the audio information, including script material and cues for the beginning and end of interviews. Notice that all times are expressed cumulatively. This makes it much easier for the director and other personnel to keep track of progress through a story. What follows is a script that is shown in the rundown as Story 304, "Course Opens":

---

304 - Course Opens

WIPE - VO/SOT	---PAT---
VO: 0 - 27	Spring must officially be here.
	That's because the municipal golf course
	opened its doors, tee boxes, and greens
	to an eager group of golfers today.
	Despite the cool temperatures and
	threat of showers, golfers were happy to
	be back on the course after the long
	winter.
SOT: 27 - 40	"It's great to be here, and I'm
CG: Brooks Garner First Day Golfer	especially impressed by the condition
	of the greens. This course will play well
	this year."
CG: Charles Overstreet Course Manager	"We worked very hard during the
	winter to smooth the greens and improve
	the tee boxes and cart paths."
	X X X

---

305 - Course Tag

TAG	
	---PAT---
READER	Other improvements were made in the
	clubhouse, where the restaurant and
	lounge were enlarged.
	X X X

incorporating local contests along with selections from the wire service lists. Then, it is a simple matter of inserting the scores as they come in. By preparing the schedule early, you also will know what scores you don't have as show time approaches. A copy of the schedule is given to the character generator operator several hours in advance of the sportscast so that the names of each team can be entered in computer memory.

Some events are affected by the weather. If the event is to be rescheduled for a later date, the event is considered "postponed." If the event is not to be rescheduled at any time, it is "canceled." An event cannot be "canceled until a later date."

Writing

Writing a TV sportscast is more complicated than preparing a radio script because clear video instructions must be included for the producer and director to follow. TV scripts are divided in half, vertically. The video instructions are on the left and the script is on the right. Depending on the station, audio instructions may be found in either column. Scripts are generally written in a narrow space so that they can be reproduced completely on the TelePrompTer™. The TelePrompTer is an electronic device that allows an anchor to read copy while maintaining eye contact with a studio camera.

Script writing on a computer is essentially identical to writing using a typewriter. Once the computer program is mastered, script writing becomes easier, faster, and neater. Computer-generated scripts have three additional benefits over those created with a typewriter: (1) the order of each story within the sportscast can be changed in seconds by the producer to make room for late-breaking stories; (2) the computer script automatically becomes part of the TelePrompTer system, eliminating the need for a mechanical TelePrompTer system and an additional person to operate it; and (3) Computer scripting can also provide for automatic closed captioning for the hearing impaired. Captioning is the appearance of the script itself on specially equipped TV sets, much like subtitles in a foreign movie.

Ad-Libbing

One of the singular skills that a sportscaster assigned to the late show must have is the ability to ad-lib. That's because not all night games are complete, nor are all highlights fed and edited in time for the 10:00 or 11:00 P.M. sportscasts. Regardless of the time zone you work in, even in Hawaii, somewhere a game is still going on. That means you

TIME-OUT 9.8

Floor Manager Signals

Cues	Signal	Meaning	Signal Description
Standby		Show about to start.	Extends hand above head.
Cue		Show goes on the air.	Points to live camera or performer.
On time		Go ahead as planned. (On the nose.)	Touches nose with finger.
Speed up		Accelerate what you are doing. You are going too slowly.	Rotates hand clockwise with extended finger.
Stretch		Slow down. Too much time left. Fill.	Stretches imaginary rubber band between hands.
Cut		Stop speech or action immediately.	Pulls index finger in knife-like motion across throat.

Cues	Signal	Meaning	Signal Description
5(4,3,2,1)		5(4,3,2,1) minutes or seconds left.	Holds up appropriate number of fingers.
½ minute		30 seconds remaining.	Forms a cross with two arms or index fingers.
15 seconds		15 seconds left.	Shows fist (which can also mean wind up).
Keep talking		Keep on talking until further notice.	Moves thumb and fingers like a bird beak.
Roll VTR		Projector is rolling. Tape is coming up.	Holds extended left hand in front of face. Moves right hand in cranking motion. Extends one, two finger(s).

Drawings by Connie Thibeau

must call upon your knowledge of the game and be able to ad-lib intelligent highlight action, sometimes even while seeing it for the first time as it goes on the air.

This is not to say that a sportscaster goes into a late show without a script. Each story has a script page prepared, even though it may contain little more than an opening sentence or line. This is done to assist the director. Without this, there would be confusion in the control room and the show would have many on-air mistakes. For example, the sportscaster knows early in the evening that she will have highlights of a Mavericks-Warriors NBA playoff game. Normally, if the result of the game were known, one might write the lead to the script this way: "The Golden State Warriors evened the playoff series with the Mavericks, posting a convincing 123–81 victory at Reunion Arena in Dallas." But because the game is expected to end minutes before going on the air, the sportscaster will write the script differently: "The Golden State Warriors flew into Dallas tonight, hoping to even the series with the resurgent Mavericks. Revenge was on their minds following Sunday's humiliating defeat in California." This is called an undated lead, because it can be used no matter who wins. It also provides some additional suspense on the part of the viewer, who may not know until the highlights are concluded as to who won. Often, this may be the only part of the script that is written. The sportscaster must ad-lib from notes or rely upon someone else, often a person in a distant city who worked to supply the highlight tape and script. The fact that most sportscasts utilizing this system go so smoothly is a credit to all individuals who work in front of and behind the camera.

Production Meetings

Networks and large-market television stations hold production meetings an hour or two before each show to coordinate efforts and discuss anything different or unusual that may occur during the program. The persons who normally attend these meetings are the director, production assistants, and the producer. Unless the producer is also the anchor, talent is not usually required at these meetings. Production assistants are essential for a successful sportscast. They pull slides, edit video, answer the phone, make calls, get scores, clear wires, separate scripts, load the TelePrompTer, and shuttle scripts and messages between the director in the control room and the sportscaster in the newsroom. During the show, these same PA's, as they are often called, operate the studio cameras (but only in nonunion shops).

The Final Hour

At many TV stations, the sports department is part of the newsroom, a large area with a dozen or more desks. If you were to visit a newsroom in the middle of an afternoon or evening, you would see a large room with only a few individuals in it. Some are reading or having a refreshment, others are chatting, and only a few seem to be working very hard. Visit that same newsroom an hour before a show, and the entire scene has changed. The atmosphere is both electric and frenetic. Phones are ringing. Reporters have returned from the field and are busy writing scripts. Photographers are editing video. Meanwhile, the sports director may be yelling for assistance. The public address system is squawking, asking that talent report to the studio to record a sports update.

The scene can get even more frantic fifteen to thirty minutes before airtime. The producer may announce that the lead story has changed. An engineer might report he is missing two videotapes that are scheduled for the show. The director will call on the public address that he needs four pages of the script. The PA's are attempting to separate the

Some sportscasters spend the majority of their time in the studio, rarely covering a game live. Here, Robin Roberts talks with Dick Vitale and former Duke star Bobby Hurley. (Source: Courtesy of ESPN/Jerry Ward)

multicopy scripts as they come off the printers and deliver them to the sports anchor, director, audio person, and producer. The anchor has gone into a dressing room to comb hair and apply makeup.

At three minutes before air time, the newsroom is suddenly empty and quiet, except for one or two persons assigned to watch the competition on monitors to see what stories they are carrying that day. The rest of the crew is deployed in the control room or the studio. The anchor is seated in place, plugging in the intercom that is attached to the ear so that the director or producer can be heard even when on the air. The talent has become accustomed to hearing someone talk in his or her ear as he or she reads copy from the TelePrompTer. It's all part of a day's work.

The MVP for This Chapter

Mr. Bill Teegins is the sports director for KWTV in Oklahoma City, presenting twice-nightly sportscasts for the CBS-TV affiliate. He is also the voice of the Oklahoma State University football and basketball Cowboys. The author expresses his appreciation to Mr. Teegins for the prompt review of this chapter at deadline time. But then, that's what professional broadcasters do on a regular basis!

10 Play-by-Play Preparations

Preparing to perform the function of play-by-play announcer for a specific sports event often begins weeks or months in advance. In the high-stakes world of network radio and television, some of this work is done for the announcer by researchers. This is especially true for major events, such as the Winter or Summer Olympic games. Researchers prepare volumes on every sport... its rules, history, and current athletes.

The announcers, both play-by-play and color, have weeks to study and digest this information. During the time of actual coverage, these books serve as valuable sources. The announcers and producers instantly know where to look for the information that may be pertinent to the event. In many cases the announcers have committed the information to memory. This is by far the best method of having information readily available. No computer has yet been designed that can match the human brain for speed in retrieving data.

In many cases, announcers attend training sessions put on by conferences and national organizations like the NCAA. These sessions, which discuss rule changes and interpretations, are not restricted to coaches and officials, as might be thought. Conferences and governing bodies want announcers to "get it right" just as much as coaches and officials. Back home, ask to attend practice sessions. You may be surprised by the welcome you receive.

For most events and at most broadcast operations, however, most announcers will not have the luxury of extended travel and training, a research staff, or months of preparation time. Normally, the staff is just one person...you. And the time devoted to preparation may be only a few days, if that. That's why you have to make the most of what is available to you. It also helps if you are organized. A sports announcer may be called upon to work two or more games over a weekend, and not necessarily in the same sport. That's why he or she must know the sports, the rules, the personalities, and the officials' signals, plus be able to shift gears from one sport to another without hesitation.

The ability to do this does not occur overnight. For most successful announcers, learning about sports probably began in childhood. The youngster listened and watched every sport and every game possible. He or she read and studied the daily newspaper and subscribed to at least one national sports publication. The student also read books on how the games are played and acquired a sense of history from sports biographies. With a tape recorder, the future announcer turned the volume down on

Students practice play-by-play using a tape recorder under real game conditions. (Source: From the collection of John R. Catsis)

Commentators have prepared for this pregame telecast, College Game Day. *(From left to right) Chris Fowler and Lee Corso talk to coaches Bill McCartney of Colorado and Lou Holtz of Notre Dame. (Source: Courtesy of ESPN)*

the TV set and practiced play-by-play techniques. Or he might have taken the recorder to a high school game; and sitting off in a corner of the stands, he called the game into the tape recorder and pretended it was a live broadcast. Later, by listening to the result, the future sportscaster compared the results with those who are associated with the networks or major local stations or teams.

Pregame Preparations

Play-by-play announcers normally know what games they will be covering months in advance of the actual event, because broadcast stations and networks must have adequate time to plan for the coverage and to sell advertising to support the broadcasts. For most stations, sports broadcasting means covering local high schools and colleges, and perhaps an American Legion baseball team. You, as the announcer, may have covered a team many times in the past and have accumulated a substantial amount of background information. You may think you have a lot of background on the team. Even so, chances are you may know little or nothing about many of the team's opponents.

Most of the readers of this book will probably begin their professional sports broadcasting careers covering high school football, basketball, and baseball. These beginning jobs are difficult for two major reasons:

1. *Inexperience*. Because everything is so new, many aspects of sports broadcasting one thought would be easy are difficult under the pressure of a live audience. This includes identifying and pronouncing players' names, describing plays, providing a steady stream of chatter, and displaying enthusiasm.

2. *Lack of information*. Nothing can hurt a broadcast more. Failure to prepare can be disastrous. In a small town with small schools, the preparation is nearly always up to the individual broadcaster. There's no assistant or service to help provide the information you need. If the high school you are covering is the school you attended, you already may know a little more about the school and its sports history than most listeners. While that may be true, you probably have accumulated little in the way of statistics and other data that will help to enhance your broadcasts. Unfortunately, many high schools have limited facilities for keeping track of these things. Few have the collegiate equivalent of a sports information department. However, there are several ways the announcer can obtain information about high school athletic teams.

Information: The Coach

The head coach of the home team you are covering should get to meet and know you well before the season begins. Make an appointment to visit at a time when both of you can talk without telephone interruptions or the pressure of pregame planning or practice sessions.

Make sure you also get to meet the coach's assistants. During the active season, you may find yourself talking to these individuals more frequently than the head coach. Assistant coaches generally love to talk. One reason may be because they are passed over by reporters who prefer to talk to the head coach. They are rarely asked to provide their expertise and opinion. But by getting to know assistant coaches, you will acquire stature in their eyes. You will also begin to understand the kinds of information you can get from them. Is the head coach the only one who will discuss certain matters? Can or will the assistants provide the same detailed information as the head coach? What is it the assistants know better than the head coach? When is the best time to contact them?

Before meeting with the coach, read as much as you can about the school, the team, the coaching staff, and its philosophy of the game. Next, make a list of questions that will provide you with added insight. There are some obvious things you need to know, such as how this team compares with last year's. Bright spots on the team. Problem areas. A word of caution on the last point: high school coaches often are less candid than college coaches in discussing negatives. Many coaches are also classroom teachers, and they realize the destructiveness of negativism upon young student-athletes. They also find themselves in closer contact with the athlete's parents. As a result, they have learned the importance of being a positive role model to every student at their school.

If this is the coach's first season at the school, you need to find out about favorite styles of play. Does the football coach prefer a strong running game? Does the basketball coach emphasize a deliberate style of play, or does she subscribe to the fast break? Even if the coach is a veteran, it's a good idea to ask if fans will be seeing anything new in the way of offensive or defensive strategies this season.

Because high school coaching staffs are smaller than those on the college and pro level, and because budgets are also smaller, there is a minimum of scouting. As a result, the coach may know little about the opponent. He may be familiar with the opposing coach's style, and prepare his own to handle it. The coach may also have heard of a couple of key players. But often, especially at smaller schools, the real learning occurs from the sideline during the game itself.

Information: Sports Editors

The sports editors of either the high school or local newspaper often have extensive background and historical information on the teams you are assigned to cover: both the home and visiting teams. The amount of information you obtain depends upon how successful you are in developing good working relationships with these individuals. Personalities have a lot to do with it . . . yours and theirs. Some sports editors, especially those associated with the local daily or weekly paper, may look upon broadcasting as competition. As a result they may be reluctant to give very much information.

For those who are cooperative, a good relationship can be made better by inviting the editors to be guests on your broadcasts. This can include a radio or TV sportscast or play-by-play of the actual event. You might just discover another great broadcast commentator who might become a member of your sports announcing team.

Information: Media Guides and Sports Information Departments (SIDs)

College Athletics

Because college athletics are big-time businesses, every effort is made to inform broadcast and print reporters. To obtain complete data on an upcoming event, a reporter should obtain information from three distinct organizations: the team, the conference, and the national body. These organizations can be broken down further:

The teams $\left\langle\begin{array}{l}\text{The home team}\\ \text{The visiting team}\end{array}\right.$

The conference $\left\langle\begin{array}{l}\text{The home team's conference}\\ \text{The visiting team's conference (if different from above)}\end{array}\right.$

The national governing body, such as the NCAA or NAIA

Division 1-A and 1-AA schools maintain Sports Information Departments (SIDs). From these, there is no shortage of information. There is a media guide for each sport, and some of the larger schools employ information specialists who concentrate solely on specific sports. Media guide books featuring a school's football or basketball team can run over one hundred pages, while some approach four hundred pages! It's often printed in color and on expensive paper. These media guides are not prepared just for working writers or broadcasters. Most schools admit that they use the guides as recruiting tools for prospective athletes. It's something recruiters can leave with high school seniors after their visit is concluded. These guides then become silent sales tools, promoting the school and its athletic program.

The various conferences and the NCAA also maintain promotion departments that publish media guides and issue weekly information by mail on each sport. It's not difficult for a member of a sports broadcasting team to get on the mailing or fax lists of any university, conference, or the NCAA. A request prepared on company letterhead is usually all it takes. It's also a good idea to send similar requests to the SIDs of all the schools your college will be playing during the upcoming season. This way you will get helpful background information that is not always possible to obtain through the local newspaper or at the last minute.

Most colleges also prepare hundreds and sometimes thousands of pages of additional statistical and background information before, during, and after each game. For example, before each game, the Sports Information Department prepares a preview look at the contest. The length varies from one to ten pages or more. The information can include the following:

- A quick preview of the upcoming game.
- Quotes from the coaches.
- Injury updates.

Media Guides

University and professional media guides are packed with information, including histories, records, player sketches, and schedules. They should be in every sports broadcaster's briefcase.

HISTORY

All-Time Fencing Honors

All-Americans

1941	Edward McNamara	Foil
1941	Richard Smith	Epee
1941	William Hoffman	Sabre
1948	Gordon Groh	Epee
1955	Richard Fixler	Foil
1983	Chris Hagen	Foil
1993	Andrew Dannhorn	Sabre

Big Ten Championships

Men: 1947   Women: 1977
1948   1978

NCAA Championships

Men's Epee: 1939
Overall: 1941

Big Ten Titles

1927	Henry Zettleman	Foil
1935	Harry Gillies	Epee
1936	Harry Gillies	Epee
1937	Tully Friedman	Foil
1939	Emery Taylor	Epee
1940	Cliff Groh	Foil
1942	Leon Lenkoff	Epee
1947	Gordon Groh	Foil
1948	Humphrey Sullivan	Foil
1948	Ralph Tykodi	Sabre
1930	Don Olander	Epee
1952	Robert Persellion	Sabre
1953	Palmer True	Epee
1977	Karen Beckman	Foil
1983	Jeff Munn	Sabre
1990	Colby Vargas	Epee

All-Time Win Charts

Women's Foil

Janel Obenchain	356-159
Chris Urban	282-104
Tracy Brown	**243-122**
Susan Rieck	234-123
Peggy Nelson	223-133
Jeanine Prokop	212-137
Karen Harris	180-146
Jenny Saunders	171-251
Bernadette Burke	152-158
Sara Heiden	**143-69**
Allison Draper	128-173

Men's Foil

Mitch Granberg	253-145
Chris Hagen	226-98
Dwight Cheu	159-70
John Van Tassel	153-118
Todd Kerschke	140-94
John Leyland	134-178
Tom Cramer	123-82
Ken Jones	116-102
Robert Lichten	**110-75**
Travis Seymour	104-112

Men's Sabre

Derek Lipscombe	199-81
Steve Hobbs	156-103
Bob Lacatena	154-106
Rob Anderson	153-105
Scott Carmichael	120-55
Chris Gaul	120-147
Joel Kickbusch	109-116
Carlos Villavicencio	**103-64**

Men's Epee

Todd Retzlaff	162-155
Colby Vargas	139-181
Jeff Brownstein	122-100
Jeff Schaff	108-131
Dan Lubin	105-82
Tom Chwojko	105-168
Greg Sumi	100-152

bold indicates current fencer minimum 100 wins

Todd Retzlaff

Janel Obenchain

Derek Lipscombe

Colby Vargas

Mitch Granberg

Chris Hagen

Source: Courtesy of Northwestern University

(continued next page)

TIME-OUT 10.1

Continued

All-Time Cowgirl Medalists

1   Val Skinner (9)
Big Eight (1979-80)
Lady Cardinal Invitational (1980-81)
Sooner Invitational (1980-81)
Nancy Lopez Invitational (1981-82)
Lady Spartan Invitational (1981-82)
Betsy Rawls Invitational (1981-82)
Sooner Invitational (1981-82)
Lady Sun Devil (1981-82)
Big Eight (1981-82)

2   Robin Hood (8)
Suncoast Invitational (1983-84)
Big Red Invitational (1983-84)
Big Eight (1983-84)
Susie Maxwell Berning (1984-85)
Big Eight (1985-86)
Betsy Rawls (1986-87)
Lady Mustang (1986-87)
Lady Sun Devil (1986-87)

3   Eva Dahllof (7)
Big Eight (1986-87)
Foley's All-College Kickoff (1987-88)
SIC Fall Classic (1987-88)
UCLA-Desert Classic (1987-88)
Big Eight (1987-88)
South Carolina Intercollegiate (1988-89)
Big Eight (1988-89)

4   Stephanie Martin (5)
Roadrunner Classic (1991-92)
Lady Cardinal (1991-92)
Guadalajara (1991-92)
Lady Mustang (1991-92)
Guadalajara (1992-93)

5   Alicia Ogrin (4)
Houston Baptist Invitational (1977-78)
Big Eight (1977-78)
Kansas Invitational (1978-79)
Big Eight (1978-79)

T6   Arantxa Sison (3)
Lady Gator (1991-92)
Big Eight (1991-92)
US-Japan (1992-93)

T6   Janice Burba (3)
Torneo Universitario Femenil de Golf (1981-82)
Cowgirl Invitational (1981-82)
Big Eight (1982-83)

T6   Marnie McGuire (3)
Guadalajara Intercollegiate (1989-90)
Lady Gator (1989-90)
Big Eight (1989-90)

T9   Charlotta Eliasson (1)
Jayhawk (1993-94)

T9   Patty Livingston Zimmer (1)
Big Eight (1976-77)

T9   Sara Killeen (1)
All-College Kickoff (1986-87)

T9   Brenda Lunsford (1)
Missouri Invitational (1978-79)

T9   Lisa Stone (1)
Big Eight (1984-85)

T9   Yoshiko Ito (1)
Guadalajara Intercollegiate (1984-85)

OSU's Big Eight Champions

1977 -- Patty Zimmer (158)	1985 -- Lisa Stone (231)
1978 -- Alicia Ogrin (154)	1986 -- Robin Hood (220)
1979 -- Alicia Ogrin (232)	1987 -- Eva Dahllof (228)
1980 -- Val Skinner (225)	1988 -- Eva Dahlof (234)
1982 -- Val Skinner (216)	1989 -- Eva Dahllof (229)
1983 -- Janice Burba (233)	1990 -- Marnie McGuire (230)
1984 -- Robin Hood (224)	1992 -- Arantxa Sison (220)

NCAA Top 20 Finishers

1982 -- Val Skinner (T7th)
1986 -- Robin Hood (T15th)
1987 -- Robin Hood (5th)
1988 -- Eva Dahllof (12th)
1989 -- Carolyn McKenizie (T11th)

Source: Courtesy of Oklahoma State University

1992-93 University of Maine Hockey Statistics

Scoring

Name	GP	G	A	Pts	+/-	Pen/Min	PP	SH	GW	FG	HT
9- Paul Kariya	39	25	75	100	+49	6/12	6	2	7	6	0
19- Jim Montgomery	45	32	63	95	+50	20/40	9	2	5	2	1
31- Cal Ingraham	45	46	39	85	+46	25/50	22	3	4	6	3
15- Chris Ferraro	39	25	26	51	+32	23/46	6	3	4	4	1
10- Mike Latendresse	40	21	30	51	+37	11/22	3	4	4	3	2
17- Peter Ferraro	36	18	32	50	+27	45/106	10	0	2	2	1
16- Patrice Tardif	45	23	25	48	+35	11/22	5	0	2	4	2
13- Dave MacIsaac	35	5	32	37	+19	7/14	3	0	2	0	0
18- Eric Fenton	31	21	15	36	+23	30/76	9	0	3	3	1
4- Chris Imes	45	12	23	35	+59	12/24	3	1	3	2	0
3- Matt Martin	44	6	26	32	+34	36/88	3	0	0	1	0
22- Kent Salfi	33	10	13	23	+20	12/24	0	1	0	2	1
25- Justin Tomberlin	34	13	9	22	+8	7/22	·5	0	1	0	0
27- Martin Mercier	39	11	8	19	+11	10/23	1	1	1	4	0
24- Lee Saunders	42	7	12	19	+31	20/40	1	1	1	0	0
14- Dave LaCouture	43	8	6	14	+8	27/78	0	1	2	0	0
11- Dan Murphy	44	0	11	11	+45	24/56	0	0	0	0	0
20- Brad Purdie	20	3	7	10	+5	7/14	1	0	0	0	0
6- Jason Weinrich	38	1	8	9	+30	21/42	0	0	0	0	0
2- Andy Silverman	37	1	7	8	+31	28/56	0	0	0	0	0
26- Chuck Texeira	13	1	3	4	+2	8/16	0	0	0	0	0
36- Jamie Thompson	10	3	1	4	-1	5/10	0	2	1	0	0
30- Garth Snow	23	0	3	3	-	3/6	0	0	0	0	0
12- Wayne Conlan	3	0	3	3	+2	0/0	0	0	0	0	0
5- Jacque Rodrigue	2	0	2	2	+4	1/2	0	0	0	0	0
1- Mike Dunham	25	0	2	2	-	0/0	0	0	0	0	0
33- Greg Hirsch	11	0	0	0	-	0/0	0	0	0	0	0
Bench						6/12					
Totals	45	292	481	773		405/901	87	21	42	39	12
Opponents	45	108	159	267		422/950	33	4	1	6	0

Goaltending

Name	GP	Min.	GA	GAA	SVS	Pct.	SO	Record
30-Garth Snow	23	1210:29	42	2.08	450	.915	1	21-0-1
1- Mike Dunham	25	1428:46	63	2.65	525	.893	0	21-1-1
33- Greg Hirsch	11	73:10	3	2.46	26	.897	0	0-0-0
Totals	45	2712:25	108	2.39	1009	.903	1	42-1-2
Opponents	45	2705:17	290(2)	6.43	1345	.823	0	1-42-2

Powerplay Efficiency
Maine: 31.9% (87-273)

Penalty Killing
Maine: 87.3% (227-260)

Score by Periods

	1st	2nd	3rd	OT	Total
Maine	83	110	98	1	292
Opponents	29	36	42	1	108

Average

	1st	2nd	3rd	OT	Total
	1.8	2.4	2.2	0.3	6.5
	0.6	0.8	0.9	0.3	2.4

Attendance

Total	249,416	Home	112,433	Road	131,983
Games	45	Games	21	Games	24
Ave.	5,543	Ave.	5,354	Ave.	5,499

28 • Maine Black Bears

Source: Courtesy of University of Maine

Media guides from teams and leagues are readily available to the professional sportscaster. Women's sports and less-publicized sports also enjoy the prestige of glossy media guides. Preparing for a game involves studying each team's media guide. (Source: From the collection of John R. Catsis)

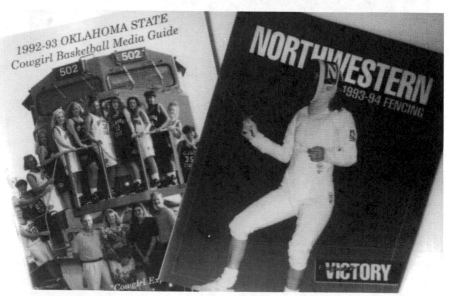

Pregame Notes

Preceeding every game, home or away, publicity departments produce thorough informational and statistical updates. These are two to ten pages or more in length.

Seawolf Sports Information
University of Alaska Anchorage
Athletic Dept. / 3211 Providence Drive / Anchorage, AK 99508
Office: 907-786-1230 / Fax: 907-563-4565
Dave Mateer, Director / Patrick Stewart, Assistant

January 2, 1995

UAA Visits Big Country, Oklahoma State In First-Ever Meeting

The University of Alaska Anchorage men's basketball team (9-4) plays its third NCAA Division I opponent in five days when it meets the Oklahoma State Cowboys (8-4) tonight in the first-ever meeting between the two schools. Both teams come into the 6,831-seat Gallagher-Iba Arena searching to end two-game losing skids. The Seawolves, who have not lost three games in a row since Dec. 29-Jan. 7 of last season, fell to Santa Clara and San Jose State at the Comerica Cable Car Classic on Dec. 29-30. The Cowboys dropped road contests at Arizona State (72-69) and at Providence (93-78) in their last two outings.

LAST TIME OUT...UAA lost two games to NCAA I foes Santa Clara and San Jose State by a combined seven points and finished fourth at the Cable Car Classic last weekend. The Seawolves led 41-40 at halftime against the Broncos of SCU, the tournament hosts, but were outrebounded 56-49-- including a 23-14 margin on the offensive glass--in a 78-75 loss. Jason Kaiser scored 28 points to lead all scorers, and Tai Riser contributed a game-high 12 rebounds to help the UAA cause. In the consolation game against the SJSU Spartans, Kaiser led UAA with 19 points as the Seawolves fell 70-66. Kaiser made the all-tournament team while Riser was named the Classic's most inspirational player.

HEAD COACH CHARLIE BRUNS... In his second season, UAA mentor Charlie Bruns (Eastern Washington '68) owns a 29-13 mark at the school and overall. The 1994 Pacific West Conference Coach of the Year, Bruns spent the previous 14 seasons on the Seawolf coaching staff as an assistant until he was elevated to the head coaching position two games into last season. He proceeded to direct the team to its third straight 20-win season, a seventh PWC conference championship in the last 12 years, and a second consecutive trip to the NCAA Division II West Regional tournament.

OPPONENT NOTES... Oklahoma State coach Eddie Sutton (OSU '58) is 104-39 in five years at the Cowboy helm. In 25 years overall, Sutton has compiled a 534-203 mark at Creighton (1970-74), Arkansas (1975-85), Kentucky (1986-89) and OSU.

COMMON OPPONENTS... Both teams have lost to Arizona and beaten Jackson State in games played at UAA's Carrs Great Alaska Shootout on Nov. 23-26. OSU handed JSU a 75-57 defeat before losing to Arizona 73-63, while UAA lost to Arizona 107-88 prior to a 96-74 victory over JSU.

TEAM STATISITCAL COMPARISON...A look at some of the squads' season statistical averages:

	FG%	3P%	FT%	PTS	OPP	REBS	OPP	TO
UAA	.488	.372	.702	92.1	76.4	43.4	40.0	16.5
OSU	.510	.370	.673	80.4	67.4	37.3	31.7	16.1

TRACKING THE SEAWOLVES...UAA has an outstanding veteran tandem in Jason Kaiser and Dana Pope. Kaiser, who claimed Pac West Player of the Year honors a year ago, is first on the squad with a 22.7 scoring average and a 6.2 rebounding clip. He also is UAA's top sharpshooter from the three-point arc with a .400 percentage on 24-of-60 attempts. Six-foot-2 senior Dana Pope (Evansville, Ind./Harrison HS), who transferred from Grand Canyon University at the end of the 1993-94 season, is making quite a statement in his initial year in the Seawolf lineup. The first-team All-Pac West forward tops the UAA team in rebounding (6.2 rpg), steals (28) and field goal percentage (.549; 112-of-204); and is second in scoring (20.2 ppg) and assists (55).

KAISER-ROLLS... Six-foot-3 senior guard Jason Kaiser (Anchorage Service High School) needs 10 points tonight to become the ninth player in Seawolf history to reach the 1,000-point plateau. His 990 points puts him in ninth place on the school's career scoring chart, and is in a position to move past Dale Bartley (1,005; 1985-88) and Todd Fisher (1,014; '88-90) into seventh all-time. Including two seasons at NCAA I Weber State, Kaiser has tallied 1,289 markers for his career. Kaiser has lived up to every bit of his preseason All-America first team billing from *Dick Vitale's College Basketball, Division II Bulletin* (Super 16), *College Sports* and *The Sporting News*.

UAA AGAINST NCAA I COMPETITION... The 'Wolves sport a respectable 31-85 record against their large-school counterparts. That includes a 1-4 mark this season as UAA defeated Southwestern Athletic Conference member Jackson State, 96-74, for seventh place at the Carrs Great Alaska Shootout, Nov. 23-26. The 22-point victory over the Tigers was UAA's largest ever against a NCAA I program, and continues a 10-year streak in which the Seawolves have beaten at least one major school each season. But undoubtedly the most memorable upset victory in UAA lore occurred during the 1989-90 campaign when it shocked then-No. 1 and unbeaten Michigan, 70-66, at the Utah Seiko Classic.

BOMBS AWAY... Senior Tai Riser, a 6-3 guard from Orem, Utah (Roosevelt HS/Utah Valley CC), etched his way into

---

Source: Courtesy of University of Alaska, Anchorage

- Anticipated starting lineups, with player numbers.
- Profiles of opposing coaches.
- Officials.
- Broadcasters and newspapers covering the game.
- Scores of previous games.
- Schedule of upcoming games.
- Other conference games that day or week.
- Information on the series rivalry between the two teams.
- Statistics relative to the rivalry.
- Year-to-date team and individual statistics.
- Record-breaking statistics.
- Thumbnail sketches of leading players on both teams.

The only limit to the kind of information and its quantity is dictated by the size of the school's staff and budget.

During halftime, larger schools distribute detailed statistics. As the reader might appreciate, it can take the better part of the intermission to calculate, photocopy, and distribute the stats to all members of the media. A broadcaster should not rely entirely on the statistics supplied by the SID. There are two reasons for this:

1. The stats are slow in coming, so if you need to fill halftime from the stadium or arena without "sending it back to the station" for music or news, you better have an interview or something interesting to talk about. This is not a problem if you keep your own stats. Even though they are unofficial, they are immediately available.
2. Keeping your own stats can provide added quality to your sportscast, and not just at halftime. That's because you are able to quickly show trends in a game through stats. For example, "That's the twelfth first down for the Tigers in this half. The Lions have had but two. But the Lions still lead, 14 to nothing."

When the game is over, the SID will prepare and distribute the final and official statistics. But once again, you may be required to conclude the broadcast well before you receive these figures. For that reason, you again will need to rely upon the statistics you or a colleague have been keeping throughout the game. And when they're in a familiar form, they are usually easier to read and comprehend as well.

Accompanying the final stats at some schools is a one-page narrative discussing key players, injuries during the game, coaches' postgame quotes, and further data on streaks or records. Some of this information will be utilized in the pregame handout for the next game.

Halftime Stats

At the halftime break of football and basketball games, publicity and sports information directors compile official statistics on the game up to that point. The example shown below for the first half is repeated for the second half of a basketball game.

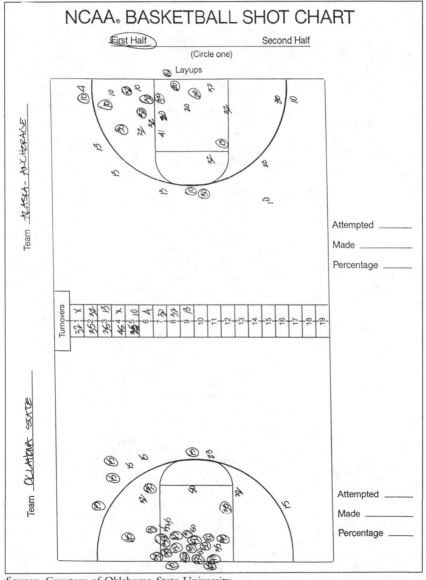

Source: Courtesy of Oklahoma State University

TIME-OUT 10.4

Final Stats

Within ten minutes following the conclusion of a game, official statistics are available. The examples shown are also provided at many arenas as halftime statistics.

```
Oklahoma State vs Alaska-Anchorage                    2nd half play by play
January 2, 1995 ' Stillwater OK                          (continued)
Gallagher-Iba Arena
```

Time	OSU	AA	Margin	Action
9:50	84	50	+34	
9:37		52	+32	Kaiser 15 ft jumper left side
9:11	87		+35	Roberts 20 ft jumper top of the key, 3 pt shot
8:43	89		+37	Miles follow off Rutherford miss
8:32				Kaiser f by Roberts (p1, t6)
8:32				OSU SUB: Skaer/Rutherford
8:22				OSU SUB: Nelson/Miles
8:12		54	+35	Kaiser 15 ft jumper left baseline
7:54	91		+37	Reeves follow off own miss
7:54	92		+38	Reeves f by Budimski (p5, t6) on the shot, shtg 1, x
7:54				AA SUB: Lentfer/Budimski
7:54				OSU SUB: Pierce/Roberts
7:43	94		+40	Skaer f by Lentfer (p2, t7) shtg 1&1, x-x BONUS
7:28	96		+42	Reeves stuff off Owens feed
7:06	98		+44	Owens layup off Owens steal
7:02				OSU SUB: Baum/Nelson Collins/Skaer
6:50		57	+41	Kaiser 21 ft jumper right baseline, 3 pt shot
6:35				JUMPBALL REEVES/LENTFER OSU Possession
6:26				Lentfer f by Reeves (p4 t7) OFFENSIVE BONUS
6:11		59	+39	Kaiser 15 ft jumper side of the lane
5:57	100		+41	Baum f by Lentfer (p3, t8) on the shot, shtg 2, x - x
5:27		61	+39	Riser f by Owens (p1, t8) shtg 1&1, x-x
5:27				OSU SUB: Nelson/Reeves
5:03				Lentfer f by Nelson (p3, t9) shtg 1&1, o
5:03				OSU SUB: Rutherford/Owens
4:52	101		+40	Baum f by Swader (p3, t9) shtg 1&1, x-o
4:40		64	+37	Kaiser 21 ft jumper left side, 3 pt shot
4:05	104		+40	Rutherford 24 ft jumper top of the key, 3 pt shot
4:02				TIMEOUT ON THE FLOOR
4:02				OSU SUB: Alexander/ Rutherford Skaer/Collins
4:02				AA SUB: Fox/Riser Pope/Lentfer
3:47		66	+38	Kaiser driving layup
3:31	105		+39	Baum f by Fox (p1, t10) on the floor, shtg 2, x-o
3:31				OSU SUB: Roberts/Pierce
3:18		68	+37	Pope 12 ft jumper left baseline
2:57	107		+39	Nelson 17 ft jumper top of the key
2:40				OSU SUB: Miles/Nelson
2:13				OSU SUB: Nelson/Baum
1:55	109		+41	Skaer reverse lauyup off Alexander feed
:22.3		70	+39	Kaiser layup off Pope feed
:5.4	111		+41	Skaer 2 ft jumper off Nelson feed
:5.4	112		+42	Skaer f by Fox (p2, t11) on the shot shtg 1, x
:.9		72	+40	Swader stuff

For the half: There were no lead changes or ties, AA never led, OSU's largest led was 44 @ 98-!
For the game: There were no lead changes & 1 tie at 2, AA never led, OSU's largest lead was
              44 @ 98-54
FINAL SCORE   112-72

Source: Courtesy of Oklahoma State University

```
OFFICIAL BASKETBALL BOX SCORE -- G A M E   T O T A L S
Alaska-Anchorage vs Oklahoma State
01-02-94 7:05 p.m.   at Stillwater, Okla.
-----------------------------------------------------------------------
VISITORS: Alaska-Anchorage
                         TOT-FG  3-PT           REBOUNDS
No.   N A M E         FG FGA FG FGA FT FTA OF DE TOT PF  TP   A TO BLK S MIN
13 RISER, Tai      f   2   9  0   5  2  2   0  0   0  2   6   1  3  0  0  29
32 POPE, Dana      f   6  15  0   0  2  2   1  3   4  1  14   1  4  0  2  33
42 LENTFER, Clint  c   0   0  0   0  0  1   0  2   2  3   0   0  1  0  0   9
10 KAISER, Jason   g  16  25  6  11  1  2   2  2   4  1  39   0  3  1  0  40
20 DENNIS, Kalu    g   2   4  0   1  0  0   2  2   4  3   4   9  2  0  1  27
04 LINCOLN, Butch      0   3  0   3  0  0   0  1   1  0   0   4  2  0  0  13
15 BUDIMSKI, Igor      0   0  0   0  1  2   0  5   5  5   1   1  2  0  0  20
30 SWADER, Jamell      3   4  1   1  0  0   1  0   1  3   7   0  1  0  0  18
41 FOX, Jeremy         0   3  0   1  1  2   1  0   1  2   1   0  2  1  1  11
99 TEAM                0   0  0   0  0  0   0  0   0  0   0   0  1  0  0   0
TEAM REBOUNDS........................................  4  0   4
TOTALS                29  63  7  22  7 11  11 15  26 20  72  16 21  2  4 200

TOTAL FG% 1st Half: 13-29  .448   2nd Half: 16-34  .471   Game:  .460   DEADBALL
3-Pt. FG% 1st Half: 3- 9   .333   2nd Half:  4-13  .308   Game:  .318   REBOUNDS
F Throw % 1st Half: 3- 4   .750   2nd Half:  4- 7  .571   Game:  .636      3

-----------------------------------------------------------------------
HOME TEAM: Oklahoma State
                         TOT-FG  3-PT           REBOUNDS
No.   N A M E         FG FGA FG FGA FT FTA OF DE TOT PF  TP   A TO BLK S MIN
32 COLLINS, Terry   f   1   3  0   0  0  0   0  1   1  3   2   1  1  0  0  18
43 SKAER, Jason     f   7   8  0   0  3  3   4  3   7  1  17   0  3  0  0  25
50 REEVES, Bryant   c  11  16  0   0  8 10   2  5   7  4  30   1  2  0  3  27
15 RUTHERFORD, Randy g   9  15  7  12  0  0   2  6   8  0  25   4  2  1  4  30
35 OWENS, Andre     g   9  14  0   0  0  2   1  1   2  1  18  13  3  0  2  28
03 MILES, Kevin         3   6  0   0  1  2   4  4   8  0   7   0  2  0  1  14
12 ALEXANDER, Chad      0   0  0   0  0  0   0  1   1  0   0   1  0  0  0   6
20 PIERCE, Scott        0   1  0   0  0  0   0  0   0  0   0   0  0  0  0  11
23 ROBERTS, Chianti     1   2  1   2  0  0   0  3   3  1   3   5  2  1  0  20
44 BAUM, Ben            0   0  0   0  4  6   0  0   0  3   4   0  0  0  0   5
45 NELSON, John         3   4  0   0  0  0   2  0   2  3   6   2  2  0  0  16
TEAM REBOUNDS..............................  1  0   1
TOTALS                44  69  8  14 16 23  16 24  40 13 112  27 17  2 10 200

TOTAL FG% 1st Half: 24-36  .667   2nd Half: 20-33  .606   Game:  .638   DEADBALL
3-Pt. FG% 1st Half: 4- 8   .500   2nd Half:  4- 6  .667   Game:  .571   REBOUNDS
F Throw % 1st Half: 6-10   .600   2nd Half: 10-13  .769   Game:  .696      1

-----------------------------------------------------------------------
OFFICIALS:  Duane Smith, Kendall Cudjoe, Eddie Jackson
TECHNICAL FOULS:
Alaska-Anchorage  - team/bench(1)
Oklahoma State    - none
ATTENDANCE: 4525
SCORE BY PERIODS:       1st  2nd  OT1  OT2  OT3  OT4   TOTAL
Alaska-Anchorage        32   40    0    0    0    0      72
Oklahoma State          58   54    0    0    0    0     112
```

Source: Courtesy of Oklahoma State University

Professional Level

At the professional level, the scenario is similar in the major leagues. The minor leagues, however, often provide far less in the way of information. And at the lowest level, such as Class D baseball, sports information may be nonexistent.

Despite all the information that is provided to the broadcaster, nothing can take the place of good, solid reporting. You should still take the time to talk to the coaches and players. Watch as many practice sessions as you are able, and ask questions. Many broadcasters are reluctant to ask questions for fear of being considered ill-informed or exhibiting a lack of knowledge in the sport. No matter how carefully you may phrase a question, some coaches may come to that conclusion. But if you get the answer you are looking for, you won't later embarrass yourself before thousands of listeners.

Self-confidence is a key to being unafraid of asking questions. Another is preparation. Read everything you can get your hands on relating to the sport and game you intend to cover. If your questions are not answered in any of the written information, chances are good that you have a solid question of which you need not be embarrassed.

Pronunciations

As soon as you obtain a roster, you should begin to verify player name pronunciations. There are five ways to obtain them.

1. The best way is to talk to each player and ask how to pronounce his or her name. There is no better source. On tricky pronunciations, repeat them back to the player until you are confident you have it right.

2. The AP and UPI provide pronunciation guides for all major professional sports teams. These are usually sent a day or two before the regular season begins. Since the lists are long and take a long time to send, the guides are transmitted during overnight hours.

3. Look at a media guide. Normally, pronunciations are found only in some media guides—those published by larger colleges and universities. These are handy sources, and generally accurate.

4. If the game you are broadcasting is also being carried by a station covering the other team, contact its play-by-play announcer. He or she is preferable to the color announcer because sometimes the color analyst is not a professional broadcaster and may not be motivated to take as much care in learning the proper pronunciations.

5. Contact the coaches. This method should be utilized as a last

TIME-OUT 10.5

AP Pronunciation Guide

A few days before the beginning of each professional major league season, the
wire services transmit a complete pronunciation list of players. The manner
of coding the correct pronunciation is much easier to learn than the conventional
dictionary system.

```
v01381nt--
r s AP-SPORTSWATCH:1993BASEB     04-05 2305
^AP-SPORTSWATCH: 1993 BASEBALL PRONOUNCER LIST (TAKE 2)
^(
                                       -----------
                                       ! SPORTS !
-------------------------------------------------------------------
  1993 BASEBALL PRONOUNVER LIST
-------------------------------------------------------------------
^(
        KEVIN MAAS -- MAHS
        JULIO MACHADO -- MAH-CHAH'-DOH
        GREG MADDUX -- MAD'-UHKS
        DAVE MAGADAN -- MAG'-UH-DUHN
        EVER/WILLIE MAGALLANES -- MAG-UH-YAY'-NEHS
        MIKE MAONANTE -- MAG-NAN'-TEE
        JOE MAGRANE -- MUH-GRAYN'
        RICK MAHLER -- MAY'-LUR
        PAT MAHOMES -- MUH-HOHMS'
        LEROY MAJTYKA -- MUH-TEE'-KAH
        MIKE MAKSUDIAN -- MAK-SOO'-DEE-UHN
        CANDY MALDONADO -- MAWL-DUH-NAH'-DOH
        ROB MALLICOAT -- MAL'-UH-KOHT
        FRED MANRIQUE -- MAN-REE'-KAY
        BARRY MANUEL -- MAN'-YOO-EHL
        KIRT MANWARING -- MAN'-WEHR-ING
        JOSIAS MANZANILLO -- HOH-SY'-EHS MAN-ZUH-NEE'-YOH
        RAVELO MANZANILLO -- RUH-VEHL'-OH MAN-ZAN'-EE-OH
        CHRIS MARCHOK -- MAR-CHAWK'
        ED MARTEL -- MAR-TEHL'
        NORBERTO MARTIN -- MAR-TEEN'
        CARLOS/CARMELO/DAVE/DENNIS MARTINEZ -- MAR-TEE'-NEHZ
        JOHN MARZANO -- MAR-ZAH'-NOH
        ED MARTEL -- MAR-TEHL'
        MIKE MATHILE -- MUH-THEEL
        PEDRO MATILLA -- MA'-TEE-UH
        LEN MATUSZEK -- MUH-TOO'-ZEHK
        ROB MAURER -- MOW'-UR
        BRENT MAYNE -- MAYN
        MATT MAYSEY -- MAY'-SEE
        LEE MAZZILLI -- MUH-ZIHL'-EE
        RANDY MCCAMENT -- MUH-KAM'-EHNT
        JIM MCCOLLOM -- MUH-KAWL'-UHM
        ODDIBE MCDOWELL -- OH'-DUH-BEE
        CHUCK MCELROY -- MAK'-IHL-ROY
        MARK MCGWIRE -- MIHK-GWY'-UR
        COLIN MCLAUGHLIN -- KOH'-LIHN MIK-LAWF'-LIHN
        MARK MCLEMORE -- MAK'-LEH-MOHR
        BOBBY MEACHAM -- MEE'-CHUHM
        LUIS MEDINA -- MEH-DEE'-NAH
        CESAR/ROBERTO MEJIA -- MUH-HEE'-UH
        FRANCISCO MELENDEZ -- MUH-LEHN'-DEHZ
```

Source: Courtesy of Associated Press

resort, because some coaches may think they know how to pronounce their players' names, but don't. After all, they are coaches, not broadcasters. As a result, they will pass the misinformation on to you. On questionable pronunciations given to you by coaches, try to get a "second opinion."

You may be surprised. Even the simplest of names may have an unusual pronunciation. Never take a pronunciation for granted.

Whenever you are given a pronunciation, don't try to remember it; rather, take notes. A proven method is to utilize the systems of both the Associated Press and United Press International. Virtually identical, pronunciations are written phonetically. You don't have to memorize the AP or UPI systems, but you should make phonetic notes by each name, no matter how innocent. For example, you may write the name Gustofsen as "GOOSE-tehf-sehn." Now you know it is not pronounced "GUS-tahf-son." The reader may think this is a fine point not worth bothering with, but the fact is that a professional will take the time to pronounce a name precisely. In the case cited above, each of the three syllables could be pronounced differently. Also note that the first syllable is in all caps, to denote where the accent goes. That way, the announcer knows it is not pronounced "goose-TEHF-sehn." The announcer should be keenly aware that one of the major ways he or she can show respect to a sports participant is by correct name pronunciation.

Sometimes, it's easier to compare a name with a word that rhymes with it. For example, a person named Knauss could pronounce the name in one of several ways. But you can write "house" next to it and underline it, knowing that the underline meant "rhymes with." It's now an easy matter to pronounce the name correctly every time. There's no excuse for pronouncing it like "gnaws" or some other word.

Proper pronunciation extends to all participants, including coaches, administrators, officials, and others. Announcers should also know how to pronounce place names as well. This includes hometowns and high schools. This is especially important in college and professional sports, where athletes can come from exotic-sounding countries. I once heard a broadcast network play-by-play announcer with decades of experience refer to the hometown of a football player as "ah-LEEF," Texas. The spelling is Alief, but the correct pronunciation is "AY-leef."

Announcers who fail to utilize proper pronunciation may "get away with it" with many listeners. But friends and relatives of the athlete will know the difference, and if they hear you botch the name, their impression of you as a professional will be unfavorable. Count on it: friends and loved ones will be listening.

Sometimes, the mistake is compounded. For example, I recall watching a college basketball game on a cable channel featuring Kansas and Nebraska. One announcer called the Jayhawk center Ostertag "AH-ster-tag," while the other called him "OH-ster-tag." This continued throughout the game. It became embarrassing. Yet, this problem never should have occurred. The day before the game, the producer and the announcers should have gone over all the pronunciations and agreed on all of them. Even during the heat of the contest, the producer should have notified the errant announcer of the correct pronunciation. In the case of this telecast, it never happened. By the way, the correct pronunciation is "OH-ster-tag."

Mispronunciations can get downright embarrassing. During a Belgium-Morocco World Cup soccer match, Enzo Seifo's surname was incorrectly pronounced by U.S. announcers as Ski-foe, which, in Italian, means "disgusting."

Spotting Boards

After compiling all the data on both teams, it is time to prepare a spotting board. Creation of the spotting board is not the job of the spotter but of the play-by-play announcer. There are three reasons for this:

1. Spotters come and go, but play-by-play announcers are normally assigned to cover one team for an entire season. The boards, therefore, are retained by the announcers for updating.
2. By creating the spotting board themselves, play-by-play announcers become more familiar with the information on it, and the way in which it is coded.
3. Since they are the ones who have to impart the information to the audience, they should be able to read their own writing!

Spotting boards have been around almost since the first football broadcast on radio. Ted Husing, one of America's earliest sports announcers, realized their lasting value and went on to invent an electric spotting board. This was nothing more than a series of light bulbs next to every player's hand-printed name. As substitutions were made, the appropriate bulb was turned on next to that player's name. The electric spotting board never caught on, even at a time of one-platoon football, when players played both offense and defense, and substitutions were rare.

Now, through the magic of computers, it would be possible to develop a spotting board that would go a step further. By simply loading a program, one might save hours of preparation time, while at the same time receiving up-to-the-minute information on starters and injuries. At this time, that device has yet to be invented.

Whatever the format, spotting boards for football are more valuable than ever, especially in this era of two-platoom play.

Spotting boards can be as different as each play-by-play announcer's style. Some are crude looking and have only basic information. Others are near works of art, using quality materials and workmanship. All are intended to accomplish the same goal: to quickly identify who is in the game and who made the key play.

For football, there are actually four spotting boards or lineups. There is one for each team's offense and one for each team's defense. The lineups can be arranged in a number of ways. Many announcers include one team's offense on the same side of a board opposite the other team's defense. Flipping the board over would reveal the reverse arrangement. This method utilizes one actual board.

The boards themselves can be made of packing cardboard, poster board, foam core, or cork. Cork may be the best because it holds thumbtacks in place well. But the cork board is expensive, and generally must be mounted with rubber cement to a firm backing such as a stiff cardboard or thin plywood. Plywood is preferred; it is less apt to be affected by wind because of its weight, and moisture does not affect the cork or the plywood. So, if you are planning to make play-by-play announcing your career, you should invest in the best, since the boards themselves can be used over and over.

A foam core board is a good choice for indoor sporting events. It is light, rigid, and holds tacks reasonably well. Foam core could be the board of choice for sports other than football, where substitutions are not as frequent. Poster board is not thick enough to hold tacks well, and if a tack is pushed too hard, it could catch on the table below it and damage the surface. The same is true of brown packing cardboard. This material is the least expensive—it is often free—and may be a sign that the announcer is an amateur who is not taking his or her responsibilities seriously.

Whatever the board, information must now be placed on it. Some announcers write directly on the board. However, most cut down 3"x5" note cards and attach them to the board, using double-stick tape, paper glue, tape, staples, or tacks. Tacks are the least preferred because they can snag, fall out, and be confused with other tacks intended to show who is in the game. In any case, it is helpful to have two different colors: one for each team.

TIME-OUT 10.6

A Typical Spotting Board

SE SHANNON COLVER 3	LT MATT JOSE 62	LG ANTHONY GREENLEE 55	C BRYAN HOPE 56	RG SCOTT WATERS 67	RT MIKE BUTLER 75	TE DEREK JONES 88

Source: Courtesy of Bill Teegins

For a football spotting board, the linemen would be placed across the top, receivers at each side on a second row, and the quarterback and running backs below the rest. You should have each position listed at least two deep; that is, for an offensive team, you should have the names and numbers of twenty-two players shown. Some announcers go three or four deep, depending upon personal preference.

The reader can now begin to appreciate the time and complexity in preparing a professional spotting board. For a typical high school or college football game, one could have cards and information for 132 players, plus those of punters and kickoff specialists.

Pens in several colors should be used for marking the spotting board. The numbers should be in a color separate from the name. The color of the numbers might match one of the school's colors for easier identification. The names themselves should be in black. One of the best pens for this job is a Sanford Sharpie™, a felt tip available with a fine point.

Avoid becoming overly creative in the selection of colored cardboard and pens. Try to achieve the strongest possible contrast between the ink and the writing surface. Remember, you will be preparing the spotting board in your home or office under well-lighted conditions, but you may be using the spotting board in a darkened broadcast booth. Good readability is important.

The information placed by each player's name is up to the individual announcer, but certain data has become universal. The number and the player's last name are printed in large numerals and letters, with the first name in smaller letters directly underneath. Under that are included the player's height, weight, year in school, hometown, and high school.

You should leave space for additional notations about each player... notes that show they are unique. These include the following:

- Was all-conference at his position last year.
- Leads the team (conference) in (sacks, tackles, catches, rushing yards).
- Is a true freshman.
- Was a walk-on last year and now has a full scholarship.
- In high school, he (complete the sentence).
- Was recruited by fourteen universities before deciding on "Ourcollege U."
- Was out last season due to an injury. (Be specific. Name the injury.)
- Is the son (brother) of _____, who _____.
- Was never expected to walk as a child, because of _____.

As you can see, there is no limit to the additional statistical and human interest information you can put on the spotting board. This data can help both the play-by-play announcer and the color analyst to make their broadcasts more interesting and exciting. Often, you will find yourself repeating much of this information without actually referring to the spotting board, except, perhaps, for specific statistical information. That's because by completing the spotting board yourself, you have committed much of this information to memory.

Other data located in other places on the spotting board could include each team's nickname, school colors, officials, coaches and their records, statistics involving the rivalry, and anything else you want to place there. There is no rule and no limit to the data you can put on a spotting board. You are only limited by space, preparation time, and enthusiasm for your chosen profession. It should become clear to the reader that the more effort one puts into spotting board preparation, the better a broadcast will sound.

While the professional announcer will try to pack as much information as possible on a spotting board, she also realizes that bigger is not usually better. Broadcast booths are crowded, and every bit of counter space is at a premium. That's why your spotting board should be as small as possible, consistent with the quality of your eyesight. I have seen some professional spotting boards showing both offense and defense that measure approximately 11 by 17 inches. I once witnessed an inexperienced person using a spotting board that was constructed out of flimsy poster board. It measured at least 20 by 24 inches. During the second half of the football game, a gust of wind ripped it out of the user's hands, out of the press box, and into the crowd below. Fortunately, no one was hurt.

When the game had concluded and the broadcast ended, the announcer was heard to exclaim, "I can't work under conditions like this." That person was displaying a clear lack of experience. For one thing, he had made the board the wrong size and from the cheapest materials. For another, ball games do not always occur under ideal weather conditions. And the vast majority of broadcast booths are not enclosed, heated, or air conditioned, even in the best of stadiums. Unless you are broadcasting from an indoor, climate-controlled arena, expect wind, rain, snow, and uncomfortable temperatures—both hot and cold. Expect the worst, and prepare yourself and your gear accordingly. That includes proper clothing for yourself and adequate protection for the equipment.

Spotting boards for other sports are far less complicated. In baseball, where the action is less rapid, information on each player can be placed on 3″ x 5″ cards and arranged in alphabetical order or in the order of the player's number. The score sheet itself is dedicated to keeping track of outs, hits, and runs.

Many other sports also lend themselves to utilizing 3″ x 5″ cards for information on participants, similar to the system used in baseball. This is especially true of sports where positions change, such as auto and bike racing and track and field.

The reader should be aware that there are as many variations to spotting boards as there are play-by-play announcers. There is no one way to design the perfect spotting board. However, all the good ones have two factors in common: They are neatly prepared and easy to read.

Spotters

The actual use of a spotting board—especially in a football game—is a shared experience between the play-by-play announcer and the spotters. In some situations, two spotters are employed: one for each team. In most cases, however, because of either budgetary or broadcast booth considerations, one spotter is utilized.

The selection of the spotter or spotters should be arranged well before the broadcast. These individuals may be hired through the following sources:

1. *The station or network.* As employees of the broadcast station or network carrying the game, these persons are often skilled in assisting the play-by-play announcer with a minimum of instruction. They understand the needs of the broadcaster in providing rapid and accurate information. And as employees, whether paid or unpaid for the event they are covering, they are motivated to do the best possible job.

Preparation comes together in a smooth telecast, where everyone works together as a team. (Source: From the collection of John R. Catsis)

2. *The SID.* Often, sports information directors for colleges and universities will have interns who can be called upon to assist broadcasters. These persons are motivated to do a good job because of their interest in sports. In some cases, they may be hired for little or no pay.

3. *Students.* If the SID is unable to provide the broadcaster spotter assistance, help can be obtained from students interested in sports. These persons can be found by contacting the sports editor of the school newspaper or the director of the school's journalism or broadcasting department.

4. *Friends.* Probably the riskiest choice. It may be tempting for the inexperienced broadcaster to promise a friend a "pass to the press box" if she will help spot a game. Chances of getting consistent quality from such an individual are slight. Often, the person forgets he is there to work. At the most critical time, he may revert to becoming a spectator and a fan.

The actual function of the spotter will be described in the next chapter.

The MVPs for This Chapter

Three Most Valuable Professionals contributed to the completeness of this chapter. They are *Dave Garrett,* voice of the New Orleans Saints of the National Football League; *Bob Barry,* sports director of KFOR-TV in Oklahoma City and voice of the Oklahoma Sooners men's football and basketball teams; and *John Walls,* sports director of KOTV in Tulsa, Oklahoma. Thank you, gentlemen.

11 Play-By-Play and Color

There is no magic to effective play-by-play or color announcing. But there are some basic skills that are not so different from those practiced by reporters in the print media. For example, Harry Heath and Lou Gelfand wrote the first definitive book on writing and editing sports in 1951. In it, they insisted that a good sports reporter should have five qualifications: (1) a sound basic knowledge of sports techniques, (2) a thorough understanding of the rules, (3) the ability to follow fast action without losing the sequence of play, (4) keenness in spotting the niceties of team play and of estimating the value of the less-publicized players, and (5) sanity about sports. These qualifications hold true today for both print and broadcast reporters.

Additionally, while print reporters must have the skills to write clearly and colorfully about the sports they cover, broadcasters must be able to use their voice to do the same. That means having a clear and understandable delivery. The quality of that voice can be enhanced through training and practice. Few persons are born with a "golden throat," nor is one needed to succeed in sports broadcasting. Although some basic techniques in voice control are essential, equally important are preparation, practice, knowledge, accuracy, quickness, and enthusiasm. We will address these points in this chapter.

Voice

There is no such thing as a perfect voice for sports, or any kind of announcing for that matter. At one time, fifty or more years ago, this was not the case. Broadcasters believed a radio voice should sound formal, as if someone were giving a speech. Fortunately for all of us, that quickly changed. Sincerity and an unaffected presentation style became acceptable. The "accent" of America's Midwest became the accepted radio voice, and to a large degree that holds true today. However, had that been a hard and fast rule, audiences would never have heard Mel Allen, Red Barber, Keith Jackson, Lindsey Nelson, or others. That's because they all had Southern accents.

Diction and Pronunciation

Whatever accent you have, you must still exhibit proper pronunciation skills. Most of the problems of modern-day broadcasters is that their mouths are lazy. It takes work to articulate the English language correctly. Saying "wearja go?" instead of "where did you go?" is a clear indication of an unprofessional announcer.

Developing a unique broadcast style is not impeded by proper annunciation. In fact, the opposite is true. Most of the top network sports announcers have clear, precise pronunciation. The result is a pleasing voice and delivery.

Negative Voice Qualities

Beyond clarity of annunciation, what constitutes a pleasing voice? That might best be answered by explaining what does not. Here are two negative examples:

- High-pitched voices can irritate the listener as almost nothing else can. This is often caused by improper breathing technique, or simply by being excited.
- A nasal voice is also caused by improper breathing. A nasal quality is the result of the sound originating in the mouth rather than from the abdomen.

In the two examples cited above, improper breathing can cause the voice to tire quickly and the vocal chords to become strained. This is especially likely to happen if the announcer is handling a fast-paced event in a noisy location, combined with a lot of drama. Unless breathing and other controls are utilized, laryngitis can result. And that's deadly for any announcer!

Losing your voice is serious and can be the result of a ruptured capillary. To hasten healing, doctors advise using a cold-air humidifier, breathing through the nose, and drinking plenty of fluids. Aspirin should be avoided because it can slow healing by increasing clotting time.

Sometimes, one can develop excessive phlegm when drinking milk or coffee with cream in it. In ordinary speech this rarely presents a problem, but under the tension of announcing, it frequently becomes necessary to clear one's throat. This can easily disrupt an otherwise good broadcast performance. Soft drinks containing carbonated water cause a different problem: gas. The easiest solution is to avoid all of these drinks two hours before going on the air. Water still is the best throat quencher and lubricant available.

Preparation and Knowledge

Several factors contribute to a broadcast voice that listeners enjoy hearing, and they all are the result of preparation—work that begins months or years before the first broadcast.

Ease of Delivery and Self-Confidence

This is best achieved in two ways. First, you must have knowledge of the sport and the specific event you are covering. If you don't know the rules and the background of the teams, you are going to have a difficult time convincing your audience you are credible. Overcoming this problem is not difficult, but it does require study. Read and learn everything you can about the sport or sports in which you wish to specialize and the teams and players who take part. Second, you must have knowledge of the English language. If your grammar is poor, or you hesitate or stutter and correct yourself frequently, you won't be able to sustain an audience. This combination is perhaps the most irritating element in announcing. Above all other factors, it marks you as an amateur. Overcoming this problem is not always easy. You may have to take remedial language courses. If you have a real stuttering problem, you should seek the professional help of a speech pathologist. Otherwise, frequent mistakes that are corrected on the air and are not the result of stuttering are the combined result of lack of preparation or lack of attention.

Evidence of Intelligence and Education

This does not mean that you should use a lot of long words that few people understand. On the contrary, simple words and simple sentences are the most effective in play-by-play and color announcing.

Reading Practice

All the preparation and knowledge in the world doesn't mean a thing unless you practice your announcing skills. The first skill that all radio and television sports announcers need to acquire is the ability to read written copy. If you have access to broadcast scripts, even if they are not related to sports, you can utilize these to improve your reading style. Of course, this means reading out loud. Even if scripts are not available, practice reading out loud from news or sports magazines or even the daily newspaper. This is an excellent way to develop skill in reading

TIME-OUT 11.1

Mike Fright

Being nervous before a broadcast is natural. Many professional announcers with years of experience still get nervous before a game. It's not unlike the feeling athletes experience.

But once the broadcast begins, the nervousness generally disappears, and the prebroadcast tension is translated into energy that enhances performance. In a few instances, however, the nervousness translates into anxiety. Broadcasters call it mike fright. And if you ever experience it, here are some suggestions on how to alleviate it.

- You can sense mike fright coming on when the pitch of your voice increases or if you find it difficult to swallow or catch your breath.
- If that happens, take a moment to stop, take a deep breath, and let it out slowly before continuing. The resulting "dead air" is less important than regaining your composure.
- Continue breathing naturally. Make sure the breaths you take are deep and regular, not short and shallow.
- Be assured of yourself. If you prepared for this broadcast, nothing should catch you by surprise or embarrass you.
- Don't think about yourself. Think about the event. Think about what you are going to say. Then say it.

unfamiliar material called "cold copy." At first, reading out loud may embarrass you, but true professionals do this all the time and think nothing of it. It shows that you care about your craft and you want to do the best possible job.

Vigor

As you practice, work on imparting vigor to your delivery, whether it is reading written material or ad-libbing. A speaker whose voice is alive exudes excitement and vitality. There is nothing dull or boring in what she is saying. A good announcer imparts the feeling that he is in good health and truly enjoys what he is doing.

Word Emphasis

A good speaker uses words to an advantage. By emphasizing some words and "playing" with others, additional vitality can be achieved. For example, you might say the ball carrier "blasted through the line." The word "blasted," should be pronounced *as* a blast. Let the listener hear the blast.

Later, the quarterback may throw a long pass. Stretch out the word "long." "He threw a looong pass."

Pauses

Pauses have dramatic effect and attract listener attention. For example, an average announcer may say "the pass is into the end zone. It is caught." A better way would be "the pass is into the end zone. It . . . is . . . *caught!* Touchdown."

Another example, this time from a sportscast: "And in a game for first place in the AFC Central Division, the Houston Oilers . . . *lost* to the Cleveland Browns.

Speed

Some sports events, like ice hockey, basketball, or boxing, involve nonstop action. These are actually the easiest types of sports to cover. So much is happening that there are fewer pauses to fill with ancillary information. Even so, the sound of any sport can be enhanced by varying the speed of delivery. A sentence at moderate speed might be followed by a short, quickly-delivered one. Speed changes can even be accomplished within a sentence. Bill Raftery, an ESPN college basketball analyst, is a master at this.

Pitch

Another way to add vitality and color to your voice is through the use of changes in pitch. Speakers who talk in a monotone voice quickly lose listener interest. A professional announcer could take the same script and make it sound more interesting by using the techniques described above, as well as changes in volume and emphasis. The voice is not unlike a musical instrument. Both can play the same monotonous note over and over again, or they can string together a variety of notes in combination with varying loudness and speed to create a work that is interesting and pleasant to listen to.

Play-by-Play Practice

The next part to practice—utilizing the principles described above—is to call a game. If your interest lies in play-by-play, practice can be accomplished in one of three ways. All should involve a tape recorder.

The easiest way to practice play-by-play is to watch a game on television with the volume turned off. Many newspapers print lineups with player numbers; these can be memorized beforehand. Because of the tremendous close-ups provided by TV, it's often an easy matter to simply read the names on the backs of player uniforms. The important key to keep in mind is to work on a smooth style with little dead air. The more you know about the sport, the teams, and the players, the less likely this is to happen. That's because you have a tremendous amount of information you want to share with your audience. This is especially important during pauses between action. Baseball announcers have learned to rely on statistics and anecdotes to cover slow periods, especially in the major leagues, where the average game now takes twenty minutes longer to play than it did in 1978. Even in football, there is a lot of "non-action." For example, the typical three-hour game contains only eleven to twelve minutes of actual play.

Another method of practicing play-by-play is to take your tape recorder to the event. Don't wait for the Super Bowl or World Series to come to town. A high school or Little League game will do just fine. Find a location that provides a good vantage point. If the sport is football, perhaps a friend can serve as a spotter.

The final method is similar to the above, except that it is part of a formalized training program such as a college course in sports announcing. Students perform play-by-play and other duties, such as keeping statistics, under the guidance of a professional instructor.

Whatever the system chosen, the student should recognize that this is only practice. Therefore, if problems occur, turn off the recorder, analyze the problem, regain your composure, and resume practicing only when ready. Later, when you listen to your work, be critical. Things to look for will be discussed later in this chapter. If possible, have a professional broadcaster critique your work. It won't take more than five minutes of listening for a pro to provide solid suggestions.

TIME-OUT 11.2

Frequently Mispronounced Words

Sports broadcasting requires accurate pronunciation skills, just like any other form of broadcasting. The most common form of mispronunciation is the failure to complete the word. For example: "gonna" for "going to"; "walken" for "walking." What follows is a partial list of words that sports broadcasters use frequently that are subject to mispronunciation.

	Correct	*Incorrect*
America	Ah MARE ih kuh	ah MUR ih kuh
Arkansas	AHR kan saw	Ahr KANS is
athlete	ATH leet	ATH eh leet
Columbus	koh LUHM bus	Klum bus
data	DAY tah	DA tah
February	FEH brew air ee	FEH boo air ee
football	FOOT ball	FUH ball
for	FOUR	FIR
get	GEHT	GIT
harass	HAIR ess	hair ASS
inquiry	in KWIR ee	IN queer ee
listener	LIHS ehn ehr	LIHS nehr
Missouri	mi ZOOR ee	mi ZOOR ah
mustache	muhs TASH	MUHS tash
New Orleans	New as in "view"	New as in "too"
	OAR lee enz	oar LEENZ
often	AWF ehn	ARF ten
Pennsylvania	Penn sill VANE ee ah	Penn sah VANE ee uh
route	ROOT	Rhymes with "shout"
Saturday	SA tuhr day	SA tah day
Sophomore	SAHF oh more	SAHF more
university	you nihv VER sih tee	you nihv VERS tee
veteran	VEHT ehr an	VEHT run
W	Duh bull you	DUHB yah

Style

As you begin to feel more comfortable at play-by-play, you will find that you are developing a certain style. This should be unique to your personality and should not be a carbon copy of an established announcer. It's all right to listen to all the good announcers and analyze their methods. It's quite another matter to attempt to emulate them. Instead, select and modify parts of their delivery techniques that you like. Be equally critical in analyzing and discarding those other portions that you believe are inappropriate for you. Don't just listen to the game these announcers are covering. Listen to how they call the game. Finally, make sure you develop your *own* style.

Some of the basic elements that good play-by-play announcers bring to a broadcast are the following:

- They try to make the event colorful and entertaining without getting bogged down in an overabundance of technicalities and statistics. Remember, many listeners just want to know who is winning.
- They try to tell stories. Sometimes, life transcends sport. For example, an athlete may be playing just after learning a parent has died. Another might be making a comeback after being told by doctors she would never compete again.

Enthusiasm

Not every sports event is filled with excitement or finds the outcome in doubt until the final moments. Even so, that does not mean you should approach the description of that event with anything less than your best. And that means an enthusiastic approach. At the same time, too much enthusiasm is artificial. Screaming is to be avoided, as it creates two negatives: (1) it can aggravate your throat and literally render you speechless from laryngitis, and (2) it tells listeners you have not had much experience. Not keeping enthusiasm under control can get you in trouble in other ways. For example, you should not describe every block as a great block or every catch as a great catch. If you do, how would you describe a block or catch that truly is extraordinary? Kern Tipps, the legendary Southwest Conference football play-by-play announcer, held a stack of 3"x5" cards that provided synonyms for words frequently used in a broadcast.

Develop a one-on-one conversational relationship with your audience. Remember, this is not public speaking. Although your voice may be heard by thousands and perhaps millions of listeners, each person is an individual. Each person wants you to be speaking directly to him or her. This is the style you should work to develop. One way to achieve this is to pretend you are announcing the game for the person sitting next to you in the broadcast booth. At the same time, you cannot revert totally

TIME-OUT 11.3

"Great" Equals...

How many ways can you say that someone made a great catch? The answer lies in a thesaurus, a reference book that provides synonyms for virtually every word in the English language. Under "great" one finds several words that might be acceptable on a sports broadcast, such as the following:

illustrious	momentous
big	excellent
gigantic	critical
enormous	majestic
important	noble
vital	grand
huge	

Don't stop there. Think of other words that might describe a great catch; words that are not listed above, such as "wonderful" or "terrific." By referring to "wonderful" in the thesaurus, the broadcaster will find additional synonyms:

extraordinary	amazing
marvelous	remarkable
astonishing	astounding

Now, let's look under "terrific." It shows the following not listed under either "wonderful" or "great":

superb	colossal
glorious	sensational
magnificent	

A broadcaster can acquire an extensive vocabulary for describing various types of game action simply by referring to a thesaurus. Then, like Kern Tipps, and Ron Franklin today, synonyms will come easily by simply keeping the cards handy. The best part is that it's a homework assignment you only have to do once in your career.

to ordinary conversation. Grammar must be correct, information must be precise, and entertainment must be prevalent.

Another danger is the opposite of enthusiasm. Disappointment in your voice can clearly be understood by the listener at home. This is especially true if the home team is not doing well. To soften this problem, some announcers interject new and less disappointing material into their play-by-play. For example, a player on a losing team may be enjoying an exceptional performance. Or the team is escaping without injury or looking forward to the next game against an easier opponent. A good announcer will always find a way to counteract a disappointing performance.

Friendliness

If you can develop a one-on-one relationship as described above, you are well on your way toward exhibiting a friendliness that all listeners want. No one wants to listen to a gruff-sounding person who takes himself too seriously and has no sense of humor. Think about the announcers on radio and TV you like the best. Chances are their voices sound friendly and their delivery is unaffected, and you think you would enjoy meeting and talking to them.

Sincerity and Honesty

You are expected to call a game as you see it. If what you describe is not actually occurring on the field, the listener will quickly wise up to the deception. Announcers who are "homers," meaning they always root for the home team, often are in danger of succumbing to this. They may hint that the reason the home team lost was not because it played poorly but rather because the visitors cheated or the officiating was bad.

Announcers who are impartial about the outcome of the event tend to take a more journalistic—and critical—approach. This would qualify as the purest form of sports announcing.

Basics of Play-by-Play

Who's Winning?

Experienced announcers insist that the most important information they can give the listener or viewer is the score. "You cannot give the score too often," they say.

Many fans do not tune in to a game from the beginning and stay riveted to an announcer's play-by-play until the end. Most, in fact, will tune in and out, both physically and mentally, whether a game is on radio or television. Therefore, at any given moment during a broadcast, someone is tuning in for an update on the score. A listener joining a game in progress can become impatient if the score is not given after a reasonable amount of time.

A personal experience serves as an example. Several years ago, I turned a radio on for the first time that evening, midway into a major college basketball game that featured a play-by-play announcer who had been working at his craft for more than thirty-five years. Both teams were shooting and scoring with frequency, yet twenty-two minutes went by before the announcer gave the score. You can imagine the frustration I felt during that time.

As a general rule, giving the score every minute would not be too often, especially on radio. In basketball, where the score can change rapidly, it should be given at least after every basket. That's not to say this is the only time to give a score. There can be a period of several minutes where no scoring occurs. That should not prevent the announcer from giving the score.

In football, the score should be given on every first down, if not more often. In baseball, the score should be given after every out. Some announcers carry a three-minute egg timer with them and use it as a guide for giving the score.

One of the recent trends of televised sports is to provide the score only as a visual. This is a disservice to many in the audience who may have the television on, but are listening rather than viewing a game. With instant replay now common on virtually every telecast, casual fans know they can listen to a game and still not miss the good plays. But they may miss knowing the score if there is no spoken reference. Television sports announcers and producers should recognize that an audible score is just as important as, if not more important than, a visual score.

A popular technique for providing scores of other games is to show them on the screen while the action of the principal game continues without interruption. Announcers should make a point of providing an audible reference to these other scores to alert the nonviewing TV listener who may have an interest in other results. NBC and ESPN, among the networks, now provide a distinctive sound whenever scores of other games are displayed.

In the instance where other games preceded the current game being broadcast, such as the first game of a baseball doubleheader or a junior varsity contest, it is important to provide that score as well. Announcers should not assume the audience knows the score of a game that may have ended hours earlier. The biggest frustration that any listener has is in not knowing.

Time Left to Play

Almost as important as the score is the time remaining to play in a period, half, game, or regulation time. For example: "Villanova leads, 84 to 80, with four-oh-two left to play in regulation." This information alerts the listener that this is a close game and the outcome is still in doubt. Sports broadcasters love close games. It means the bulk of the audience will stay to the end. For the account executive, it means spots remaining to be run will not be of diminished value to their client advertiser. For the announcers, it means tension and excitement come naturally because of the close score.

In the case of baseball, announcers should tell the audience what inning the game is in. "Bottom of the ninth. One out. Runners on second and third. Rangers down by one." No baseball fan could possibly tune out at this point!

Other sports have different methods of determining when the competition will end. For example, in golf it's the number of holes left to play. In tennis, it is match point. In racing, it's the number of laps remaining. Whether a game is close or a blowout, time remaining is vital for listener comprehension.

The pinnacle for aspiring sports broadcasters is to work a Super Bowl for a national network. (From left to right) Chris Mortensen, Chris Berman, Tom Jackson, and Joe Theismann cover Super Bowl XXVII in 1993. (Source: Courtesy of ESPN)

Down and Distance

In football, three additional elements of information are required after every play: (1) Where is the ball? (2) What down is it? and (3) How far for a first down or touchdown? "First and ten for the Jacksonville Jaguars on their 20 yard line." "Third and two for the Fighting Irish on the Buckeye 22."

Since American football fields have two of every yard line except the 50, it is important for the viewer or listener to know on whose side of the field the ball is located in addition to the down. Football fields that are often the sites of regular TV coverage have an arrow next to the yard marker, pointing to the nearest goal line. For the viewer, this helps identify which side of the field the ball is on. At other stadiums, and especially on radio, it is vital for the announcer to inform the audience exactly where the ball is, what down it is, and how many yards to go for a first down.

Additionally, when a team achieves a first down or touchdown, it must be announced the moment it is confirmed. This is the most important piece of information that can be given during a play. For example, "Denson is up to the 30, the 35—he's got the first down—the 40, and brought down around the 42." "Aikman throws into the end zone. Touchdown! Michael Irvin with the TD catch." Notice that the touchdown information preceeded the name of the pass catcher.

Radio Play-by-Play

Play-by-play is best learned and perfected on radio. That's because in radio, the play-by-play announcer is the principal source of information for the listener. The color analyst is of secondary importance.

In television, the reverse is true. Since the viewer can see the action unfolding, the role of the color analyst to describe why it happened is more important than play-by-play.

That's why play-by-play on radio continues to be a fulfilling and exciting way to earn a living. And a good radio play-by-play announcer can more easily make the transition into television. The reverse is not nearly so easy to achieve.

Description, Description, Description

Beyond the caveats about score and time remaining, the most important factor that a radio play-by-play announcer must remember is that he or she is the eyes of the listener. Beginners often forget this. As a result, the listener is denied accurate descriptions of what is going on.

Radio is the purest form of sports broadcasting. Here, Tom Dirato and Bill Teegins prepare to go on the air from their courtside seats at an Oklahoma State University basketball game. (Source: From the collection of John R. Catsis)

Perhaps the biggest sin among novices is forgetting that the principal function of the job is to describe the action and not be a fan.

How often have you heard something like this? "Here's a long pass into the end zone. Oh, wow! Unbelievable! Listen to the crowd. They can't believe it either." So what happened? Was it caught for a touchdown? Was the pass dropped? Was it intercepted? Was there a terrific defensive play? There is no way to know. As a result, the listener is frustrated, and perhaps more than a little disappointed with the announcer.

These problems are not limited to football. What examples have you experienced in other sports?

Who's Got the Ball?

Many announcers, even experienced ones, assume the radio listener is familiar with the players of both teams. As a result, it is often impossible for the casual fan to know what is going on. For example: "Jones with the jumper. No good. Rebound by Brown. Pass to Smith. Long shot from the corner. No good. Grabbed by Winslow." Who has the ball? Did the ball ever change hands? How many times? There is no way of knowing. Here is a better way to describe the action: "Jones with the jumper. No good. Rebound by Brown for St. Ignatius. Pass *downcourt* to Smith. Long shot from the corner. No good. Grabbed by Winslow for Pius." Notice that the names of both schools were added for clarity and that "downcourt" was further added to emphasize that the action was reversing itself. "Outlet pass" also would have helped to clarify the action as much as "downcourt." These are but two examples of how accurate words used in each sport can help to develop greater understanding on the part of the listener.

Can you come up with other examples for other sports? If not, analyze the play-by-play of accomplished radio sportscasters. What are their poor habits? In what areas are they especially skilled?

In football, the outcome of passes or other plays such as field goal attempts are important; so are shots and rebounds in basketball. When a player shoots, the listener wants to know if it was good or not. Everything else, like the play under the basket, or a brilliant pass, is secondary. The same is true of rebounds. All of that can be explained after the listener knows if a shot was successful.

To summarize, the critical elements of any action should be told first. Don't leave your audience in suspense. There's always time later to go into detail with explanations of how or why it happened.

Names

Two or more players with the same last names can add an extra challenge to any event. In these instances they must always be fully identified by both first and last name regardless of whether they play on the same or opposing teams. That's the only time you should use both first and last names on a frequent basis. To do otherwise results in a habit that is both hard to break and annoying to the listener. And in games involving a lot of rapid action, it wastes time.

When calling a game for radio, numbers are immaterial to the listener. Perhaps you have heard, "the pass was caught by number 20." Unless a radio listener has a program, which is unlikely, this information is meaningless. A beginning announcer tends to use numbers as a crutch, because he has not taken the time to memorize the players' names, or he is working without a spotter and is attempting to find the player's name on the spotting board, or both. On television, of course, where viewers can easily see a player's number, this can have the opposite effect and can assist in more clearly identifying a particular player.

Cliches

Sports is loaded with cliches, and it's tough to resist using them, especially during the excitement of calling a game. Kern Tipps was well-known for using the term, "ran through a hole big enough for a Mack truck." Marv Albert refers to three-point shots in basketball as being from "downtown." Dan Patrick of ESPN uses "nothing but the bottom of the net" frequently in describing basketball highlights. These professionals created these terms and phrases as their trademark. If you were to use them, they would immediately become cliches. They would also mark you as an amateur.

Someone once said, "Create your own cliche." That statement

TIME-OUT 11.4

Cliches

Cliches and sports seem to go together. The problem is, they shouldn't. Cliches are methods of expression used by announcers who cannot come up with creative new descriptions of their own. As stated elsewhere, certain sports cliches are often identified with specific announcers. Using them accomplishes two things, neither of which is good: (1) it marks you as an amateur, and (2) it promotes the other person.

The following article by Rachel Shuster shows how silly sports cliches can be. You might enjoy reading this out loud.

Cachet gives way to cliche

It's time to fish or cut bait.

You don't have to be a Rhodes scholar to figure out that today's sports lingo is nothing to write home about. Listening to athletes and commentators, the name of the game is to let it all hang out.

Reggie White, wearing his emotions on his sleeve, waits for a sign from God to determine his new NFL home.

We just want him to take the bull by the horns and steer clear of no-man's land.

On to greener pastures.

Wouldn't it be a feather in the cap if Jack Nicklaus or Ray Floyd, neither one a spring chicken, shot the lights out and wrapped up another Masters title?

Or is Fred Couples going to rise to the occasion and end up higher than a kite with his second Masters in a row?

remains true today. By creating your own clever phrases or synonyms, you can look forward to the ultimate compliment when you hear others copy you! A word of caution, however. A pet term or cliche could become "old hat" if repeated too often. I recall hearing one announcer describing a football game in which players were getting "hammered" on nearly every play. After a while, a listener will tune out the play-by-play and begin to count the number of "hammers" in the broadcast.

Propriety

Profanity and other questionable language have no place in a professional sports broadcast. There are times, however, when this is

---

The plot thickens.

Whomever people wanted to ice the NCAA men's basketball title, one thing's as good as gold: Everyone will be jumping on the bandwagon of the winner today, giving credit where credit's due.

Deja vu all over again.

This is also when baseball fans go bananas 'cause it's anybody's game at the start of the season. Except the shoe's on the other foot for the expansion Florida Marlins and Colorado Rockies, who probably will have a tough row to hoe.

But you know those pitching-rich Atlanta Braves will take no prisoners. Uh-uh. They look like a million bucks. (Now there's a really old cliche, given sports' economic realities. Got to be as dead as a doornail.)

The New York Yankees, in some circles, are being touted to win it all, and you can take that to the bank. Or can you?

It won't be a walk in the park or a day at the beach for my boys in pinstripes. The Boss is back, and we all know George Steinbrenner is one tough cookie. Couldn't stop him with a Mack truck, although you feel like hitting him over the head with, "George, if it's not broke, don't fix it."

A controversy-free season will take a miracle.

The Pittsburgh Pirates waved the towel to the most thoroughbred talent, namely Barry Bonds, Doug Drabek and Jose Lind. The Pirates could drop off the face of the earth, although you can't ever count them out with manager Jim Leyland in the saddle.

(continued next page)

TIME-OUT 11.4

Continued

The defending champion Toronto Blue Jays also lost a ton of folks, and many feel that takes the wind out of their sails. But it also could be a blessing in disguise, to compete without the pressure on their backs.

Time will tell, because when the going gets tough, the tough get going.

Speaking of going, Marge Schott can't be a happy camper. The Cincinnati Reds owner not only can't rule the roost for her use of naughty words, she also faces a tough haul next season when smoking is shown the door at Riverfront Stadium.

Could be the straw that breaks the Camel's back. (Or is her brand True? Only the hairdresser knows for sure.)

And I wonder who's going to be dishing out that World Series trophy at season's end. The owners have dodged a bullet so far without a commissioner in the bag, but the excuses are getting pretty thin. Then, too, you can lead a horse to water but you can't make him drink.

Still, isn't it time to separate the men from the boys?

Hockey got a shot in the arm with Mario Lemieux's return to the Penguins, and now it's Katy-bar-the-door time for the rest of the Patrick Division (soon to be the new and improved Atlantic zone, minus Pittsburgh).

It's do or die, time to go for broke, wrap up a playoff spot and begin the second season.

Then, as Charles Barkley would say, it's off to the races.

Those pro basketball stars have been busy bees, too, duking it out like there's no tomorrow. Went to a basketball game and a hockey game broke out.

Shaquille O'Neal, a little wet behind the ears, still has to learn to turn the other cheek. You know, if you can't stand the heat, get out of the kitchen.

As for Greg Anthony, off the bench as fast as greased lightning, he turned out the lights and found the party over. And that's all she wrote about that.

So our lingo's gone down the tubes, and we don't see much light at the end of the tunnel.

But hey, as it is written, Rome wasn't built in a day.

P.S. *Deja vu* MEANS "all over again." Thus, when one says "Deja vu all over again," it loosely translates to "all over again all over again."

Source: Copyright © 1993, USA TODAY. Reprinted with permission.

difficult to avoid. Live interviews are one such instance. Another is action caught by a microphone along a sideline. If an obscenity should occur, it is the responsibility of the audio operator to immediately turn off that microphone or turn down the pot. It is also up to the announcer not to draw undue attention to it.

Professional announcers are rarely heard to utter obscenities. But questionable taste can be another matter. For example, during a cable telecast of a Nebraska-Oklahoma State basketball game several years ago, the color announcer referred to a player injury as having been caused by being "popped in the family jewels area." "Groin" would have been more accurate, and certainly more acceptable.

In another instance, a baseball announcer was talking about gametime weather conditions. He called it a "hot and sultry night," adding that the fans were packed into the stadium. He hoped out loud that all were friendly, because by the end of the evening, he announced, they might be "smelling pretty bad."

Television Commentary

As mentioned earlier, the color analyst is the more significant member of a television announcing team for many sports events. That's because the viewer can see what is happening and depends on the play-by-play announcer as a spotter. The color announcer, on the other hand, explains the nuances of the game, or why a particular play developed as it did.

TIME-OUT 11.5

Tips from a Pro

ESPN announcer Ron Franklin says the most important quality a sports announcer can have is trustworthiness. This includes the trust of your audience, your colleagues, and the participants of the event you are covering.

This trust has enabled Franklin to be told of trick plays that will be attempted during certain times of a football game. One major college coach who has won a national championship often discloses to Franklin the first twenty or so offensive plays his team proposes to use at the beginning of a game. This is kept secret in the booth until just before each play is to be run. The producer in the production truck is then notified to isolate a camera on a certain player who will be instrumental in the play. The color analyst keys in on the special elements of the play to better describe it moments later on instant replay. In each play-by-play broadcast, says Franklin, "you're taking an exam and you'd better well pass it."

Intimate knowledge of a sport is extremely important for effective color announcing. That's one reason why most color analysts were former athletes or coaches. Not only are they knowledgeable, but also they often are more believable because they participated in the sport they are analyzing. The other reason is that they bring a marquee quality to the broadcast.

However, having played or coached is not the sole prerequisite for becoming an effective color commentator. The same effective delivery techniques discussed earlier in this chapter are important, although perhaps not to the degree expected of a play-by-play announcer.

The TV commentator also has technology as an assistant. Instant replay, different camera angles, slow motion, and the Telestrator™ are useful accessories in helping the viewer develop a greater appreciation of the game and its subtleties. The commentator who develops a professional relationship with this equipment will become more effective.

Good commentators, whether on radio or television, can also point out bad habits that drive coaches crazy. For example, many years ago I could always predict when a Northwestern University quarterback was going to pass. For pass plays only, he always lined up with his right foot farther back than his left, as if this helped him drop back more quickly. Recently, analyst John Madden noted that passes occurred whenever certain quarterbacks licked their fingers before a pass.

The examples just given are easy to understand. And good commentary tends to be simple. Getting too analytical can harm a broadcast. That's one reason Madden and others like him are so good. They may have coached the game, but their explanations are given in a way that even the novice fan can understand them.

Radio Commentary

Radio commentary is more difficult than television for two reasons: (1) the radio commentator does not have the assistance of TV technology to help explain a play, and (2) the radio commentator must serve entirely as the eyes of the audience. Therefore, vivid and accurate description is as important as that provided by the play-by-play announcer. A radio commentator must also be careful in providing statistics. Too much, too quickly, can overwhelm the listener.

A skilled radio color analyst provides a valuable balance and sense of excitement to any sports broadcast. This is accomplished by explaining a play with additional detail not covered by the initial play-by-play description. For example: "It resulted in a touchdown because Williams cleared the way with a tremendous block on Standish back on the 43."

This kind of explanation adds to the description of the play-by-play announcer, whose job it is to follow the ball or principal action. The color analyst, on the other hand, does not have to follow the ball or the puck. He or she can look for action downfield or down the ice.

Although most television color commentators come from the sport they cover, this is generally not the case in radio. Many quality analysts are broadcasters who know the sport, the teams, and the players extremely well. They attend practice sessions and talk to coaches. They are students of the game. A good radio color commentator has two basic qualities, both of which come under the general heading of teamwork:

1. *Timing.* This means knowing when to talk and when to stop. In fast-moving sports like ice hockey or basketball, this is especially important. Commentary is usually limited to that brief moment when the action is moving to the other end of the court. One color commentator who understands timing is Dick Vitale. He generally limits his comments to one sentence during those periods.
2. *Non-duplication of play-by-play.* A good color commentator does not merely repeat, with different wording, what the play-by-play announcer just said. To do so would diminish the value of the play-by-play. A color analyst must watch the game differently and provide exciting insight not otherwise apparent. While a play-by-play announcer is expected to follow the football, the color analyst should adjust his vision to provide a wide-angle view, looking for key blocks or significant defensive moves.

Objectivity

Commentators and announcers often find it difficult to be objective. This is especially true if they are being paid to cover a particular team throughout its season. Even so, give credit for great plays, even if by the opponent. If the home team is playing poorly, don't try to hide it. Avoid blaming poor performance on the officiating. Most coaches admit that officiating—good or bad—rarely gives the victory to a team that otherwise would have lost. This is not to say that you should not comment on officiating. But be careful. Make sure you know the rules as well as the official. On questionable calls, let the viewer or listener determine how the official performed. If you do comment, don't say the official made a "great" call or a "poor" call. The official did neither of these. Instead, he or she made the "correct" call or "wrong" call. There is no grade that is partially right or partially wrong, like B- or C+. In officiating, the call is either right or wrong. Duane Smith, a longtime Big 8 basketball official, says that broadcasters, who are normally located at center court and at floor level, have the worst seat in the house for watching a game and judging the performance of officials.

It's not just officiating calls that broadcasters can miss. In baseball, it's the type of pitch thrown. Gary Ward, who has coached college baseball for two decades, says broadcasters misidentify 20 percent of the pitches thrown.

Second-Guessing

One of the annoying habits of some inexperienced color announcers is to continually second-guess players and coaches. This often occurs when strategy is not successful. For example: "I would have called a pass. The Wildcats saw the draw coming, all the way." Or: "I would put my best ball handler into the game now, instead of going after rebounding strength." Or: "I don't know why Lasorda is calling for a left hander from the bullpen. I'd have called for a right hander."

Second-guessing might be considered fun, but in most instances it is unprofessional. First, you are not the coach. Second, you may have overlooked an element that is not clearly apparent at the time, such as an undisclosed injury. Third, when a truly questionable decision is made, it will not have any impact upon the listener if you had been second-guessing throughout the game.

Second-guessing officials can also be a touchy situation. If instant replay clearly shows the official made a mistake, you should report it. In these instances, most officials will support your verdict. But neither should you dwell on it. After all, everyone makes mistakes, and the vast majority of officials are sincere, dedicated persons who are neutral about the outcome of a game or match. They only want to be accurate.

The Baseball Challenge

Baseball provides an additional challenge to announcers because of the slowness of the game. Extensive preparation is the only solution. There are no shortcasts. By doing homework, a broadcast will sound smooth and have a minimum of dead air. Most professional baseball announcers will put in a full workday preparing for and broadcasting each game.

Other Sports

While much of this textbook concentrates on the so-called major sports, many announcers will find themselves being asked to cover sports that

TIME-OUT 11.6

Announcing Baseball

Good baseball announcers have strong organizational skills and are detail-oriented. That's because keeping track of statistics is vitally important to a successful baseball broadcast. Before every game, a professional play-by-play announcer will go through the following informational checklist:

1. Gathering basic information
   a. Annual media guides
   b. Media notes from each team, highlighted by a colored marker pen
   c. Pregame conversations with players, coaches, managers, and other broadcasters
2. Detailing starting pitchers, often on 3" x 5" cards
   a. Records for the year
   b. Types of pitches each throws
3. Obtaining starting lineups
   a. Note recent hitting streaks
   b. Note previous game performance for each player on both teams
   c. Reference season-to-date records for each player, highlighting significant games
4. Gathering general information on the opposing team
   a. Home and road records
   b. Recent team trends and streaks
   c. Overall team trends

   Armed with this information, properly organized, a professional baseball announcer experiences no shortage of interesting material to talk about and keep the broadcast moving.

receive less attention. For example, a few radio stations cover wrestling tournaments. These situations are generally limited to towns where major universities field highly competitive teams on a regular basis.

Whatever the game played, chances are that somewhere it is being described in a radio broadcast. The opportunities for radio sports play-by-play are endless.

Keeping Track

Besides keeping up with the action, both play-by-play and color announcers have other responsibilities:

1. They must be aware of and follow instructions of the game producer. This includes breaking for commercials or introducing a reporter outside a locker room.
2. They are often expected to keep certain statistics for themselves. This is true of virtually all events, except, perhaps, for those covered by national networks. And even in those instances, some announcers prefer to keep some statistics themselves as a method of providing up-to-the-moment information.

TIME-OUT 11.7

Keeping Statistics

Keeping track of scoring and essential statistical material is an important part of any sports broadcast. Although "official" statistics are provided in many instances, they are usually available only at the conclusion of periods, at halftime, or at the end of the game or event.

For professional sportscasters, that's not good enough. That's why they have developed methods of keeping track of action beyond the customary scorekeeping available to fans. There is no single method of keeping track. Different sportscasters use different methods. Some statistics are kept by the play-by-play announcer and some by the color analyst. The assignments are often decided by the announcers themselves, as there is no hard and fast rule over who keeps track of what.

What follows are two examples of statistical data often kept by announcers during the broadcasts of football and basketball games. These examples are not represented as complete, by any means. Each broadcaster will make additional notes and use abbreviations different from those shown. You will want to add your own custom touches to these scorekeeping methods.

Football

Keeping track of first downs, scoring drives, and other information is easy once you master the method described below. The only special equipment required are two different colored pens. Each should match the colors used in identifying each team on the spotting board.

Additionally, several sheets of lined notebook paper have been scored in advance, with vertical lines, to separate the downs. Thereafter, whenever a play is run, a brief notation is made under the appropriate "down" column.

Both Announcers

Whether you are the color analyst or the play-by-play announcer, a smooth broadcast is one where neither interrupts the other, both pronounce the players' name identically, and each brings different information to the broadcast.

Both announcers should remember that they are not just talking to each other. It's a three-way conversation, with the most important

	1	2	3	4
	10-20	10-20 TT 15		
①	10-35 Ⓟ	8-37	8-37	
②	10-46	7-49 Ⓟ DY		
④③	10-o42 —	THOMAS 42-run, 8 plays, 80 yards (Jones), BULLDOGS, 7-0		
	10-18 (Smith)	5-25		
①	10-30 P	10-30		
②	10-40	2-48		
③	10-o39	4-33 McKEEVER, 33-pass, 8 plays, 82 yards, 7-6		
	10-13 P — DAVIS, int. pass, 13 yards (Rowley) WILDKITS 13-7 4:31 1st			

(continued next page)

TIME-OUT 11.7

Continued

Explanation:

Line 1. On first down with ten yards to go on the Bulldogs' (offensive team's) 20 yard line, there is no gain. On second down, still on the 20, Thomas makes a fifteen-yard run. In this case, "TT" is the abbreviation for Terry Thomas.

Line 2. The circled numeral 1 indicates the team has made one first down so far in the game. The ball is on the 35; first down, with ten yards to go. A two-yard pass, indicated by the circled P, results in second down, eight yards to go on the 37 yard line. After no gain, it is now third and eight.

Line 3. The circled numeral 2 shows the Bulldogs have made their second first down of the game. It is now first and ten on the 46, as the result of a nine-yard run on third down. On second and seven from the Bulldog 49, there is a completed pass to Donny Young (DY).

Line 4. The pass results in the third first down of the game. The ball is now on the opponent's (o) 42 yard line, first and ten. On that play, Thomas runs 42 yards for a touchdown. The TD run also earns the team credit for its fourth first down. One can now quickly add up the total plays of the drive, which are eight. And a quick glance shows that the team had only one third-down situation. (Jones) kicked the extra point to make the score 7–0.

Line 5. The Wildkits (opposing team) now have the ball. They are first and ten on their own 18 yard line, following the kickoff and a runback by Smith. After a seven-yard run, it is now second and five from the 25.

Line 6. On the second down, there was a five-yard run, resulting in the first first down of the game for this team. Therefore, it is now first and ten from the 30. Following an incomplete pass, as shown by the uncircled P, it is now second and ten from the 30.

Line 7. The Wildkits earned their second first down of the game on a ten-yard run. As a result, it is now first and ten from the 40. An eight-yard run makes it second and two from the offensive team's 48 yard line.

Line 8. The team earned a third first down, and is now first and ten from its opponent's 39 yard line as a result of a thirteen-yard run. On first down, there is a six-yard gain, making it second and four from the opponent's 33. From there, on second down, McKeever caught a pass and scored. The eight-play drive did not see any third down plays for the Wildkits. The extra point was missed and the Bulldogs continued to hold the lead, 7–6.

Line 9. Following the kickoff it is first and ten for the Bulldogs on their own 13. On the first play, the pass is intercepted and run back for a touchdown. This time, Rowley kicked the extra point and the Wildkits took the lead, 13–7, with 4:31 left to go in the first quarter.

Basketball

It is very easy to follow action throughout a basketball game and keep track of scoring runs and three-point plays. Here, a writing instrument of a single color will serve quite well. Several sheets of lined paper have been scored as shown below. Normally, this running score is kept by the color analyst. The play-by-play announcer keeps the traditional box score, which tracks individual scoring and fouls.

Explanation

The game opened with Reeves scoring on a lay-up, with 19:02 left in the first half.

Exactly one minute later, Heller scored on an eighteen-foot shot (18) to tie the game.

NOTES	TIME	COWBOYS	TIGERS	TIME	NOTES
Reeves L	19:02	2			
			2	18:02	Heller-18
Sutton 3-35	17:41	5			
Thompson 3	17-31	8			
Rutherford 3	17:11	11			
Burley 3	17:01	14			
			4	16:34	Crudup -S
Collins - T	16:20	16			

(continued next page)

TIME-OUT 11.7

Continued

The Cowboys then went on a twelve-point scoring run within a forty-second time span, marked by successive three-pointers, one of them by Sutton, which was from about 35 feet away from the basket.

That made the score 14–2, Cowboys, before Crudup ended the run with a slam (S) for the Tigers.

Collins then followed with a tip-in (T) for the Cowboys.

This explanation is identical to the manner in which the color announcer would recap the game during a time-out or at the end of the half or the game.

Baseball

Most fans are familiar with the traditional baseball score sheet. Each defensive player is given a number as follows:

1—pitcher	6—shortstop
2—catcher	7—left field
3—first base	8—center field
4—second base	9—right field
5—third base	

From this point, many announcers develop their own code. What is important is that the announcer be able to read his or her own score sheet to be able to recap during the game broadcast.

Before each game, announcers update batting and pitching information for each player and maintain it in a three-ring binder. In baseball play-by-play, the name of the game is recap, recap, and recap.

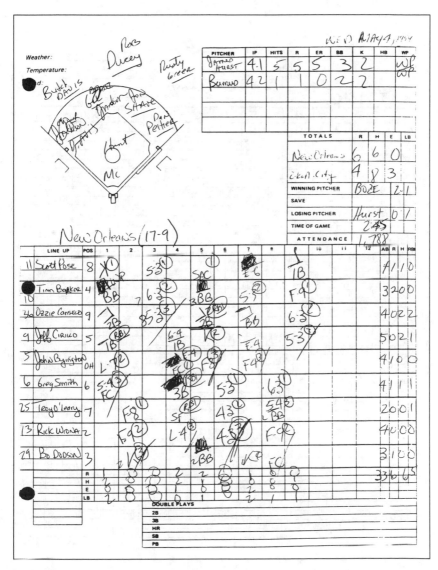

Source: Courtesy of Brian Barnhart

(continued next page)

TIME-OUT 11.7

Continued

NOTES:

CAREER:

GAMES 3 errors on 4/20/94

AVG.

HR

SLAMS

SB

RBI

"NAME BENJI GIL

AGE 21

BORN IN 15 6 72

HOME TOWN

YRS. IN MAJORS

BATTING

W/L GM	GAME	DATE	OPP	D/N	HOME/ROAD	POS	AB	R	H	2B	3B	HR	HR OFF	RBI	BB	SO	HP	SH/SF	SB/CS	TB	AVG	E
L 10 4	#1	4-7	NASH/N		H	SS	3	0	0	0	0	0		0	0	1				0	.3	0 3
L 4 2	#2	4-8	NASH/N		H	SS	4		1	0	0	0		0	0	0				1	.9	1-7
L 2 0	#3	4-9	NASH/N		H	SS	3	0	0	0	0	0		0	0	1				0	.3	1-10
W 2-1	#4	4-10/11	BUF/N		H	SS	3	0	1	1	0	0		1	0	0				1	.3	2-13
W 6 0	#5	4-11	BUF/N		H	SS	3	1	2	0	0	0		0	0	0				2	.3	4-16
W 4-3	#6	4-12	BUF/N		H	SS	3	0	0	0	0	0		0	0	0				0	.3	4-19
L 3-2	#7	4-14	LOUIS/N		R	SS	4	0	1	1	0	0		1	0	1				1	.4	5-23
W 7-7	#8	4-15	LOUIS/N		R	SS	3	1	1	0	0	1	BRERRE (2R)	2	1	0	HP			3	.6	26
L 3-0	#9	4-16	LOUIS/N		R	SS	3	0	1	0	0	0		0	0	1				1	.7	29
W 8-5	#10	4-17	INDY/N		R	SS	4	0	0	0	0	0		0	0	1				0	.4	7 33
W 13 6	#11	4-18	INDY/R		R	SS	5	1	4	2	0	1	MATHRE (SOLO)	1	0	0				4	.5	11-38
L 4 2	#12	4-19	IND/N		H	SS	3	0	0	0	0	0		0	1	0				1	.3	12-41
L 7-5	#13	4-20	LOUIS/N		H	SS	4	1	1	0	0	0		0	0	0				1	.4	13-45
L 4 2	#14	4-21	LOUIS/N		H	SS	4	0	0	0	0	0		0	0	2				0	.4	13-49
W 6 2	#15	4-22	LOUIS/N		H	SS	3	1	1	0	0	0		0	0	2				0	.3	13-52
L 11-4	#16	4-23	INDY/N		H	SS	4	1	1	0	0	0		1	1	2				1	.4	14-56
L 2-0	#17	4-24	IND/N		H	SS	4	0	0	0	0	0		0	0	1				0	.3	14-59
L 5-2	#18	4-25	IND/N		H	SS	4	0	1	0	0	0		0	0	2				1	.4	15-63
L 12-11	#19	4-26	OMA/N		R	SS	3	0	0	0	0	0		1	1	1		SF		0	.3	15-66
W 3-1	#20	4-30	OMA/N		H	SS	2	1	1	0	0	0		0	1	0				1	.2	16-68
L 6-1	#21	5-1	OMA/H		H	SS	4	0	1	0	0	0		0	0	2				1	.4	17-72
L 3-2	#22	5(01)	NASH/N		H	SS	3	0	0	0	0	0		0	0	0				0	.3	17 75
L 2-0	#23	5 5(02)	LOU 9/N		H	SS	3	0	1	0	0	0		0	0	1			Sb	0	.3	17-78
L 6-4	#24	5-4	DON/N		H	SS	2	0	2	1	0	0		0	0	0				2	.2	19-80
W 6-2	#25	5-5	NO/N		H	SS	4	2	2	0	0	0	TAYLOR (SOLO)	1	0	0				2	.4	21-84
L 7-3	#26	5-6	NN/N		R	SS	3	0	1	0	0	0		0	0	0				1	.3	22-?
W 10-9 (10)	#27	5-7	OMA/N		R	SS	4		1	0	0	1	KNEBER (SOLO)	3	1	0		SF		4	.23	91
W 11-10	#28	5-8	OMA/D		R	SS	5	1	2	0	0	1	NICHOLS (SIAM)	5	0					5	.25	96
W 6 0	#29	5-10(1)	NO/D		R	SS	4	0	0	0	0	0		0	0	0				0	.26	100
L 2-1 (8)	#30	5-10	NO/D		R	SS	2	0	0	0	0	0		0	1	0				0	.26	102
W 8-7 (6)	#31	5-11	NO/N		R	SS	4	0	1	0	0	0		0	0	1		SF		1	.27	106
L 2-1	#32	5-13	NASH/N		H	SS	4	1	1	0	0	0		0	0	0				1	.28	106
L 3-1	#33	5-14	NASH/N		H	SS	3	0	0	0	0	0		0	0	1				0	.28	113
L 7-3	#34	5-15	BUFF/N		H	SS	4	0	0	0	0	0		0	0	1				0	.28	117
L 9-3	#35	5-16	BUFF/N		H	SS	3	0	0	0	0	0		0	1					0	.28	120
W 7-4	#36	5-17	NN/N		H	SS	4		1	1	0	0		0	0					1	.29	124
L 3-2	#37	5-18	NN/N		H	SS	4		1	1	0	0		0	0	0				1	.30	128
W 4-3 (11)	#38	5-20			R	SS	3	0	0	0	0	0		0	0	2				1	.31	133
L 6-5 (10)	#39	5-21	NASH/N		R	SS	3	0	0	0	0	0		0	1	2		SAC		0	.31	136
L 7-4	#40	5-22	NN/N		R	SS	4	0	1	0	0	0		1	0					1	.3?	?
L 6-1	#41	5-23	NN/N		R	SS	4	0	0	0	0	0		0	0	1				0	?	?
L 5-0	#42	5-25	BUFF/N		R	SS	3	2	0	0	0	0		0	1					0	.32	147
W 12-5	#43	5-27	NO/N		R	SS	5	2	1	0	0	0		0	0					1	.33	152
L 5-4	#44	5-28	NO/N		R	SS	4	0	0	0	0	0		0	2	0				0	.33	152
L 7-2	#45	5-29	NO/N		R	SS	3	0	0	0	0	0		0	2	0				0	.33	158

Source: Courtesy of Brian Barnhart

PITCHING

WINS _____ RLL _____
LOSSES from Texas 4/25/94
BB   To Texas 5/22/94   NAME James Hurst
STRIKEOUTS from Texas 5/25/94
INNINGS PITCHED _____   AGE _____
SAVES _____   BORN IN Fast, slider, change
SHUTOUTS _____   HOME TOWN _____
COMP. GMS. _____   YRS. IN MAJORS _____

W/L GM	1M GM	GAME	DATE	OPP	D N	CG SHO	ST	REL	INNS	H	ER	R	W	SO	HR	HR BY	W	L	ERA	ENT/GM	LV/GM
R)	2.12·11	#19	4·26	laa/N					0.0	1	0	0	0	0	0					9th	END
H)	2·6·1	#21	5·1	atlana/D					0.2	0	0	0	2	0	0					6th	7th
H)	1·6·4	#24	5·4	N.Y/N			x		4.1	5	5	5	3	2	0					START	5th
R)	W·1H·0	#28	5·8	sm/D					1.2	5	5	6	1	3	2	McGwire(24) Bossy(38)					8th	9th
H)	·13·1	#33	5·14	N·sH/N					0.2	5	7	7	2	0	0					6th	6th
R)	L·6·5(a)	#39	5·21	NASH/N					1.1	0	0	0	0	1	0					9th	9th
R)	w·10·5	#44	5·27	N.Y/N					1.0	2	0	0	1	1						9th	FINISH
R)	·7·0	#46	5·29	col·D					1.0	3	3	3	2	0	1					6th	8th
H)	L·H·9	#48	6·1	N.Y/N					2.1	4	2	3	2	2	0					10th	FINISH
H)	W·3·3(10)	#51	6·4	iaa/N				x	1.0	1	0	0	0	0	0					10th	FINISH
									·1	1					1						
H)	w·12·9	#58	6·10	N·D/N					2.0	0	0	0	0	0	0					7th	9th
R)	13·4(11)	#63	6·14	cin/N					0.2	1	3	3	1	0	0					7th	7th
R)	w·9·5	#64	6·16	louis/N					2.1	1	1	1	1	3	0					7th	FINISH
R)	8·2	#66	6·18	louis/N					1.0	3	2	2	0	0	0					8th	END
H)	L·9·5	#68	6·21	lou/N					0.2	1	0	0	1	0	0					9th	END

Source: Courtesy of Brian Barnhart

listener being each member of the audience. Inside jokes or references known or appreciated only by those working on the broadcast do not have a place.

Good announcers are like good athletes. They both share the same five positive attributes:

1. They pay attention to the job at hand. They forget about personal problems and concentrate on a successful performance.
2. They strive to improve. Great athletes and announcers are achievement motivated. They practice, practice, and practice.
3. They know their limitations. They may not be able to pitch a doubleheader or announce two games in one day. That's OK.
4. They have mental toughness and learn from their mistakes. Giving the wrong winner of a race is not a catastrophe (provided the error is corrected).

TIME-OUT 11.8

Expressions Made Famous by Famous Sports Announcers

Marv Albert	"From downtown."
Mel Allen	"How about that?"
Red Barber	"From the catbird seat."
Chris Berman	"Back, back, back, back, back, back, back, back, back."
Andres Cantor	"Goooooooaaaaaal! Goooooooaaaaaal!"
Harry Caray	"Holy cow."
Howard Cosell	"Tell it like it is."
Ron Franklin	"Oh, my goodness."
Ernie Harwell	"Long gone."
Keith Jackson	"Whoa, Nellie."
John Madden	"His light is on but nobody's home."
Graham McNamee	"Good evening, ladies and gentlemen of the radio audience."
Don Meredith	"Turn out the lights, the party's over."
Al Michaels	"Do you believe in miracles? Yes!"
Johnny Most	"Havlicek stole the ball! Havlicek stole the ball!"
Brent Musberger	"You are looking live . . ."
Dan Patrick	"Nothing but the bottom of the net."
Dick Vitale	"Awesome, baby."
Bert Wilson	"We don't care who wins as long as it's the Cubs."

5. Great announcers and athletes are goal-oriented and have developed strategies to achieve those goals. For many, performing before a large audience may be one of those goals.

In the final analysis, a great sports announcer is made, not born. He or she practices, analyzes, and studies.

The MVPs for This Chapter

Mr. Ron Franklin, college football and basketball announcer for ESPN, is thanked for providing additional wisdom that has been incorporated in this chapter.

Mr. Brian Barnhart, voice of the Oklahoma City '89ers Triple-A team, is thanked for his extensive assistance on baseball announcing tips and techniques.

Appendix: The National Academy of Television Arts and Sciences

Emmy Award Winners for Sports Programming

1976–1977

Live Sports Special: 1976 Summer Olympic Games, Montreal, ABC
Live Sports Series: The NFL Today/NFL Football, CBS
Edited Sports Special: A Preview of the 1976 Olympic Games, ABC
Edited Sports Series: The Olympiad, PBS
Director: Chet Forte, NFL Monday Night Football, ABC
Personality: Frank Gifford, ABC

1977–1978

Live Sports Special: Heavyweight Title Fight, Ali/Spinks, CBS
Live Sports Series: The NFL Today/NFL Football, CBS
Edited Sports Special: Ballooning Across the Atlantic, CBS
Edited Sports Series: The Way It Was, Syndicated
Director: Ted Nathanson, AFC Championship Football Game, NBC
Personality: Jack Whitaker, CBS

1978–1979

Live Sports Special: Super Bowl XIII, NBC
Live Sports Series: NFL Monday Night Football, ABC
Edited Sports Special: The Flight of Double Eagle II, 1978, ABC
Edited Sports Series: The American Sportsman, ABC
Director: Harry Coyle, 1978 World Series, NBC
Personality: Jim McKay, ABC

1979–1980

Live Sports Special: 1980 Winter Olympic Games, Lake Placid, ABC
Live Sports Series: NCAA College Football, ABC
Edited Sports Special: Gossamer Albatross, CBS
Edited Sports Series: NFL Game of the Week, Syndicated
Director: Sandy Grossman, Super Bowl XIV, CBS
Personality: Jim McKay, ABC

1980–1981

Live Sports Special: Kentucky Derby, ABC
Live Sports Series: PGA Tour, CBS
Edited Sports Special: Wide World of Sports 20th Anniversary Show, ABC
Edited Sports Series: The American Sportsman, ABC
Personality, Play-by-Play: Dick Enberg, NBC
Personality, Commentary: Dick Button, ABC

1981–1982

Live Sports Special: NCAA Basketball Championship Final, CBS
Live Sports Series: NFL Football, CBS
Edited Sports Special: Indianapolis 500, ABC
Edited Sports Series/Anthologies: The American Sportsman, ABC
Personality, Play-by-Play: Jim McKay, ABC
Personality, Commentary: John Madden, CBS

1982–1983

Live Sports Special: The 1982 World Series, NBC
Live Sports Series: CBS Sports Presents the NFL, CBS
Edited Sports Special: Wimbledon Tennis Tournament, NBC
Edited Sports Series/Anthologies: The American Sportsman, ABC

Program Achievement: The American Sportsman, "Triumph on Mt. Everest,"
ABC; Football in America, PBS; Wide World of Sports, "Great
American Bike Race," ABC
Sports Journalism: SportsBeat, ABC
Personality, Play-by-Play: Dick Enberg, NBC
Personality, Commentary: John Madden, CBS

1984–1985

Live Sports Special: 1984 Summer Olympics, Los Angeles, ABC
Edited Sports Special: Road to the Super Bowl '85, Syndicated
Edited Sports Series: The American Sportsman, ABC
Program Achievement: The American Sportsman 20th Anniversary Show, ABC;
Closing Ceremonics, 1984 Summer Olympics, ABC; Wide World
of Sports 1984 Year-End Show, ABC
Sports Journalism: Sports Features, Dick Schaap, ABC; Sports Sunday, Joe
Valerio, CBS; 1984 Summer Olympics Segment Features, Steve
Skinner, ABC; SportsBeat, Howard Cosell, *et al.*, ABC; Race Across
America, Roone Arledge, *et al.*, ABC
Personality, Play-by-Play: George Michael, NBC

1986–1987

Live Sports Special: Daytona 500, CBS
Live Sports Series: NFL on CBS, CBS
Edited Sports Special: Wide World of Sports 25th Anniversary, ABC
Edited Sports Series: Wide World of Sports, ABC
Personality, Play-by-Play: Al Michaels, ABC
Personality, Commentary: John Madden, CBS

On July 13, 1988, the first Sports Emmy Awards were televised, covering outstanding achievements in 1987.

1987

Live Sports Special: The Kentucky Derby, ABC
Live Sports Series: NFL Monday Night Football, ABC
Edited Sports Special: Paris Robaix Bike Race, CBS
Edited Sports Series: Wide World of Sports, ABC
Personality, Play-by-Play: Bob Costas, NBC
Personality, Commentary: John Madden, CBS
Individual Achievement: Dick Schaap, 20/20: "To An Athlete Dying
Young," ABC

1988

Live Sports Special: Games of the XXIV Olympiad, Seoul, NBC
Live Sports Series: 1988 NCAA Basketball, CBS
Edited Sports Special: Road to the Super Bowl '88, NFL Films
Edited Sports Series: Wide World of Sports, ABC
Sports Journalism: Games of the XXIV Olympiad, NBC
Program Achievement: World Triathlon Championships, CBS; Iditarod Trail
        Sled Dog Race, ABC; 48 Hours: Showdown at Cheyenne, CBS
Personality, Play-by-Play: Bob Costas, NBC
Personality, Commentary: John Madden, CBS
Individual Achievement: Harry Coyle, Director, NBC

1989

Live Sports Special: Indianapolis 500, ABC
Live Sports Series: NFL Monday Night Football, ABC; Speedworld, ESPN
Edited Sports Special: Trans-Antarctica! The International Expedition, ABC
Edited Sports Series: This Is the NFL, NFL Films
Program Achievement: Sportsworld, The Championship, NBC
Sports Journalism: 1989 World Series Game #3 Earthquake Coverage, ABC
Personality, Play-by-Play: Al Michaels, ABC
Personality, Commentary: John Madden, CBS
Individual Achievement: Geoffrey Mason, *et al.*, ABC
Lifetime Achievement: Jim McKay

1990

Live Sports Special: Indianapolis 500, ABC
Live Sports Series: NCAA Basketball Tournament, CBS
Edited Sports Special: Road to the Super Bowl XXIV, Syndicated
Edited Spots Series/Anthologies: Wide World of Sports, ABC
Sports Journalism: Outside the Lines, Autograph Game, ESPN
Program Achievement: "Let Me Be Brave," CBS
Personality, Play-by-Play: Dick Enberg, NBC
Personality, Commentary: John Madden, CBS
Lifetime Achievement: Lindsey Nelson

1991

Live Sports Special: The NBA Finals, Lakers vs. Bulls, NBC
Live Sports Series: NCAA Basketball Tournament, CBS
Edited Sports Special: Wide World of Sports 30th Anniversary Special, ABC

Edited Sports Series/Anthologies: This Is the NFL, NFL Films
Sports Journalism: Outside the Lines: Steroids—Whatever It Takes, ESPN
Special Program Achievement: Play-by-Play: A History of Sports Television, HBO
Personality, Play-by-Play: Bob Costas, NBC
Personality, Commentary: John Madden, CBS
Lifetime Achievement Award: Curt Gowdy, Sr.

1992

Live Sports Special: The Breeders' Cup, NBC
Live Sports Series: NCAA Basketball Tournament, CBS
Edited Sports Special: Games of the XXV Olympiad, Barcelona, NBC
Edited Sports Series: MTV Sports, MTV
Sports Journalism: Outside the Lines: Portraits in Black and White, ESPN
Special Program Achievement: In This Corner, Boxing's Legendary Heavyweights,
    HBO; Games of the XX Olympiad: Tragedy in Munich, NBC
Personality, Play-by-Play: Bob Costas, NBC
Personality, Commentary: John Madden, CBS
Lifetime Achievement: Chris Schenkel

1993

Live Sports Special: 1993 World Series, CBS
Live Sports Series: NFL Monday Night Football, ABC
Edited Sports Special: Road to the Super Bowl, NFL Films
Edited Sports Series/Anthologies: This Is the NFL, NFL Films
Program Achievement: Outside the Lines, ESPN
Sports Journalism: SportsCenter: Houston Football, ESPN; Outside the Lines:
    Mitch Ivey Feature, ESPN
Personality, Play-by-Play: Dick Enberg, NBC
Personality, Commentary: Billy Packer, CBS
Lifetime Achievement: Pat Summerall

1994

Live Sports Special: NHL Stanley Cup Finals, ESPN
Live Sports Series: NFL Monday Night Football, ABC
Edited Sports Special: Lillehammer '94, 16 Days of Glory, Disney/Cappy
    Productions
Edited Sports Series/Anthologies: MTV Sports, MTV
Special Program Achievement: Arthur Ashe, Citizen of the World, HBO

Sports Journalism: 1994 Winter Olympic Games: Mossad Feature, Rick Gentile,
    et al., CBS
Personality, Play-by-Play: Keith Jackson, ABC
Personality, Commentary: John Madden, Fox
Personality, Studio Host: Bob Costas, NBC
Lifetime Achievement: Howard Cosell

Index